D0387152

A CABINET
❧ OF ❧
GREEK
CURIOSITIES

A CABINET

 OF

GREEK
CURIOSITIES

STRANGE TALES

AND

SURPRISING FACTS

FROM THE

CRADLE OF WESTERN CIVILIZATION

J. C. McKEOWN

OXFORD
UNIVERSITY PRESS

OXFORD
UNIVERSITY PRESS

Oxford University Press is a department of the University of Oxford.
It furthers the University's objective of excellence in research,
scholarship, and education by publishing worldwide.

Oxford   New York
Auckland   Cape Town   Dar es Salaam   Hong Kong   Karachi
Kuala Lumpur   Madrid   Melbourne   Mexico City   Nairobi
New Delhi   Shanghai   Taipei   Toronto

With offices in
Argentina   Austria   Brazil   Chile   Czech Republic   France   Greece
Guatemala   Hungary   Italy   Japan   Poland   Portugal   Singapore
South Korea   Switzerland   Thailand   Turkey   Ukraine   Vietnam

Oxford is a registered trade mark of Oxford University Press
in the UK and certain other countries.

Published in the United States of America by
Oxford University Press
198 Madison Avenue, New York, NY 10016

Library of Congress Cataloging-in-Publication Data
McKeown, J. C.
A cabinet of Greek curiosities: strange tales and surprising
facts from the cradle of western civilization /J.C. McKeown.
pages.   cm.
Includes bibliographical references and index.
ISBN 978-0-19-998210-3 (alk. paper)
1. Greece—Social life and customs. 2. Greece—Civilization. I. Title.
DF78.M35   2013
938—dc23   2012036875

1 3 5 7 9 8 6 4 2

Printed in the United States of America
on acid-free paper

For Jo
sine qua non

~~✦~~

I have to report what is said, but I do not have to believe it all without discrimination (Herodotus *Histories* 7.152).

People believe what is either true or probable; therefore, if they believe something that is implausible and not probable, it must be true, for it is not its probability or plausibility that makes it seem true (Aristotle *Rhetoric* 1400a).

The only people who are skeptical about wonders are those who have not had anything wonderful happen in their own lives (Pausanias *Guide to Greece* 10.4).

Someone I know who had spent a great part of his life immersed in reading gave me a book that he himself had written, packed with information amassed from a wide and varied range of abstruse texts. I took it eagerly and shut myself away to read it without interruption. But, my God, it was just a collection of curiosities! . . . I lost no time in returning it to its author (Aulus Gellius *Attic Nights* 14.6).

CONTENTS

PREFACE

THE ANCIENT Greeks were a wonderful people. They gave the Western world democracy and drama, and many forms of art and branches of science would be inconceivable without them. "The safest general characterization of the European philosophical tradition is that it consists of a series of footnotes to Plato" may be a slightly unsafe overstatement, but the abiding influence of Greek philosophy is undeniable. Who can even speculate what our lives would be like without the improbable victories at Marathon and Salamis?

The idea that the Greeks were a wonderful people has always been with us, for they were not shy about asserting their own special status in the world: they were Hellenes, and everyone else was a barbarian, a term that usually carried negative connotations. Greece had the great good fortune to remain more or less intact when it was absorbed into the empire of a people with a massive and, at least in the early generations after the conquest, well-deserved inferiority complex about intellectual and artistic matters. The Greeks therefore had no difficulty preserving their high opinion of themselves, and they would be gratified by the still prevailing tendency to idealize them. This tendency comes not just from our admiration for what they actually achieved, but also from a desire to create a past utopia in which things were better than they are now. This was the Greece imagined by the romantic movement that dominated European thought in the 18th and 19th centuries. J. J. Winckelmann, the father of modern classical archaeology and a towering figure in that movement, saw no need to set his wonderful Greeks in context by actually visiting Greece. Wilhelm von Humboldt, the Prussian minister of education early in the 19th century, caught the spirit of the age perfectly when he declared that "if every other part of history enriches us with its human wisdom and human experience, then from the Greeks we take something more than earthly—something almost godlike." Such was the vision that inspired Lord Byron to fight and die for Greek freedom in the 1820s.

Idealism held sway unchallenged for far too long. Eventually Ulrich von Wilamowitz-Moellendorff, perhaps the greatest of the early modern Greek philologists, was moved to complain: "I once heard a prominent scholar regret that these papyri [*Greek Magic Papyri*] were found, because they deprive antiquity of the noble splendor of classicism." He (sc. UvW) added, "They unarguably do so, but I am glad of it. For I don't want to admire my Greeks, I want to understand them, so that I can judge them properly." Wilamowitz was standing up for truth against the imaginative exploitation of the classical past by such luminaries as Nietzsche and Wagner (adhered to by Adolf Hitler, who maintained that "the Hellenic ideal of culture must remain preserved for us in its paradigmatic beauty"). The thoroughly unscholarly regret expressed by Wilamowitz's "prominent scholar" resonates back to antiquity. In the heyday of their intellectually vibrant democracy in the 5th century B.C., the Athenians voted to chop off the right thumbs of all their prisoners from Aegina, to brand the Athenian owl on the foreheads of all their prisoners from Samos, and to kill all the male inhabitants of Mytilene; writing more than six centuries later, Aelian wished not simply that the Athenians had not passed such brutal decrees, but that no record had been preserved of their having done so (*Miscellaneous History* 2.9).

Nearly everything in this book illustrates the not-quite-so-wonderful aspects of Greek life and thought. As in the companion volume *A Cabinet of Roman Curiosities* (Oxford University Press, 2010), my aspiration here is simply to entertain. Nevertheless, over the course of many years, while accumulating the material presented here I have found my perspective on the Greeks changing gradually but remorselessly. I used to dismiss each individual little quirk and oddity as an aberration, not fitting into the noble and inspiring, or at least dignified and rational, world of Homer, Euripides, Plato, and Aristotle. But the more quirks and oddities I gathered, the more difficult it became for me to keep that world in focus. Did a werewolf win the boxing event at the Olympic Games? Did officials armed with canes ensure order among the spectators during Athenian dramatic performances, or only during pig-imitating contests? Did Greeks wear as an amulet promoting virility the penis of a lizard caught while mating? Did anyone really believe that Pythagoras flew about on a magic arrow?

In some ways I hope to show in this book how much the Greeks were like us. Politicians were regarded as shallow and self-serving; fat people resorted to implausible methods of weight control; Socrates and the king of Sparta used to entertain their children by riding around on a stick pretending it was a horse; and jokes were in circulation that seem gruesomely familiar: "There were twin brothers and one of them died. Someone met the surviving twin and asked him, 'Was it you or your brother who died?'" (Philogelos *Joke Book* 29).

On the other hand, much of the book shows how very different the Greeks were from us. Shipping companies no longer safeguard their vessels from lightning by wrapping the hides of seals or hyenas around the mast; prisoners are not released on bail so that they can enjoy dramatic festivals; no one sows pieces of copper in the expectation that they will sprout and grow; voters are not paid to vote, nor are they herded to the polls by means of a rope dripping with red paint; and scapegoats are not thrown from cliffs to ward off evil, much less fitted out with feathers and live birds to give them a sporting chance of survival.

Some material is included because it concerns particular people. It is interesting that Euripides had bad breath, that Sophocles was very handsome and an excellent ballplayer, that Aeschylus (according to Sophocles) wrote his plays while drunk, that his brother lost an arm while trying to hold back one of the Persian ships at Marathon, and that he died when an eagle dropped a tortoise on his head. The earnest Skeptic philosopher Sextus Empiricus observed that "there is nothing sophisticated in recording that, for example, Plato's real name was Aristocles and he rather decadently wore an earring when he was young" (*Against the Professors of Liberal Studies* 1.258). He is quite right, of course, but sophistication is not everything. There is a perennial fascination in comparing and contrasting the rich, the powerful, and the famous with ordinary folk; as Diogenes Laertius records, "When Diogenes the Cynic was asked whether philosophers eat cake, he replied, 'We eat everything that other people eat'" (*Lives of the Philosophers* 6.56). It may not be particularly remarkable that Euripides suffered from halitosis, but we do perhaps gain a surprising perspective on that icon of Western intellectual achievement when we learn that he persuaded the king of Macedon to hand over to him for a whipping the person who had teased him about his bad breath.

The austere historian Polybius criticizes his predecessor Timaeus for arguing that poets and prose writers reveal their own nature by what they choose to emphasize in their works, and that on this principle it is possible to infer from the frequent banquets in the Homeric poems that Homer himself was a glutton (*Histories* 12.24). Polybius suggests that if such deductions are valid, one might draw some rather negative conclusions about Timaeus's own personality, given that his work "is full of dreams, marvels, incredible tales, and silly superstitions, and displays an effeminate interest in curiosities." Neither athletics, nor mathematics, nor philosophy holds any special fascination for me; even so, whole chapters of this book are devoted to these topics simply because the Greeks were so preoccupied with them. One important aspect of Greek life may, however, be particularly conspicuous by its absence: because there is so much that might be said about Greek medicine, it has been isolated for treatment in a forthcoming volume of its own.

Polybius would not enjoy this book. He reports that *some historians claim that there are two Greek cities in which neither snow nor rain ever fall on the statue of Artemis, even though it stands in the open air. Throughout my work I have resisted such assertions and rejected them with disgust, for they are impossible, not just improbable, and believing them is a sign of childish simplemindedness* (*Histories* 16.12). Those who share Polybius's ideals should read no further. But there may be readers with the cast of mind to wonder if these statues, despite being thought to be weatherproof, had little umbrellas over them, standard issue for Greek statuary to protect them from bird droppings; such readers may care to turn to p. 197.

One further limitation in the book's serviceability should perhaps also be acknowledged here. The *Geoponica* (*Farm Work*), a 10th-century Byzantine manual, draws on lore at least half a millennium old to assure us that intoxicated people can be restored to sobriety if they drink vinegar, eat radishes or honey-cakes, wear garlands of many types of flowers, or discuss topics in ancient history (7.33). It would be a fine thing if I could claim that reading this book might have such a useful application, but I have little faith in that last remedy.

Many of the beliefs and opinions reported here are certainly misguided and incorrect. In most cases, however, the truth or falsehood of the statement is irrelevant, and the interesting, amusing, and possibly even thought-provoking point lies in the simple fact that someone in antiquity thought fit to record it at all. Even though I am not concerned to establish truth and dispel falsehood, the normal goal of scholarly research, I might perhaps add an afterword to one of the seemingly more bizarre assertions made by the elder Pliny and reported in *A Cabinet of Roman Curiosities*: that kissing a she-mule on the nostrils will stop sneezing and hiccups. I have subsequently acquired a she-mule and now believe that, however weird it may seem, this remedy has at least some efficacy: being so close to such a large animal perhaps distracts and relaxes the diaphragm, thereby relieving hiccups. I have yet to find anyone willing to try this experiment as a cure for sneezing.

It may perhaps surprise some readers that so many Roman writers are quoted in a book about Greek life. It is quite understandable that we should associate Greek culture most immediately with Homer, Sappho, and the dramatists and philosophers of 5th- to 4th-century B.C. Athens, but Greece was part of the Roman Empire for about as long as the period from Homer to the conquest. Most surviving Greek literature dates from the Roman era, and it is inevitable that Roman writers should have a lot to tell us about Greece. The elder Pliny occasionally expresses contempt for Greeks; even so, in the first book of his *Natural History*, where he catalogs the sources from which he draws his material, he names 146 Romans, but 327 Greeks. Marcus Aurelius may have been a Roman emperor, but he wrote his *Meditations* in

Greek, and Aelian, whose Greek collections *On Animals* and *Miscellaneous History* are quoted frequently in this book, was born near Rome and may never have left Italy.

It is astonishing how persistently the same information was copied faithfully by author after author over the centuries. Photius, the 9th-century patriarch of Constantinople and the Byzantine world's nearest approach to a one-man *Reader's Digest*, is altogether justified in remarking rather despondently that "they all say the same things about the same things" (*The Library* 106*b*). He is referring to compilers of agricultural manuals, but the same complaint might be applied much more broadly. In quoting primary sources, I follow the practice established in *A Cabinet of Roman Curiosities*. I refer either to the best-known source, to the most coherent, or simply to the passage in which I happened to note it. To avoid cluttering the text and to ensure that the reader does not suppose that this book has academic pretensions, I frequently do not cite sources at all. When ancient authorities are quoted directly, this is indicated by either italicization or quotation marks. Such quotations should not, however, be assumed to be verbatim: details not relevant to the point being made are often omitted, and extra information is sometimes added to clarify the context. Almost all Greek words and phrases quoted in the book have been translated and also, where appropriate, transliterated, because it would appear that substantially more people in the United States are currently learning Klingon, the language of an alien race in *Star Trek*, than are learning classical Greek, the language of Sophocles and Plato.

Greek culture is so diverse and spans so many centuries that no one can hope to master all aspects of it. I have therefore been shameless in exploiting the expertise and patience of many colleagues and friends, who have generously answered my numerous queries or read through some or all of the typescript. I am particularly grateful to William Aylward, Mary Beard, Jeffrey Beneker, Paul Cartledge, Raffaella Cribiore, James Diggle, John Dillon, Simon Goldhill, John Marincola, Silvia Montiglio, Christopher Pelling, Barry Powell, Richard Stoneman, John Yardley, and Sophie Zermuehlen. I have spent many stimulating afternoons discussing the book with Debra Hershkowitz, who has greatly improved it with her knowledge and acumen. I am indebted also to Amber Kleijwegt for her careful reproductions of ancient graffiti. An author could not hope for better editorial guidance than I have once again received from Stefan Vranka, and I am very grateful also to Sarah Pirovitz, Marc Schneider, and Sharon Langworthy for their help in the preparation of this book for publication.

This book is dedicated to my wife, Jo. Many books are dedicated to wives and husbands in gratitude for their moral support and tolerant encouragement through the many long, dark hours of intellectual torment and self-doubt involved in the writing process. Although it is certainly true that not every Greek author gives me much pleasure to read (Aristotle, Aelius Aristides, and all of the Philostrati spring readily to mind), and most ancient commentaries on classical authors are by and large as tedious as they are difficult, nevertheless, the compilation of this book has been hugely enjoyable. My wife may have a slightly different perspective, judging by the substantial number of items she culled Scylla-like from various drafts.

I have of course acquiesced in the culling. Even so, I rather wish that Greek rhetorical strategies were still in vogue, for then I could resort to the crafty trick of *paraleipsis* ("[the pretense of] leaving things to the side") and lament that there is no room to speculate, for example, why the Cyclops Polyphemus was a one-eyed monster, given that his father was Poseidon and his mother was a sea nymph (Aristotle *frg.* 172), whether it is more likely that there is an even number of stars or an odd number (Plutarch *Table Talk* 741c), why its Greek name, στρουθοκάμηλος (*strouthokamelos*), suggests that the ostrich is a cross between a sparrow and a camel (Galen *Properties of Foodstuffs* 6.702), or whether the Greeks ever devised a more wonderfully vigorous term of insult than κατωμόχανος (*katomochanos*): "with an ass so flabby you could sling it over your shoulder" (Hipponax *frg.* 28).

A CABINET
✾ OF ✾
GREEK
CURIOSITIES

· I ·

FOOD AND DRINK

*Aristotle said that human life is like a cucumber—
bitter at both ends*

(***Gnomologium Vaticanum*** 143).

I am told that, to prevent the stomachs of red mullet from bursting during the cooking process, really skillful chefs kiss them on the lips (Aelian *On Animals* 10.7). Cooking mullet was a serious art: Seneca fulminates against gourmets who would not trouble to sit with a dying father, brother, or friend, but avidly watch a mullet's death throes, as it is killed right there in the dining room to ensure freshness (*Natural Questions* 3.17).

Galen (*On the Powers of Foods* 6.664) notes some unusual types of food:

> *Some people serve bear, and also lion and leopard, though these are much worse than bear.*

> *Many people also eat panther meat—indeed, some doctors recommend it.*

> *Plump young puppies, especially if they have been castrated, are a popular food in many countries.*

> *Hunters serve fox meat in the fall, when the foxes have grown fat on grapes.*

One way to tell a good cheese from a bad one is by belching: a good cheese gradually loses its distinctive characteristics, whereas a bad one does not.

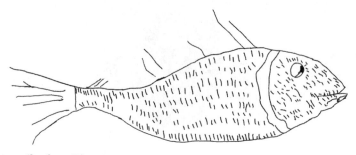

A graffito from Olympia.

Since a bad cheese does not readily change, it is harder to digest (Galen *On the Powers of Foods* 6.699).

People have sometimes felt ashamed at slaughtering land animals, which make pitiful cries and in so many cases have lived with them and shared their food supply. Sea creatures, on the other hand, are entirely different and exist in a quite alien environment. It is as if they were born and lived in some other world. Neither their appearance, nor their voice, nor any service they do for us argues against our eating them. We do not feel any affection for them. The world where we live is like Hades to sea creatures (Plutarch *Table Talk* 669d).

If, as they say, even plants have a soul, what sort of life will we have if we neither kill animals nor chop down plants? (Porphyry *On Abstinence from Killing Animals* 1.18).

An orator from Sidon was talking with two friends. One of his friends said it was not right to slaughter sheep, since they provide us with milk and wool, and the other one said it was not right to slaughter cows, since they provide us with milk and plow our fields. The orator said it was not right to kill pigs either, since they give us their liver, their udder, and their kidneys to eat (Philogelos *Joke Book* 129).

Pythagoras was not only one of the most influential pre-Socratic philosophers, but also a vigorous advocate of vegetarianism:

> *Pythagoras ordered his followers not to eat beans, because they cause flatulence.*

He maintained that abstaining from beans ensures that such visions as appear to us in sleep are gentle and not disturbing.

Aristotle says that Pythagoras prohibited the eating of beans because they are testicle-shaped, or because they look like the gates of the Underworld, or because they are used to register votes in oligarchical regimes.

Pythagoras was murdered by his political opponents, who were able to catch him only because he insisted on running around a field of beans rather than trample the crop.

(Diogenes Laertius *Lives of the Philosophers* 8.24, 8.34, 8.39)

If you put a bean into a new pot and cover it with manure for forty days, you will find it has been transformed, and looks like a human being with flesh on his body. That is why the poet says, "Eating beans is the same as eating one's parents' heads" [*Orphic Fragments* 291] (John the Lydian *On the Months* 4.42).

Empedocles of Acragas was a follower of Pythagoras and abstained from animal food. When he was victorious in the Olympic Games, he fashioned an ox out of frankincense, myrrh, and other expensive perfumes, and shared it out among those who had come to the festival (Suda s.v. *Athenaeus*).

A man from Cyme [where people were proverbially stupid] *was selling honey. A customer sampled it and said that it was excellent. "Yes," agreed the man from Cyme, "if a mouse hadn't fallen into it, I wouldn't be selling it"* (Philogelos *Joke Book* 173).

To attack luxury and remove the desire for wealth, Lycurgus introduced his third and finest decree: the Spartans should have their meals together in groups, all eating the same strictly regulated foods, rather than dining

An ear of barley, with a mouse on the leaf.

at home, lounging on expensive couches at expensive tables, fattened in the dark by slaves and cooks, just like gluttonous animals, inviting ruin, both physical and moral, and giving themselves up to every craving and excess that requires a lot of sleep, hot baths, lots of idle time, and high daily maintenance (Plutarch *Life of Lycurgus* 10).

Athletic trainers always say that intellectual conversation at dinner spoils the food and makes the head heavy (Plutarch *Advice on Preserving One's Health* 133*b*).

The sophists Anchimolus and Moschus lived healthily on a diet of figs and water, but their sweat was so pungent that everyone avoided them at the public baths. . . . A Theban athlete grew exceptionally strong on a diet of goat's meat, but was laughed at because his sweat was very foul smelling (Athenaeus *Wise Men at Dinner* 44*c*, 402*c*).

Milon of Croton used to eat twenty pounds of meat and an equal amount of bread, along with two gallons of wine. At Olympia he lifted a four-year-old bull onto his shoulders and carried it around the stadium, and then he butchered it and ate it all by himself in one day (Athenaeus *Wise Men at Dinner* 413*e*).

Milon of Croton and Titormus of Aetolia had a competition, to see who could eat a whole ox first (Athenaeus *Wise Men at Dinner* 412*f*).

Zeno of Citium, the founder of Stoicism, said that the dead ought to be given to the living as food, rather than be thrown onto a funeral pyre (Zeno *frg.* 253).

Smindyrides of Sybaris is said to have been so decadent that, when he went to Sicyon as a suitor for the tyrant's daughter, he took with him one thousand chefs, one thousand bird catchers, and one thousand fishermen (Aelian *Miscellaneous History* 12.24; for Smindyrides, see also p. 249).

Philoxenus of Cythera once prayed to have a throat that was five feet long, "so that," he said, "I can swallow for as long a time as possible, and enjoy everything I eat at one and the same time" (Machon *Anecdotes* 10).

It is said that Philoxenus and Gnathon the Sicilian were so keen on delicacies that they used to blow their noses over the dainty morsels to put off the other diners and so be the only ones to gorge themselves on the food that was served (Plutarch *Whether "Live in Obscurity" Is a Good Precept* 1128*b*).

A glutton accustomed his hand to heat by dipping it into the hot water at the baths, and he did the same for his mouth by gargling with hot water. It was said moreover that he used to bribe the cooks to serve the food especially hot. The purpose of all this was that he alone could enjoy the food while no one else was able to follow his example (Athenaeus *Wise Men at Dinner* 5*e*).

A person with no social graces will describe, right in the middle of a meal, how he was cleaned out top and bottom by drinking hellebore, and how the bile in his feces was blacker than the soup served for dinner (Theophrastus *Characters* 20).

THE CAKE STALL

Alcibiades sent Socrates a large and beautifully prepared cake. Xanthippe, Socrates's wife, was very annoyed, regarding the cake as a provocative gift from a beloved to his lover, so she threw it out of the basket it came in and trampled on it. Socrates laughed and said, "Then you won't be getting a piece of it either" (Aelian *Miscellaneous History* 11.12).

King Philip of Macedon was once invited to dinner out in the countryside. His host, who had expected him to come with just a few followers and had prepared for dinner accordingly, was alarmed to see him arrive with a large retinue. Philip saw the problem and sent word discreetly to each of his companions to leave room for cake. In expectation of more to come, they ate sparingly, and so there was enough for everyone (Plutarch *Advice on Preserving One's Health* 123f).

Dreaming about cakes made without cheese is a good omen, but cheesecakes signify deceit and trickery (Artemidorus *Interpretation of Dreams* 1.72).

Anything sacrificed to the Nymphs in the temple of Asclepius must be sacrificed on the altars. It is forbidden to throw cakes or anything else [i.e., any other offering] *into the temple springs* (*Lois Sacrées des Cités Grecques* 152).

Top pastry-cooks devise every conceivable variety of cake, each one distinctive not only in its ingredients but also in the way it is made and in its shape, so as to have a seductive appeal both to taste and to sight. . . . They ingeniously invent countless confections to make life luxurious, decadent, and not worth living (Philo of Alexandria *On Drunkenness* 213). Filo pastry derives its name not from Philo, but from φύλλον (*phyllon*), "leaf."

In the third book of his commentary on the poems of Alcman, Sosibius says that there is a type of cake called a cribane *that is breast-shaped* (Athenaeus *Wise Men at Dinner* 115a).

WINE

As today, some regions had a reputation for producing particularly good wine, the best being thought to come from Greece and Campania, the region south of Rome. However, the general quality of wine, which was regularly mixed with water, even seawater, or with honey and occasionally perfume, seems questionable. Whereas the classical Greek word for wine, οἶνος (*oinos*), is related to the Latin *vinum* and the English *wine*, the modern Greek word, κρασί (*krasi*), means literally "the thing mixed," reflecting the old custom.

Why do those who drink diluted wine suffer worse hangovers than those who drink undiluted wine? Is it because diluted wine, being lighter, penetrates further into the body and is consequently harder to drain out? Or is it because it is not possible to drink so much undiluted wine, and those who try to do so are more prone to throw it up? (Ps.-Aristotle *Problems* 871a).

Just as we call the mixture "wine" even though there is more water in it than wine, so we should say that the marital property and the house belong to the husband, even if it is the wife who contributes the larger share (Plutarch *Advice on Marriage* 140f).

As part of his plan to escape from the Cyclops's cave, Odysseus made him drunk with neat wine; wine was normally diluted with twenty parts water (Homer *Odyssey* 9.209). Homeric heroes were partial to wine with goat's cheese grated into it, along with a sprinkling of barley (*Iliad* 11.638). Bronze cheese graters have been found in the graves of several 9th-century B.C. warriors on the island of Euboea.

On the island of Cos, large amounts of seawater are added to wine, a custom that arose when a slave stole some wine and added seawater to top up the jar (Pliny *Natural History* 14.78).

Since leopards are so partial to wine, hunters in the Libyan desert catch them by mixing twenty jars of sweet eleven-year-old wine with water from a spring, and then concealing themselves under goatskins or their nets. The leopards are attracted to the spring both by their thirst and by the aroma of the wine. At first they leap about like a troupe of dancers, but gradually they feel sleepy and lie sprawled on the ground (Oppian *Hunting with Dogs* 4.320ff.).

Filling her bucket with wine and milk, Chloe had a drink to share with Daphnis (Longus *Daphnis and Chloe* 1.23).

When mice fall into the wine vat they cause an unpleasant smell, so put a flat board into the vat, so that any mouse that falls in can run up it (*Farm Work* 6.1).

Odysseus escapes from the Cyclops's cave, slung under his ram.

*If you throw warm bread or an iron ring into the vat, it will draw off the poison with which the wine has been tainted by any venomous creature (*Farm Work *7.27).*

Those who get into the vat to tread the grapes should have scrupulously clean feet. They should neither eat nor drink in the vat, nor should they

get in and out frequently. If they must get out, they should not go off barefoot. They should wear clothes, including undergarments, because of the sweat generated (Farm Work 6.11).

Some people who want to trick buyers soak an empty cup in fine old wine with a very appealing bouquet. This quality lingers in it for a long time and gives the impression that it comes from the wine poured into it subsequently. And so they deceive those who taste it. Some wine merchants are even more unscrupulous and lay out cheese and nuts in the winery to persuade customers to eat them, thus confusing their sense of taste. (I record this, not as something we should do, but to ensure we are not duped) (Farm Work 7.7).

Those who are addicted to wine grow old before their time, and many such people become prematurely bald or gray haired (Plutarch Table Talk 652f).

In order to counter the headaches caused by drinking too much wine, Dionysus is said to have tied a band around his head. . . . They say that this is the origin of the custom whereby kings wear a crown [διάδημα (*diadema,* literally "a thing tied around")] (Diodorus Siculus *The Library* 4.4).

Why does the semen of drunkards tend not to be productive? Is it because the elements that make up the body have become moist? For moist seeds are not productive, unlike those that are firm and solid (Ps.-Aristotle *Problems* 871a).

Why do women very seldom get drunk? Aristotle suggests that those who drink fast, absorbing large amounts at one go, rarely get drunk, since the wine does not stay long in their system, being forced through by the pressure of such large draughts. Observation shows that women generally drink this way (Plutarch Table Talk 650a).

Those who get drunk on wine fall on their faces, whereas those who have drunk beer lie flat on their backs. Wine causes headaches, whereas beer stupefies (Aristotle *frg.* 106).

Mendaean is the wine that the gods themselves piss on their soft couches (Hermippus *frg.* 82, in a catalog eulogizing vintage wines).

Why is it that tipsy people behave badly, rather than those who are very drunk? Is it because they have not drunk so little as to be like sober people, nor so much as to become helpless? Sober people exercise good judgment, and very drunk people make no attempt to do so. Those who are tipsy, because they are not entirely drunk, do try to exercise judgment, but they do it badly and are quick either to despise people or to suppose that they themselves are being sneered at (Ps.-Aristotle *Problems* 871a).

SYMPOSIA

(Where men get tight with loose women.)

Herodotus's "agonies for the eyes" as a description of beautiful women is open to criticism, but in mitigation one may note that those whom he represents using the expression are barbarians, and drunk (Ps.-Longinus *On the Sublime* 4.4). At *Histories* 5.18, Herodotus describes the Persian ambassadors being entertained at the Macedonian court as complaining that it would be better to have no women at the dinner than that they should only be allowed to look at them. Plutarch reports that Alexander the Great used the same phrase to describe Persian women (*Life of Alexander* 21).

The parasite Chaerophon came uninvited to a wedding party and reclined at the far end of a couch. When the women regulators counted the guests and told him to run away, since there was one person present in excess of the legal maximum of thirty, he replied, "Count again, but start with me this time" (Athenaeus *Wise Men at Dinner* 245a). The women regulators [γυναικονόμοι, *gynaeconomoi*] were officials who oversaw public order, with authority to intrude even into private gatherings.

Numerous trick drinking cups have survived. Some have a very shallow bowl and appear more capacious than they actually are (when the host is stingy); some have a secret inner section from which the cup is surreptitiously replenished (as the thirsty host drinks); and some have a hole in the bottom, apparently so designed that the unwary drinker is drenched when a plug attached to a string is pulled out.

Empedocles of Acragas, the pre-Socratic philosopher who established the influential theory of the four elements (earth, air, fire, and water), once attended a banquet at which *the symposiarch ordered the guests either to drink or to have their wine poured over their heads. Empedocles made no protest at the time, but the next day he had both the host and the symposiarch condemned in court and executed. This was the beginning of his career in politics* (Timaeus *frg.* 134).

Forfeits at drunken symposia sometimes get out of hand—ordering stutterers to sing, bald men to comb their hair, or lame men to dance on a greased wineskin. To make fun of Agapestor, the Academic philosopher, who had a withered leg, all the drinkers were required either to drain their wine cups while standing on their right legs or pay a fine. But when it was Agapestor's turn to set a forfeit, he ordered everyone to drink the way they saw him drinking. Then he put his weak leg into a narrow pot and drained his wine cup. Everyone else tried to do the same, but without success, and so they paid the fine (Plutarch *Table Talk* 621e).

The Seleucid king Antiochus VIII Grypus (Hook Nose) used to give lavish banquets at which *each guest had to get up on a camel and drink his wine, after which he was given the camel, the trappings on the camel, and the slave that looked after it* (Posidonius *frg.* 72a).

A drunk arrives at a symposium straight from his bed, where he has been sleeping off the previous night's excesses. . . . There, with his eyes dimmed by alcoholic tears, he can scarcely recognize the other drunks. One guest is

Antiochus VIII.

taunting his neighbor for no good reason; another wants to fall asleep but is forced to stay awake; another is spoiling for a quarrel; another wants to avoid a fuss and go home, but is kept there by the doorkeeper with blows, under orders from his master to stop him leaving; yet another guest has been thrown out and is supported by his slave as he totters off, dragging his cloak through the mud (Rutilius Rufus *On Figures* 2.7, drawing on Lyco of Troas, head of the Peripatetic school in the 3rd century B.C.).

Eggs hatch when birds incubate them, but sometimes they hatch spontaneously in the ground, as in Egypt, with the mother birds burying them in manure heaps. It is said that there was once a serious drinker in Syracuse who used to put eggs under the mat he was reclining on and then keep drinking steadily until he hatched them (Aristotle *History of Animals* 559a).

To ensure against drunkenness, even when drinking much wine:

> *Roast and eat a goat's lung*
> *or, before eating anything else, eat five or seven bitter almonds*
> *or eat some raw cabbage*
> *or wear a garland of ground-pine branches*
> *or, while taking your first cup, recite this line of Homer: "Three times from the Idaean mountains counselor Zeus thundered"* [*Iliad* 8.170; it is not clear why this line might be thought to have special power].
>
> (*Farm Work* 7.31)

Life without celebration is a long road without an inn (Democritus *frg.* 230).

> *If a cucumber is bitter, just throw it away. . . .*
> *Don't go on to complain "Why do such things exist*
> *in the world?"*
>
> (Marcus Aurelius *Meditations* 8.50).

· II ·

CHILDREN AND
EDUCATION

The breeding of children is a self-inflicted grief
(**Ps.-Menander** *Sayings* 70).

A mother's love is always stronger than a father's, for she knows the children are hers; he only thinks they are his (Euripides *frg.* 1015).

A famous letter (*Oxyrhynchus Papyrus* 744) from an anxious expectant father in Roman Egypt, dated June 17, 1 B.C. (i.e., about the same time as King Herod's massacre of the innocents, St. Matthew 2:16–18) includes the following lines:

> *Greetings from Hilarion to his dear Alis, and to his dear Berous and Apollonarion. We are still in Alexandria. Don't worry if I stay here when everyone else returns home. Please look after our little child. As soon as we are paid I shall send you the money. If—please god!–you have a baby, let it live if it is a boy, but expose it if it is a girl. You told Aphrodisias "Don't forget me." How could I forget you? So please don't worry.*

People used to take a pot full of honey with a sponge blocking the aperture and put it in children's mouths to keep them quiet and to stop them from crying to be fed (Scholion to Aristophanes *Acharnians* 463).

When a child puts his hand into a clay pot with a narrow neck to get the figs and nuts in it, what happens is that, if he fills his hand full, he cannot get them out of the pot, and starts crying, but, he can get them out if he lets go of a few of them. You should likewise give up your desires: do not want many things, and you will get what you do want (Epictetus *Discourses* 3.9).

King Agesilaus of Sparta was exceptionally fond of children. It is said that he used to play with his children by getting astride a stick as if it were a horse. When one of his friends spotted him playing this way, Agesilaus asked him not to tell anyone until he had children of his own (Plutarch *Life of Agesilaus* 25). The same story is told about Socrates.

In the game called "Bronze Fly," one child is blindfolded with a ribbon, and then the others turn him around. He shouts, "I'll hunt the bronze fly," and the others reply "You'll hunt it, but you won't catch it," and they hit him with strips of papyrus until he catches one of them (Pollux *Onomasticon* 9.123).

Lawgivers who try to legislate against children's screaming tantrums are misguided, for such behavior helps them grow and is healthy physical exercise. Exertion like this helps children in the same way as retaining the breath strengthens those who are in training (Aristotle *Politics* 1336a).

Of all creatures, the boy is the hardest to handle. Since the fountain of reason is not yet properly adjusted in him, he is crafty, sly, and the most obstreperous of animals. He therefore has to be held in check with many bridles, as it were (Plato *Laws* 808d).

Life expectancy being so low, the Greeks felt the need for a word specifically denoting a child with both parents still alive: ἀμφιθαλής (*amphithales*, meaning literally "blooming on both sides").

In Persia, a boy is not shown to his father until he is five years old. Before then, he lives with the women. The rationale is that, should he die while he is being reared, he will not cause his father any grief. I think this is a good custom (Herodotus *Histories* 1.136). Surprisingly little is known about Herodotus's personal life; might his final comment here reflect his own experience?

Children are born with resemblances to their parents not only in congenital features but also in acquired characteristics. There have been cases of children born with the outline of a scar where their parents have scars, and there was a child at Chalcedon with an indistinct birthmark showing the same letter with which his father had been branded on the arm (Aristotle *On the Generation of Animals* 721b). Some people deduced from this that semen is formed in all parts of the father's body. The same phenomenon was thought to occur in plants: *If you scratch letters on a nut and plant it, the tree that grows from it will bear nuts with the same letters* (Ps.-Alexander *Problems* 5.1).

Lycurgus could see the misguided arrogance in the way people breed their bitches and mares with the best pedigree sires, either paying their owners for the breeding or asking for it as a favor; on the other hand, they lock up their wives and keep guard over them, insisting that they have children with themselves alone, even if they are witless, or too old, or sickly (Plutarch *Life of Lycurgus* 15).

EDUCATION

Children need distractions. Since they can't stay still, the rattle is a fine invention; people give it to little children so that they don't break anything in the house. A rattle suits infants, and for older children education is equivalent to a rattle (Aristotle *Politics* 1340b).

There are three types of student: the golden, the silver, and the bronze. The golden student pays and learns, the silver student pays but does not learn, the bronze student learns but does not pay (Bion of Borysthenes *frg.* 78).

Large numbers of people, mad keen to recruit pupils for the various schools, were always lurking at the Piraeus docks, lying in wait for newcomers, but

A 4th-century B.C. terra-cotta pig-shaped rattle.

the captain took all his passengers straight on to Athens, . . . where he knocked at the door of his old friend, the sophist Prohaeresius, and presented him with enough students to fill a school, at a time when wars were being fought to enroll even just one or two young boys (Eunapius *Lives of the Sophists* 10.1).

Why is it that we are more sensible when we grow older, but learn more quickly when we are younger? (Ps.-Aristotle *Problems* 955*b*).

Education is a possession that cannot be taken away from anyone (Ps.-Menander *Sayings* 2).

Aristotle used to say that education was an ornament in prosperity, a refuge in adversity (Diogenes Laertius *Lives of the Philosophers* 5.19).

When the people of Mytilene gained control of the sea, they punished those of their allies who had revolted from them by not allowing their children to learn to read and write or to have any education at all; for they regarded a life of uncultured ignorance as the severest of all punishments (Aelian *Miscellaneous History* 7.15).

Even if education has no other merits, attending school at least keeps pupils who have any sense of decency away from wrongdoing, whether by day or by night (Plutarch *frg.* 159).

Advice on listening to lectures, however pointless they may be:

- *Sit up straight, without lolling or sprawling.*
- *Look straight at the speaker in an attitude of active interest.*
- *Maintain a calm and inscrutable expression, free not only from arrogance and impatience, but also from any other thoughts and preoccupations.*
- *Do not frown superciliously or look disgusted.*
- *Do not let your eyes wander.*
- *Do not shift about in your seat or cross your legs.*
- *Do not nod, or whisper, or smile to anyone.*

(Plutarch *On Listening to Lectures* 45c)

When Dionysius the tyrant of Syracuse (ruled 367–357 and 346–344 B.C.) was sent into exile, he taught children in Corinth, for he was quite incapable of living without exerting power (Cicero *Tusculan Disputations* 3.27).

Without flogging, no one can be educated (Ps.-Menander *Sayings* 573).

They say that, whenever he taught anyone anything, Protagoras told the student to fix a price he thought the instruction was worth, and he would accept that amount (Aristotle *Nicomachean Ethics* 1164a). Diogenes Laertius, however, reports that *Protagoras was the first sophist to demand payment from his students, fixing his fee at a hundred minae* [ten thousand drachmas, an astronomical amount, equivalent in the mid-5th century B.C. to payment for service on an Athenian jury for thirty thousand days] (*Lives of the Philosophers* 9.52).

If boys had the chance to make fun of their teachers and insult them, there is nothing they would rather do (Dio Chrysostom *On Personal Appearance* 10).

When the Socratic philosopher Antisthenes saw the Thebans giving themselves airs after they had defeated the Spartans at the Battle of Leuctra [in 371 B.C.], *he said they were just like little boys prancing around after thrashing their tutor* (Plutarch *Life of Lycurgus* 30).

Libanius was a 4th-century A.D. sophist and teacher of rhetoric, from a family that had fallen on relatively hard times. (He himself survived being struck by a bolt of lightning while reading Aristophanes's *Acharnians*.) He resisted both the onset of Christianity and the corrupting effects of Latin literature. Despite the following outbursts on the difficulties of schoolteaching, not only was he very influential, but he also had rather an endearing personality, as appears here and there in his vast surviving works:

> *The students nod to each other about charioteers, or mime-actors, or horses, or dancers, or about some gladiatorial fight; some just stand there like blocks of stone, others pick their noses . . . Anything is preferable to paying attention to their teacher* (*Oration* 3.12).

> *A schoolteacher is a slave not just to his pupils, but also to all their many attendants, and to their fathers, and to their mothers, and to their nurses, and to their grandfathers. If he doesn't turn his young pupils into the sons of gods (no matter if they are blockheads) by overcoming their nature by his art, all sorts of accusations pour in against him from every side* (*Oration* 25.46).

> *You, my students, would rather handle snakes than touch your work books* (*Oration* 35.13).

> *Make sure that your son has books. If he has no books, he is like someone trying to learn archery without a bow* (*Letter* 428).

To this day Agathius has caused no trouble either to the teachers or to the other students. I am always happy to see him come into the classroom and enjoy hearing his declamations. Some of the other students are quite good at declaiming, but are so surly and so proud of the way they cause disruptions that I curse myself for being a teacher whenever they show up for class (*Letter* 1165 [from a school report]).

When Gelon [who became tyrant of Gela and Syracuse in the early 5th century B.C.] *was still a little boy, a wolf came into the school where he was sitting and snatched his writing tablet. Gelon ran out after the wolf and his tablet, just before an earthquake shook the school to its foundations, killing all the other children and their teacher* (Timaeus *frg.* 95).

A teacher wanted to have a sleep and, since he had no pillow, he told his slave to give him an earthenware pot instead. When the slave said that pots are hard, he told him to fill it with feathers (Philogelos *Joke Book* 21).

A teacher with a country home many miles away knocked the number seven from the milestone to bring the house closer to the city (Philogelos *Joke Book* 60).

While he was going up a steep hill on his way back home, a teacher said with surprise: "When I came this way before, the road went downhill; how come it's suddenly changed now and goes uphill?" (Philogelos *Joke Book* 88).

Everyone was amazed at how similar two twin brothers were, but a teacher said, "This one isn't as much like that one as that one is like this one" (Philogelos *Joke Book* 101).

When asked how the educated differed from the uneducated, Aristotle said, "In the same way as the living are different from the dead" (Diogenes Laertius *Lives of the Philosophers* 5.19).

The root of education is bitter, but the fruit is sweet
(Isocrates *frg.* 19).

· III ·

WOMEN

It is reasonable that men who were cowardly or
criminal should be born again as women
(**Plato** *Timaeus* 90e).

Women had very little public life in Greek society and were appallingly undervalued. This chapter might almost better have been entitled "Misogyny." Consider the following selection of *Sayings*, attributed to the comic poet Menander:

- *A woman knows nothing except what she wants to know.*
- *Don't trust your life to a woman.*
- *It isn't easy to find a good woman.*
- *It's better to bury a woman than to marry her.*
- *Don't trust a woman even when she's dead.*
- *A woman who flatters you wants something.*
- *Even women can behave reasonably.*
- *Sea, fire, and woman as the third evil.*
- *A bad woman is a treasure store of bad things.*
- *A woman is the wildest of all wild animals.*
- *When there's no woman around, nothing bad happens to a man.*
- *A woman is silver-coated dirt.*

One type of woman god created from a long-bristled sow. Everything in her house lies in disorder, stained with mud, rolling around on the floor, while she herself, unwashed, sits on the dunghill in unwashed clothes and grows

An octopus on a 4th-century B.C. coin from Syracuse.

fat (Semonides *frg.* 7.2–6; the first of ten types of women, nearly all of which are very negatively portrayed).

The people of Mytilene [her hometown on the island of Lesbos] *honor Sappho, even though she is a woman* (Aristotle *Rhetoric* 1398b).

As she danced, the girl threw up twelve hoops one after the other, judging just how high to throw them so that she could catch them in time to the music. Socrates said, "The girl's performance is just one of many proofs that women are not naturally inferior to men; they lack only sense and strength." . . . Then a round board studded with swords fixed upright was brought in, and the dancer leaped in and out of the circle of swords. The audience was afraid she might get hurt, but she performed confidently and without being harmed (Xenophon *Symposium* 2.8).

Women should marry when they are about eighteen years old, and men at thirty-seven, since that is when they are in the prime of life, and they will both grow old together when their time for child production is over (Aristotle *Politics* 1335a).

Women are more compassionate than men, more easily moved to tears. But they are also more prone to envy, grumbling, criticizing, aggression, depression, pessimism, shamelessness, deceit, trickery, resentment. They are more wakeful than men, more hesitant, harder to rouse to action, and they need less food. Men are braver than women, and more ready to help others. Mollusks demonstrate this difference: when a female cuttlefish is struck by a trident, the male helps her, but if a male is struck, the female flees (Aristotle *History of Animals* 608b).

Where women are treated badly, as in Sparta, almost half of that society is deprived of happiness (Aristotle *Rhetoric* 1361a; a perhaps surprisingly enlightened remark).

Socrates: *Is there anyone to whom you entrust more important matters than to your wife?*
Critobulus: *No one.*
Socrates: *Is there anyone with whom you have fewer conversations than with your wife?*
Critobulus: *Not many people, if any.*
(Xenophon *Household Management* 3.12)

The woman called "mother" is not the parent of a child; she's just the one who fosters the newly sown embryo. The parent is the one who mounts her, and she merely preserves the young offshoot, as a stranger would (Aeschylus *Eumenides* 658ff.).

We see the moon shining bright when it is far from the sun, but when it is near to the sun, it disappears and is hidden. A virtuous woman, on the other hand, should be most visible when she is with her husband, but stay hidden at home when she is not with him (Plutarch *Marriage Advice* 139c).

A woman ought not to make friends of her own. She should be content to share acquaintance with her husband's friends (Plutarch *Marriage Advice* 140d).

Theophrastus records that the Ephors fined King Agesilaus for marrying a small woman. "She will provide us," they said, "not with kings, but with kinglets" (Plutarch *Life of Agesilaus* 2).

When he married a small woman, a Spartan said, "One should choose the smallest of evil things" (Plutarch *On Brotherly Love* 482a).

In Sparta all the girls and all the young men who were unmarried used to be locked in together in a dark room, and whichever girl each young man grabbed hold of, that was the girl he married, without a dowry. Lysander [the Spartan general who brought the Peloponnesian War to an end]

was fined for abandoning the girl he got this way and scheming to marry another girl who was far prettier (Athenaeus *Wise Men at Dinner* 555c).

Why are male creatures generally larger than females? Is it because they are warmer, and therefore more prone to growth? Or because they are complete, whereas women are incomplete? Or because males mature slowly, females quickly? (Ps.-Aristotle *Problems* 891b).

> *Seeing a woman being taught to write, Diogenes the Cynic said, "What a sword is being sharpened!"*
>
> *Seeing a woman giving advice to another woman, Diogenes said, "An asp is being given poison by a viper."*
>> (*Papyrus Bouriant* 1 folio 6, from a book of exercises to be copied by schoolboys; a version of the second statement is found in Ps.-Menander *Sayings*).

Theophrastus says that it seems essential to teach women to read and write, enough to be useful in managing household affairs. A more advanced level of education makes them lazy, talkative, and meddlesome (Stobaeus *Anthology* 2.31.31).

St. Jerome expresses clear opinions in favor of celibacy at *Against Jovinian* 1.47, drawing on *About Marriage*, a "golden book" attributed to Theophrastus. For example:

> *A wise man should not marry, above all because it gets in the way of the study of philosophy. It is not possible to devote oneself to one's books and to a wife.*
>
> *Married ladies need expensive clothes, gold, jewelry, maids, furniture of all kinds, litters, and gilded carriages.*
>
> *Then there are the endless complaints all night long:*
>> *"So and so is better dressed when she goes out in public."*
>> *"Why were you looking at the woman next door?"*
>> *"What were you talking about with my maid?"*
>> *"What did you bring me from the market?"*

We can't choose a wife; we have to accept the one that we happen to get. If she is bad-tempered, or stupid, or ugly, or arrogant, or malodorous— whatever faults she has, we find out about them after the wedding. Horses, donkeys, dogs, the lowliest of slaves, clothing, pots, wooden chairs, cups, and earthenware jugs—we try out all such things as part of the buying process. A wife is the only thing not put on display, in case she should seem unsatisfactory before the wedding.

Thargelia of Miletus, who was a very beautiful and wise woman, was married fourteen times (Hippias *frg.* 4).

Crocodile dung is good for giving women's faces a bright and shining complexion. . . . Some dealers deceitfully sell the droppings of starlings fed on rice as a cheap imitation (Dioscorides *Medical Material* 2.80).

A wife should endure whatever befalls her husband, whether through misfortune or mistake, if he is ignorant, or sick, or drunk, or has dealings with other women. This sort of lapse is permissible for men, but never for women, who are punished for such behavior. It is the law, and a wife should respect it without complaining. A wife should also tolerate her husband's anger, his meanness with money, his grumbling about life, his jealousy, his accusations, and any other natural defects he may have. This passage is attributed to Plato's mother, Perictyone, at Stobaeus *Anthology* 4.28, but it is definitely spurious; it may have been written in the 4th or 3rd century B.C., and there is a very high probability that, like all but the tiniest fraction of Greek literature, it was written by a man.

It may be that many people think it inappropriate for a woman to engage in philosophy, or ride a horse, or make a speech in public. . . . A woman should not leave the house either at dawn or at dusk. She should go out, accompanied by one or, at most, two maidservants, when the market is full of people, and when she has something specific to see or something specific to buy for the household (Phintys, daughter of Callicratidas, *On the Proper Behavior of Women* [ca. 400 B.C.], quoted at Stobaeus *Anthology* 4.23).

Phidias sculpted Aphrodite with her foot on a tortoise, signifying to women that they should stay at home and keep silent. A woman should talk either to her husband or through her husband, and she should not be offended if, like a piper, she makes a more impressive sound by means of a tongue that is not her own (Plutarch *Marriage Advice* 142d).

Beauty contests for women were held regularly in some cities. Listing several such events, as well as one for men at Elis, Athenaeus comments, "Theophrastus says somewhere that there are contests for women in modesty and household management, just as there are among the barbarians" (*Wise Men at Dinner* 610a). It would be interesting to know how a modesty contest was judged.

At *On Invention* 1.51, Cicero reports a conversation between Aspasia and Xenophon's wife (after which she asked Xenophon equivalent questions and elicited the same reactions):

> *"Tell me, please—if your neighbor had better gold jewelry than you do, would you prefer to have hers or your own?"*
>
> *"Hers," she said.*
>
> *"Suppose she had more expensive dresses and other such feminine finery than you have; would you prefer your own or hers?"*
>
> *"Hers, of course," she replied.*
>
> *"All right, then, suppose she had a better husband than you have; would you prefer your own husband or hers?"*
>
> *At this point, the woman blushed.*

In the tense times before the decisive Greek victory at Plataea in 479 B.C., *Lycidas, a member of the Athenian Council, proposed that the assembly should give a hearing to an ambassador sent by the Persians. (He made this proposal either because he had been bribed or because he really thought it was a good idea.) His fellow councilors and those outside the meeting place stoned him to death. . . . When the Athenian women learned what was happening, they went to Lycidas's house and stoned his wife and children as well* (Herodotus *Histories* 9.5).

There is a story that the Amazons dislocate the joints of their own male offspring when they are still very young, either at the knees or at the hips. The purpose is said to be to make them lame, so that they will not plot against the women. They exploit them as craftsmen, in sedentary jobs such as shoemaking and brass working. I do not know if this is actually true (Hippocrates *On the Joints* 53).

The Graeae, "the Old Women," were three sisters who shared a single eye, a single ear, and a single tooth. Perseus forced them to help him in his attack on Medusa by intercepting the eye as it was being handed from one of the sisters to another. Pythagoras suggested that the myth was inspired by the remarkable readiness with which women lend each other articles of clothing or jewelry without a witness to the transaction and without recourse to legal proceedings to get them back (Iamblichus *On the Pythagorean Way of Life* 55).

Fishing with poison is quick and easy, but it makes the fish inedible and worthless. Likewise, when women use love-potions and magic spells on

Circe tries to give a potion to Odysseus.

their husbands, gaining control of them through pleasure, they find themselves living with dull-witted and brainless shells of men. Circe derived no benefit from the men she turned into pigs and donkeys with her drugs, whereas she was passionately in love with Odysseus, who lived with her in full possession of his senses (Plutarch *Marriage Advice* 139a).

When Hecuba says of Achilles, "I wish I could take hold of his liver and eat it," the expression might seem unacceptably exaggerated, if we did not already know about her sufferings. In fact this is an appropriate thing for an old woman to say when her child has not simply been killed, but also maltreated after death and left unburied (Scholion to Homer *Iliad* 24.212, after Achilles kills Hecuba's son Hector in a duel).

STEPMOTHERS

Bees derive honey from thyme, the most bitter and arid of plants. Likewise, sensible people often draw benefit and profit from the most awkward situations. We really should try to do this, like the man who threw a stone at his dog, but missed it and hit his stepmother; "Not so bad!" he said. For we can change Fortune when it does not suit us (Plutarch *On the Tranquility of the Mind* 467c).

Do not marry again when I am dead, I beg you, for a stepmother is hostile to the former children, no more gentle than a viper (Euripides *Alcestis* 309).

When Aesop was asked why wild plants grow quickly, whereas those that people sow or plant grow slowly, he replied, "Because the earth is mother to wild plants, but stepmother to the others" (*Gnomologium Vaticanum* 125).

You know how everyone thinks that stepmothers, however good they may be in other respects, hate their stepchildren. This is considered to be a mania shared by all women (Lucian *The Disowned Son* 31).

He does not use the word "stepmother," since that has negative connotations. Instead he says "one's father's wife" (Theodoretus *Interpretation of the Fourteen Letters of St. Paul* 82.261 [on *First Corinthians* 5.1]).

A dream involving one's stepmother is not good,
whether she is alive or dead

(**Artemidorus** *Interpretation of Dreams* 3.26).

· IV ·

SEX

People derive as much pleasure from scratching
themselves as they do from having sex
(**Democritus** *frg.* 127).

What man could derive more pleasure from sleeping with the most beau-
tiful woman than from staying awake to study what Xenophon has
written about Panthea, or Aristobulus about Timoclea, or Theopompus
about Thebe? (Plutarch *A Pleasant Life Is Impossible on Epicurean Prin-*
ciples 1093*c*). Xenophon tells the uplifting tale of the noble Panthea at
The Education of Cyrus 6.1; the other accounts are lost.

Tiresias once saw two snakes mating. He wounded one of them and was
changed into a woman. Apollo prophesied that, if he saw two snakes mating
again and wounded one of them, he would be turned back into a man.
Tiresias watched for an opportunity, did what the god said, and was turned
into a man again. Zeus had an argument with Hera, maintaining that
women derive more pleasure from sex than men do, whereas Hera claimed
the opposite. They agreed to ask Tiresias, since he had experience of both
sexes. He said that men get 10 percent of the pleasure, women 90 percent.
This angered Hera, who stabbed him in the eyes, making him blind, but
Zeus gave him the gift of prophecy and a life span of seven generations
(Dicaearchus of Messana *frg.* 37).

Throwing apples was a ploy in seduction, since the apple is sacred to Aphrodite (Scholion to Aristophanes *Clouds* 997).

> *An incantation to be recited three times over an apple:*
>
> *I shall throw apples [at . . .]. I shall give this charm, always appropriate and edible for mortals and immortal gods. Whatever woman I give this apple to, whatever woman I throw it at and hit with it, may she go crazy with love for me, forgetting all about everything else, whether she takes it in her hand and eats it . . . or lays it in her lap. May she not stop loving me. Queen Aphrodite, born on Cyprus, make this charm work perfectly.*
> *(Supplementum Magicum Graecum 72.1)*

Those who are not decadent or immoral should regard sexual intercourse as justified only if it takes place within marriage and for the procreation of children, as the law ordains. Sexual intercourse in pursuit of pleasure alone is unjustified and illegal, even within marriage (Musonius Rufus *Discourse* 12).

To deprive a woman of sleep: take a living bat and draw in myrrh on its right wing the figure indicated below [a not particularly mysterious figure sitting on a high couch], *and on its left wing the seven names of the god and also the words "May so-and-so, the daughter of so-and-so, not sleep until she agrees to sleep with me," and then release it* (Greek Magical Papyri 12.376).

To have an erection whenever you wish: mix up crushed pepper in honey and smear your thing (Greek Magical Papyri 7.185). There is a hole (caused by a worm) in the middle of the last word in the papyrus, which actually reads π[. . .]μα. πράγμα (*pragma*, "thing," used here as a euphemism) is a modern conjecture to repair the damage. Other scholars prefer πέλμα (*pelma*, "sole of the foot"). I do not know whether any practical experiments have been done to solve this textual problem.

The Indian had a quite amazing plant. It was not for eating. A man who rubs his penis with it allegedly gets an erection powerful enough for him to

have intercourse with as many women as he wants. Some men said that by this means they had managed twelve times, but the Indian himself, who was a big, strong fellow, said he had once managed seventy times, though his sperm came in mere drops and was eventually bloody. He also claimed that women become unusually eager for intercourse when they use this drug. If this is true, it is extremely powerful (Theophrastus *Enquiry into Plants* 9.18). Theophrastus does not actually identify the plant.

Grind the ashes left after burning a deer's tail and then make a paste of the powder by adding wine. Smear this paste on the testicles and penis of an animal being put to stud, and you will stimulate its desire to mate. Smearing olive oil on its genitals counteracts the stimulus. The same procedure works for humans as well (*Farm Work* 19.5).

On a lapis lazuli, engrave an ostrich with a fish in its mouth. Put under the stone an orchid seed and a sliver of the gizzard in the ostrich's stomach. Close the amulet and wear it to ensure a completely sound digestion. It also causes an erection and fosters interest in sex. It is especially effective in causing an erection for men who are already old and for those who want to have frequent sexual intercourse. It also makes the wearer seductive (*Cyranides* 1.18).

The testicles of a weasel can both ensure and prevent conception. If the right testicle, reduced to ashes and mixed in a paste with myrrh, is inserted into a woman's vagina on a small ball of wool before intercourse, she will conceive immediately. But if the left testicle is wrapped in mule-skin and attached [we are not told how] *to the woman, it prevents conception. The following words have to be written on the mule-skin:* "ioa, oia, rauio, ou, oicoochx" [these groups of letters are meaningless]. *If you are skeptical, try it on a bird that is laying eggs; it will not lay any eggs at all while the testicle is attached to it* (*Cyranides* 2.7).

A fibula is a little ring that tragic and comic actors have inserted into their penis, to prevent them from having sexual intercourse, for fear that they might lose their voice (Scholion to Juvenal *Satires* 6.379).

A terra-cotta model of a sandal with the word ΑΚΟΛΟΥΘ[Ε]Ι (*AKOLOUTH[E]I*, "follow [me]") picked out in the nails on the sole. Presumably a prostitute might wear such sandals.

PROSTITUTES

Moirichus wanted Phryne to sleep with him, but when she demanded a high price, he complained, "But didn't you sleep with some foreigner recently for far less?" She replied, "Just you wait then until I actually want to fuck you, and I'll accept far less" (Machon *Anecdotes* 18.450).

Many women even have figures in erotic postures engraved on the soles of their sandals so that they can leave an impression of their obscene thoughts on the ground as they walk along (St. Clement of Alexandria *Paedagogus* 2.11.116).

The tears of a politician and the tears of a prostitute are equally sincere (Ps.-Menander *Sayings* 584).

The prostitute Metiche had the nickname "Waterclock" because she would have sex until all the water had run out of the jar (Athenaeus *Wise Men at Dinner* 567c).

In his treatise Prostitutes at Athens, *Apollodorus says that Phanostrate's nickname was "Doorlouse," because she used to stand at the door delousing herself* (Suda s.v. *Phanostrate*).

The following are more names or noms de guerre adopted by prostitutes:

Aedonion	Little Nightingale
Aix	Goat
Boidion	Little Cow
Chelidion	Little Swallow
Cochlis	Snail
Conopion	Mosquito
Corone	Crow
Cynna	Bitch
Dorcas	Gazelle
Hys	Sow
Leaena	Lionness
Leontion	Little Lionness
Lyce	She-Wolf
Melissa	Bee
Moscharion	Little Calf
Myia	Fly
Phryne	Toad
Sepia	Squid
Strouthion	Little Sparrow
Tigris	Tigress

To Thinabdella from Pelaeas and Socraton, the collectors of the tax on prostitutes: You have our authorization to have intercourse with anyone you wish here on the date given below—Year Fourteen, Phaophi 10 [October 7, A.D. 111] (*Wilcken Ostraca* 1157, written in Greek at Elephantis in Roman Egypt).

In Ptolemy Philadelphus's great parade at Alexandria, the objects on display included *a gold phallus one hundred and eighty feet long, painted in various colors and bound with golden garlands. At its tip, it had a gold star nine feet in circumference* (Athenaeus *Wise Men at Dinner* 201e). It is not the phallus per se, but its size, that is remarkable. A phallus, as a fertility symbol, was appropriate to festivals in honor of various deities: *Since they happen to be Athenian colonists,* [the people of Paros are] *to send a cow and a suit of armor to the Panathenaea, and a cow and a phallus in commemoration to the Dionysia* (from an inscription, dated

A woman carrying a phallus. Note the eye near the top of the phallus, intended to ward off evil.

to 372 B.C., found on the slope of the Athenian acropolis; Rhodes and Osborne *Inscriptions* 29).

Chrysippus of Soli is considered to be an ornament to the Stoic sect of philosophers because of his many wise treatises, but he misinterprets the Samian painting in which Hera is portrayed performing an unspeakable act for Zeus. The revered philosopher says in his writings that matter receives the words of god as seed and keeps them within herself, for the adornment of the universe, Hera representing matter and Zeus representing god in the Samian painting (Origen *Against Celsus* 4.48). Origen is discussing an allegorical interpretation of Hera fellating Zeus on a mural in her temple on Samos, a portrayal that puzzled many Greeks.

At the Scira [an Athenian festival for women], *participants used to eat garlic, to ensure that they abstained from sexual intercourse, and so as not to smell of perfume* (Philochorus *frg.* 89). An inscription records the generous provision for buying garlic for the women of one Attic deme for the Scira (*Greek Inscriptions* 2² 1184.15).

Why is it not appropriate to make love while barefoot? Is it because the inner parts of the body, when we are intent on sex, should be warm and moist? . . . Being barefoot causes dryness and cold, making it difficult or impossible to have sexual intercourse (Ps.-Aristotle *Problems* 877a).

Why do people whose eyelashes drop out have a strong sex drive? Is it for the same reason as with bald men? (They both involve the same region of the body.) . . . The answer is that lust chills the upper parts of the body, which have little blood; nourishment is not digested there, and being starved of nourishment, the hair falls out (Ps.-Aristotle *Problems* 878b).

Why are people ashamed to admit that they want to have sexual intercourse, whereas this is not the case with drinking or eating or other such things? Is it because most of our desires are for things we must have, some of them actually being essential for life, whereas sexual desire is a non-vital indulgence? (Ps.-Aristotle *Problems* 880a).

The Cyrenaic school of philosophy maintains that we should not indulge in sexual intercourse in the light, but rather under a veil of darkness, so that our minds do not repeatedly kindle desire by picking up images of the sexual act through having seen it clearly (Plutarch *A Pleasant Life Is Impossible on Epicurean Principles* 1089a).

Pausanias refers to a temple of Black Aphrodite in Arcadia, noting that the goddess *is so called because humans, unlike animals, generally have sexual intercourse during the night rather than in the day* (*Guide to Greece* 8.6).

The philosopher Favorinus was a eunuch, but he was so passionate about sex that he was prosecuted for adultery by an ex-consul (Philostratus *Lives of the Sophists* 489).

Sexual intercourse has never done anyone any good, and we should be content if it does us no actual harm (Epicurus *frg.* 62).

The athlete Cleitomachus was admired because he always stood up and went away whenever anyone started talking about sex (Plutarch *Table Talk* 710e). By contrast, Pliny reports that *when athletes are sluggish, sexual intercourse restores their strength* (*Natural History* 28.58), but this was very much a minority view in antiquity.

What is "plucking" and "radishing"? Well, listen. A poor man who was caught committing adultery was laid out in the middle of the marketplace and had hot ashes sprinkled over his genitals, the hair being thus removed. Then the end of a radish was thrust into his orifice, making it wider (Scholion to Aristophanes *Wealth* 168). A fish, specifically a mullet, might be used in the latter procedure, a more awkward alternative because of the spines.

Astyanassa was the slave of Menelaus's wife, Helen. She discovered the sexual positions and wrote about methods of intercourse. Philaenis and Elephantis imitated her, portraying such outrageous things in dances (Suda s.v. *Astyanassa*). Fragments of Philaenis's manual have survived on *Oxyrhynchus Papyrus* 2891, but they are brief and barely legible. Under the heading "On Seductions," the introductory words, "The seducer should be scruffy and not comb his hair, so that the woman can't see that he's at work," are hardly very salacious.

Africanus says that the Gorgon plant grows mostly underground but that, if a girl has sexual intercourse near it, it shoots up to watch and observes what is going on with considerable curiosity. It is also very easy for Africanus to restore a woman's virginity even if she has had intercourse with many men (Michael Psellus *Opusculum* 32). The Gorgon plant has not

The stump of one of two monumental *phalloi* in the sanctuary of Dionysus on Delos, with a phallus-bird sculpted in relief on the base.

A nymph with an ithyphallic satyr.

been securely identified, and the restoration of virginity is not discussed in the surviving portions of Africanus's works.

Much thought was given on Crete to legislation intended to encourage the useful practice of eating sparingly, and homosexuality was introduced to prevent too high a birth rate through intercourse with women; whether rightly or wrongly, there will be another opportunity to consider (Aristotle *Politics* 1272*a*).

> *Sexual intercourse is a brief attack of apoplexy*
> (**Democritus** *frg.* 32).

· V ·

ANIMALS

Why do all animals have an even number of feet?
Is it because movement other than jumping is not
possible unless one foot is stationary?

(Ps.-Aristotle *Problems* 893*b*).

Hares became so numerous on the island of Astypalaea that the inhabi-
tants consulted the oracle about them. The Pythia replied that they should
breed dogs and hunt the hares. More than six thousand were caught in one
year. This plague happened because someone from the island of Anaphe
had introduced two hares, just as someone from Astypalaea had earlier
released two partridges on Anaphe; the partridge population grew so big
that the inhabitants of the island were in danger of having to move away
(Hegesander *frg.* 42).

An evil viper once bit a Cappadocian, but the snake itself died, when it
tasted his poisonous blood (Demodocus *Greek Anthology* 11.237).

To determine how long they live, Alexander the Great attached collars
to a large number of deer. When they were captured a hundred years
later they still showed no signs of old age (Solinus *The Wonders of the*
World 19.18).

Some people hate particular animals, such as weasels, beetles, toads, and snakes (Plutarch *On Envy and Hatred* 537a). Spiders might seem conspicuously absent from this list. Arachnophobia is a pure Greek term, but it is a modern coinage. Spiders are rarely mentioned in surviving ancient texts as an object of fear. Lucian's reference to spiders in the yarn he spins at *True History* 1.15 is exceptional: *Endymion's army had about sixty million infantry, including many huge spiders, each bigger than one of the Cycladic islands, that had been ordered to spin a web between the moon and the morning star.*

The Psylli [an African tribe] *often filled Italy with poisonous creatures from other countries so that they could make money at the expense of other people's misery* [by getting rid of them]. *They tried to introduce scorpions, but they could not survive the climate north of Sicily* (Pliny *Natural History* 11.89). Pliny was probably referring to a particularly nasty species, for there are nowadays some twenty-seven species of scorpion ranging quite far north in Europe.

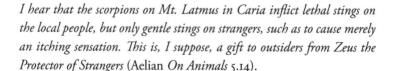

There are said to be so many scorpions on the second stage of the road from Susa to Media that, three days before he travels along it, the King of Persia commands everyone to hunt for them, and he gives rewards to the person who catches the most (Aelian *On Animals* 15.26). *The region around Susa is so hot that at noon in the summer lizards and snakes cannot cross the street quickly enough to avoid being burned to death when they are half-way across* (Strabo *Geography* 15.3.10).

I hear that the scorpions on Mt. Latmus in Caria inflict lethal stings on the local people, but only gentle stings on strangers, such as to cause merely an itching sensation. This is, I suppose, a gift to outsiders from Zeus the Protector of Strangers (Aelian *On Animals* 5.14).

Anyone who is stung by a scorpion should sit on a donkey, facing backward toward its tail, for this transfers the pain to the donkey and makes it fart (*Farm Work* 13.9).

When he was being bitten by many fleas, a fool put out the light, saying, "You can't see me any more" (Ps.-Lucian *Greek Anthology* 11.432).

If you are ever in a place where there are fleas, say, "Och! Och!" [with a long *o*, rhyming with "joke"] *and they will leave you alone* (*Farm Work* 13.15).

Perhaps not many countries nowadays would feature a scorpion on their coinage.

Bugs are useful, because they wake us up, and mice motivate us not to leave all our possessions lying around untidily (Chrysippus *frg.* 1163).

Mice are said to nibble iron and gold. That is why gold miners cut them up and extract the gold (Photius *The Library* 278.528).

If a mouse cannot reach the oil in a lamp with its tongue, it inserts its tail and then licks the oil off it (Timotheus of Gaza *On Animals* 38).

Take a piece of paper and write on it: "I conjure any mice caught here to do me no harm and to allow no other mouse to do so either. I grant you such-and-such a piece of ground (and you specify which piece of ground). But if I catch you still here, I swear by the Mother of the Gods, I shall cut you into seven pieces." When you have written this, attach the paper to a rock where the mice are, with the writing facing outward, before sunrise (*Farm Work* 13.5). The author feels moved to add: *I have written this for the sake of completion, but I hope it has no validity. I reject these practices and advise everyone else to do the same, paying no attention to any such ridiculous measures.*

Weasels give birth through their ears, though some say through their mouths (Timotheus of Gaza *On Animals* 39).

Weasels occur on one side of the road that runs across the island of Pordoselene, but not on the other (Aristotle *History of Animals* 605b).

The blood of the chameleon, and likewise that of green frogs, is thought to remove the hairs on the eyelids (Dioscorides *Medical Material* 2.79).

The people of Pergamum paid a substantial sum for the skin of a basilisk, to ensure that a temple decorated with murals by Apelles was kept free of spiders' webs and birds (Solinus *The Wonders of the World* 17.53).

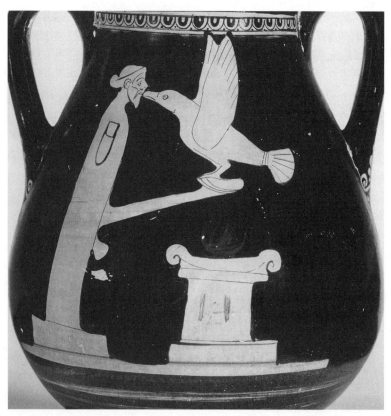

A bird perched on a herm.

There is an island in the Black Sea on which countless birds nest and look after a shrine dedicated to Achilles. Every day at dawn they fly out to sea, and when their wings are drenched with seawater they fly quickly back to the shrine. They sprinkle it with the water and then sweep the floor with their wings (Arrian *Voyage Around the Black Sea* 21).

Indian dogs are said to be a cross between tigers and bitches. Not on the first interbreeding, but on the third. The first cross is said to be a fierce creature. They take the bitches out to a lonely spot. Many get eaten, if the tiger is not in the mood for mating (Aristotle *History of Animals* 607a).

I hear that there was once a flying pig near the city of Clazomenae, and that it devastated the whole countryside. That is why there is a famous region there called "The Place of the Winged Sow." If anyone thinks this is just a myth, that's fair enough, but I don't regret recording what I have heard said about any animal (Aelian *On Animals* 12.38).

Why are pigs particularly sensitive to the cold when they are being fattened? Is it because, just as with fat people, the fatter they become, the further they are away from their internal source of heat? (Ps.-Alexander *Problems* 4.138).

In Arabia, there is an amazing breed of sheep with a tail no less than five feet long. If they were allowed to drag their tails along the ground, they would develop ulcers from the friction. In fact, however, the shepherds are skilled enough at carpentry to make little carts that they fasten under each sheep's tail (Herodotus *Histories* 3.113).

A pig with wings on a two drachma coin minted at Clazomenae in the early 5th century B.C.

This was not the only device used by shepherds. Varro notes that because ewes less than three years old are unsuitable for breeding, they sometimes wear chastity belts, *little baskets made of reeds or some other material, fitted over their reproductive organs* (*Country Affairs* 2.1), though he does comment that *it is easier to look after them if they are pastured away from the rams.*

In the same passage, Varro refers to the practice of putting little leather jackets on "Greek sheep," a breed associated particularly with the south of Italy, to protect their especially fine and expensive wool. They were allowed to graze only in pastures from which all brambles and other bushes had been cleared, and their jackets had to be removed regularly to prevent them from overheating (Columella *On Farming* 7.4).

Sleeping among sheep is not as warm as among goats, for goats are less restive and come up close to people (Aristotle *History of Animals* 606a).

Hedgehogs shake vines with their paws and then roll around to impale the fallen grapes on their spines, so that they can take them to their young. When I was a boy, I once saw a hedgehog that looked like a walking bunch of grapes (Plutarch *On the Cleverness of Animals* 972a, in a dialogue discussing whether land or sea animals are more intelligent; the discussion reaches no clear conclusion).

Hedgehogs are easier to catch than to keep hold of; money is like that, too (Aelian *Miscellaneous History* 4.14).

In the only surviving fragment of a work entitled *On Antipathy and Sympathy*, Nepualius lists various interesting observations on natural history:

- *Storks put a tortoise bone and the leaves of a plane tree in their nests because of the bats.*
- *Owls put a bat's heart in their nests to prevent ants from removing their eggs or their hatchlings.*

A terra-cotta hedgehog with grapes attached, found in the Athenian agora. That hedgehogs do transport grapes in this way is a securely attested fact.

- *If you put a bat's heart close to an ants' nest, the ants will not come near it, and they die.*
- *Warm goat's blood dissolves diamonds.*
- *Neither horses nor cows walk on anything you smear with lion fat.*
- *A horse goes numb if it treads on the fresh tracks of a wolf.*
- *Lions are afraid of roosters, especially white ones.*
- *If anyone smears himself with rooster fat, this turns aside a lion's charge.*
- *If you smear yourself with elephant fat, no wild animal will come near you.*

There are two ways to catch long-tailed monkeys. They are imitative creatures that tend to run off up the trees. So when hunters spot one sitting in the trees, they put out a bowl of water where the monkey can see it, and rub their eyes with the water. Then they put out a bowl filled with birdlime rather than water and go off and watch from a distance. The animal jumps down and smears itself with the birdlime. When it blinks, its eyelids stick together, and the hunters run up and seize it. That is one way of catching monkeys, and here is another: the hunters put on baggy trousers and move away, leaving behind other pairs of pants that are smeared on the inside with birdlime, and then the monkeys are easily caught when they put them on (Strabo *Geography* 15.1.29).

About four hundred names for Greek and Roman dogs are known. They are almost never human names. The longest list is given by Xenophon at *Hunting* 7.5: forty-seven names for hunting dogs, all just two syllables long, to make it easy to give them commands. For example:

Actis	Sunshine
Alce	Strength
Bia	Force
Bremon	Roarer
Caenon	Killer
Chara	Joy
Hebe	Youth
Hybris	Violence
Lochus	Ambush
Lonche	Spear
Phlegon	Flaming
Phonax	Bloodthirsty
Phylax	Guard
Psyche	Soul
Rhome	Vigor
Sperchon	Rushing
Stibon	Tracker
Thymus	Bravery

Cattle recognize their herdsman's voice, and understand when he calls them by name, and respond to what he tells them to do (*Farm Work* 17.2). Cows sometimes have Egyptian names in papyrus documents written in Greek in Roman Egypt.

No names for cats are known from either Greece or Rome.

According to Procopius (*History of the Wars* 7.29.9), a whale, given the name Porphyrius, caused trouble in the waters around Constantinople for more than fifty years, sinking ships and carrying off sailors. It evaded all attempts by the emperor Justinian to catch it, but eventually beached itself while pursuing an unusually large pod of dolphins.

Although he suppresses the names of generals in the Carthaginian army, Cato records that the elephant that fought most bravely in their battle line was called Syrus [the Syrian]. When Antiochus the Great tried to ford a river, Ajax, the elephant that normally led the troupe, refused to go across. Antiochus announced that the first elephant to cross would be made troupe leader. Patroclus dared to go first and was rewarded with a silver harness (an elephant's greatest delight) and all the other emblems of leadership. Ajax preferred to starve himself to death rather than endure his disgrace (Pliny *Natural History* 8.11).

Ajax's name was perhaps unlucky, for it is difficult not to recall that the Homeric hero with that name, who was distinguished by his large size, committed suicide, unable to bear the shame when the arms of Achilles (made after Hector despoiled Patroclus's corpse) were awarded to Odysseus, not to him.

A female Indian elephant named Nicaea took care of its keeper's infant child when his wife died, rocking its cradle with its trunk whenever it cried (Aelian *On Animals* 11.14). This elephant belonged to the army of Antigonus Gonatas, king of Macedon, whose elephants were panicked during the siege of Megara by pigs hurled over the wall after they had been doused with oil and set on fire (Aelian *On Animals* 16.36).

An elephant with an ornamental belt, on a coin of Apollodotus I of Bactria. The inscription reads ΒΑΣΙΛΕΩΣ ΑΠΟΛΛΟΔΟΤΟΥ ΣΩΤΗΡΟΣ (*basileos Apollodotou* [illegible] *soteros*, "King Apollodotus Savior").

Nicon, an elephant in the army of King Pyrrhus of Epirus (ruled 306–302 and 297–272 B.C.), rescued its wounded rider, who had fallen off in a battle in the streets of Argos. Picking him up with its trunk, it laid him across its tusks and trampled friend and foe to bring him to safety (Plutarch *Life of Pyrrhus* 33).

A fighting cock called Centaur fell in love with Secundus, the wine-pourer of Nicomedes, the king of Bithynia (Athenaeus *Wise Men at Dinner* 606b). Centaur is also one of only two known names of fighting cocks portrayed on 5th-century B.C. Athenian vases. The other is Aeacides ("descendant of Aeacus" = Achilles).

In the game of quail knocking, they provoked the birds by scratching and poking them. Then they drew a circle on a board like a baker's tray and set the quails on it to fight each other. The quail that flinched and fell outside the circle was the loser (Pollux *Onomasticon* 9.107).

At Patras, in honor of Artemis, the goddess of hunting, they throw edible birds onto a fire while still alive, along with all sorts of other sacrificial victims, even wild boar and various species of deer. Some people actually bring wolf and bear cubs, or even fully grown wolves and bears. I have seen animals, including a bear, forced to the outside of the pyre by the first blast of the flames, and some actually getting away thanks to their own strength. But those who threw them on bring them back at once to the fire. There is no record of anyone being hurt during this ceremony (Pausanias *Guide to Greece* 7.18).

Pythagoras captured the she-bear that was ravaging the Daunian region. He stroked her for a long time and fed her by hand with barley cakes and fruit. Then he released her, after making her swear not to touch a living creature ever again. She went straight off into the mountains and the woods and was never again seen attacking even the humblest animal (Porphyry *Life of Pythagoras* 23).

A hunter charged by a wild boar should fall facedown and grab hold of any plants growing beneath him. If the beast attacks him when he is lying

*in that position, it cannot get a hold on his body because of the way its
tusks curve upward; but if he is standing up, he will definitely be gored*
(Xenophon *On Hunting* 10.13).

It is a serious difficulty in reading ancient accounts of natural history,
whether written in Greek or in Latin, that it is often impossible to
determine precisely the flower, fish, animal, or bird being referred to.
For example, Aristotle observes that "the most powerful species of
hawk is the Three-Testicle" (*History of Animals* 620a), but the species
is no longer identifiable.

*It is thought that no animal is more timorous than the chameleon, and
that this is why it changes color. But it does have tremendous power over
sparrowhawks. It is said to draw down any sparrowhawk that flies over-
head, rendering it a helpless victim for the other animals to rip apart*
(Pliny *Natural History* 28.113, drawing skeptically on Democritus).

*Observers say that the hawk flies upside down, like a man swimming on
his back* (Aelian *On Animals* 10.14).

Falconry was imported from the east in the Byzantine period. There
are several admirably detailed manuals on the breeding and care of
hawks and other such birds. *If your hawk snores and is in pain and
cannot eat, it has picked up a throat inflammation. Give it meat sprinkled
with iron filings, and it will be cured* (Demetrius of Constantinople
Hawk Wisdom 151).

*As long as a pair of eagles stays together, every second one of their offspring
is an osprey. Ospreys produce black eagles and vultures. That is not the end
of the line of vultures, for black vultures produce great vultures, and these
are sterile, as is indicated by the fact that no one has ever seen a great
vulture's nest* (Ps.-Aristotle *On Marvelous Things Heard* 835a).

*When cranes rest for the night, three or four of them keep watch while the
others sleep. So as not to fall asleep during their watch, they stand on one*

leg, holding a stone firmly and carefully in the foot that is raised up. If they ever fail to notice that they are slipping off into sleep, the stone falls and makes a noise, and this forces them to wake up (Aelian *On Animals* 3.13). Similar stories are told about Aristotle and Alexander the Great.

Apsethus the Libyan trained a large number of parrots to say "Apsethus is a god." He then released them, and they persuaded the Libyans that he was a god. But a Greek shrewdly saw through the so-called god's trick. He caught many of the same parrots and taught them to say instead, "Apsethus put us in a cage and forced us to say 'Apsethus is a god.'" When the Libyans heard the parrots' change of tune, they gathered together and burned Apsethus to death (Hippolytus *Refutation of All Heresies* 6.8).

To teach a parrot to talk, you should speak to it from behind a mirror. The parrot is tricked into thinking that it is listening to another parrot and rapidly imitates what it hears (Photius *The Library* 223.215b).

Short-necked birds with crooked talons and flat tongues tend to be mimics. The Indian bird, the parrot, is like this. And it becomes particularly obstreperous when it drinks wine (Aristotle *History of Animals* 597b).

Some say that, if a fledgling swallow is blind, its mother cures its affliction with greater celandine (Dioscorides *Medical Material* 2.180). "Celandine" is derived from χελιδών (*chelidon*, "swallow") because, as Dioscorides says, its growing season begins and ends with the arrival and departure of swallows in summer.

They say that around the Sea of Azov wolves work as a team with the fishermen in catching fish, and if ever the fishermen do not give them a share in the catch, they destroy their nets while they are laid out on the ground to dry (Aristotle *History of Animals* 620b).

Cuttlefish escape capture by discharging the contents of their ink sacs, in imitation of Homer's gods, who often take up stealthily in a dark cloud those whom they wish to save (Plutarch *The Cleverness of Animals* 977f).

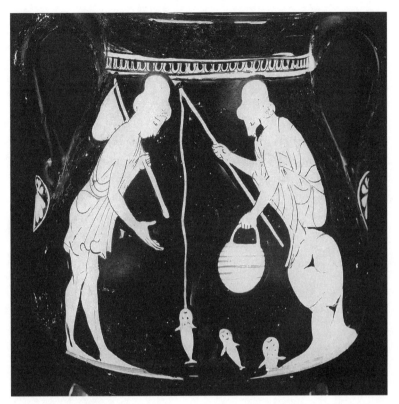

An old couple fishing.

We do not eat lions or wolves, even though that would be a way of defending ourselves against them. We leave such beasts alone, but slaughter tame and harmless creatures, those without stings or teeth to bite us, animals that Nature seems to have produced for the sake of their beauty and grace (Plutarch *On Eating Meat I* 994*b*).

♀

Mongooses are deadly enemies to crocodiles. . . . They lie in wait for them, and when the crocodiles are sunning themselves with their jaws open, they rush into their gaping mouths and emerge from their dead bodies after gnawing their way out through their entrails and stomachs (Strabo *Geography* 17.39). When Pliny tells this tale, he vividly describes the mongoose as "hurling itself like a spear through the crocodile's jaws" (*Natural History* 8.89).

A logical problem: *If a crocodile snatches your child when it finds him wandering beside the river and promises to give him back to you if you can say correctly whether it intends to give him back or not, what will you say it intends to do?* (Lucian *Ways of Life for Sale* 22).

Why do beasts of burden not belch, nor cattle, nor any horned animal, nor birds? Is it because their stomachs are so dry, expending moisture quickly and filtering it through? It is when moisture is retained and becomes aerated that belching occurs. Because animals with manes have long necks, their breath rushes downward, and so they are particularly prone to passing gas. Birds and horned animals neither belch nor pass gas (Ps.-Aristotle *Problems* 895a).

Elephants are said to be immune to other ailments, but they are troubled by flatulence (Aristotle *History of Animals* 604a).

Why does no animal have a pleasant smell except the panther, at which other animals are said to enjoy sniffing? (Ps.-Aristotle *Problems* 907b). No discussion of this peculiarity of panthers is offered.

A man-headed bull being crowned by Victory.

Only humans have understanding. Other creatures have perception, but they do not have understanding (Alcmaeon of Croton *frg. 1a*).

Only humans have a sense of rhythm (Plato *Laws* 653*e*).

Only humans can count (Aristotle *Topics* 142*b*).

Only humans can be tickled, because they have delicate skin and because they are the only animals that laugh (Aristotle *On the Parts of Animals* 673*a*).

Human beings, bats, and elephants are the only animals to have breasts on their chests (Clearchus *frg.* 110).

- *Only humans stand upright.*
- *Only humans have hands, which are responsible for most of the advantages that make us happier than creatures that move on all fours.*
- *Only humans can speak.*
- *Other animals have sexual urges only at particular times of the year, but human beings have them continually until old age.*
- *What race of living creatures other than humans worships gods?*

    (Xenophon *Memoirs of Socrates* 1.4)

Lack of hairiness is what particularly sets human beings apart from animals. If man is the holiest of all animals, and the holiest of men are those who have had the good fortune to lose their hair, then a bald man would be the most divine creature on earth

(Synesius *In Praise of Baldness* 5).

· VI ·

ATHENS

Athens, with its massive hinterland, Attica, is slightly larger than Luxemburg and almost as large as Rhode Island, dwarfing most other Greek *poleis*. Some outstanding classicists rarely venture outside 5th- and 4th-century B.C. Athens, with all the wealth of literature, history, and philosophy that it offers. Such Athenocentricity in modern scholarship would be more problematic, were it not in fact to some extent justified. The intellectual output of other great *poleis*, such as Sparta, Thebes, Argos, Corinth, and Syracuse, was negligible or nonexistent for centuries at a time, and the Greeks themselves acknowledged the special position held by Athens:

- After recounting how the tyrant Pisistratus regained power in Athens by the simple ruse of dressing a tall and handsome peasant girl as Athena in her full armor and riding with her into the city in a chariot, while heralds announced that the goddess was bringing him back, Herodotus expresses surprise that the trick worked, given that the Greeks have always been more intelligent than barbarians, and that the Athenians have a reputation for being more intelligent than other Greeks (*Histories* 1.60).
- Athens is described as "the Greece of Greece" (Ἑλλάδος Ἑλλάς, *Hellados Hellas*) in *Greek Anthology* 7.45, an epitaph for Euripides attributed to the historian Thucydides.

- Heraclides Criticus, in the 3rd century B.C., says that "when it comes to the pleasures and refinements of life, Athens excels all other cities by as much as all other cities are different from farms" (*Description of Greece* 1.4). He then adds the warning: "You have to watch out for the prostitutes in Athens; otherwise, while you are enjoying yourself, you may be ruined without realizing it."
- Although he was a scholar in Alexandria, which might claim intellectual preeminence in the Greek world, Philo of Alexandria admits: "I regard the Athenians as having a sharper intellect than any other Greeks—what the pupil is to the eye or reason is to the soul, that is what Athens is to Greece" (*Every Good Man Is Free* 140).
- *It seems well said of Athens that it produces good men who are outstandingly excellent and bad men who are supremely wicked, just as it produces the sweetest honey and the deadliest hemlock* (Plutarch *Life of Dion* 58).

Athens is the only state that has flourished as a democracy. The Athenians achieved greatness with that form of government, for they outdid all other Greeks in native intelligence and showed the highest regard for established laws (Pausanias *Guide to Greece* 4.35).

At the height of its prosperity the Athenian democracy was financed by the harsh exploitation of untold thousands of slaves in the silver mines at Laurium and by the subjection of the tribute-paying allies. The whole citizen population of Mytilene was condemned to death or slavery for trying to secede in 427 B.C., only to be spared at the last moment; there was no such reprieve for the people of Melos in 416.

Our present system of government is the same as it nearly always has been in the past. Some people call it a democracy, whereas other people call it whatever they like. It is actually an aristocracy approved of by the masses (Plato *Menexenus* 238c). Socrates is said to be reporting a funeral speech in honor of the Athenian war dead, purportedly written by Aspasia, Pericles's mistress.

In theory, Athens was a democracy, but in practice it was ruled by just the one leading man (Thucydides *History* 2.65, referring to the dominant influence of Pericles in the heyday of the Athenian empire).

Thucydides the historian is not to be confused with his namesake, the leader of the oligarchic opposition to Pericles. *When asked by King Archidamus of Sparta whether he or Pericles was the better wrestler, Thucydides* [the politician] *complained, "Whenever I throw him, Pericles argues that he hasn't fallen, and he gains the victory by convincing those who have actually seen him falling"* (Plutarch *Life of Pericles* 8).

To ensure attendance at the assembly, shops were closed, streets not leading to the meeting place were blocked off, a rope soaked in bright red paint was used to herd citizens to the assembly, and those who did not arrive in time to avoid the rope were fined. Sometime early in the 4th century B.C., payment for attendance at the assembly was introduced.

Slave: *Do you come from a genteel family?*
Sausage-seller: *God, no! From a worthless one.*
Slave: *Lucky you! That'll give you a great advantage in politics.*
(Aristophanes *Knights* 185–86).

Plutarch expresses great admiration for the openness and vigor of the Athenian democracy at *Advice on Government* 799d:

> *The Carthaginians were surly and sullen and did not tolerate frivolity in the running of the state. They would never have agreed to an adjournment of the assembly if Cleon requested one because he had made a sacrifice and was expecting guests to dinner, but the Athenians granted it, laughing and clapping their hands.*
>
> *Nor, if a quail escaped from under Alcibiades's cloak while he was addressing their assembly, would the Carthaginians have eagerly joined in the hunt for it and given it back to him, as the Athenians did.*
>
> *They would have put both Cleon and Alcibiades to death for insolent and frivolous conduct. After all, they exiled Hanno for aspiring to tyranny because he had a lion carry his baggage when he was on military campaigns.*
>
> *If the Thebans had captured Philip of Macedon's messengers, who were carrying a letter from him to Olympias, I do not think that they would*

have refrained, as the Athenians did, from opening the affectionate private correspondence of an absent husband to his wife.

I am quite sure that the Spartans would not have tolerated the insolent buffoonery of Stratocles, who persuaded the Athenians to celebrate a victory with sacrifices and, when it was reported that they had in fact been defeated and everyone was angry with him, he then asked what harm he had done the Athenian people: had they not, thanks to him, been happy for three days?

I fully agree with the observation that no man who throws himself into politics, relying on the good faith of the people, ever has a happy death (Pausanias *Guide to Greece* 1.8.3). Pausanias is commenting on the suicide of Demosthenes, who took poison hidden in a reed pen when abandoned by the Athenians to the mercy of the Macedonians.

Gangs of young men from respectable families prowled the streets of Athens, looking for trouble. One such gang called themselves the *Ithyphalloi* (the Erect Phalluses); another, the *Triballoi*, named after a wild Thracian tribe, used to eat food set out for the goddess Hecate and the pigs' testicles offered to the gods as a purification before the assembly met (Demosthenes *Against Conon* 14, 39).

A graffito of a wild Thracian.

It is the responsibility of the King Archon to set up on both banks of the Ilissus a notice prohibiting the soaking of animal skins in the river upstream from the shrine of Heracles, as well as the tanning of hides and the throwing of waste material into the river (Greek Inscriptions I³ 1.257, a fragmentary marble slab found southeast of the Acropolis in the 1920s). This environmental ordinance is datable to sometime between 450 and 420 B.C. and possibly had some effect, if we may judge by the famously idyllic opening of Plato's *Phaedrus* (which has a dramatic date just a few years later), in which Socrates and Phaedrus come to sit beside the "delightfully pure and clear" stream of the Ilissus.

But any improvement will not have been permanent; commenting on the *Collection of Rivers* by the 3rd-century B.C. scholar-poet Callimachus, Strabo observes that *he says that he laughs at the notion of a poet writing that the Athenian girls "draw pure liquid from the Eridanus," a stream that even cattle would keep away from* (*Geography* 9.1.19).

When Socrates's friends were going along the Hermcarvers' street by the law courts, they met with a large herd of pigs all covered in mud and jostling each other because there were so many of them. There was nowhere to stand aside, so some of the men were knocked over and others were spattered with mud (Plutarch *On the Spirit of Socrates* 580e). Socrates himself had been warned by his "spirit" not to go that route.

Diogenes the Cynic was famous for living in a terra-cotta jar, but he was not the only one: *because of housing shortages, the people who came into Athens from the countryside during the Peloponnesian War lived in jars and in caves* (Scholion to Aristophanes *Knights* 792).

The market officials must ensure that the broad streets traversed by the processions in honor of Zeus the Savior and Dionysus are leveled and cleared as well as possible (*Greek Inscriptions* 2² 380). Leveling and clearing presumably consisted of removing deep strata of detritus and garbage.

The Athenians awarded Choerilus of Samos a gold coin for each line of his poem celebrating their victory over Xerxes (Suda s.v. *Choerilus*; for a different tale about Choerilus, see p. 77).

The Athenians gave Pindar a gift of ten thousand drachmas for one line of poetry in praise of Athens (Isocrates *The Exchange of Property*

166). In what may be another version of this same incident, an anonymous *Life of Pindar* reports that the Thebans fined Pindar for writing, "O splendid and great-citied Athens," and that the Athenians paid the fine on his behalf.

Herodotus received a gift of ten talents from the Athenians for flattering them in his *Histories* (Plutarch *On Herodotus's Spitefulness* 26).

Demosthenes paid Isaeus ten thousand drachmas for private lessons in public speaking (Plutarch *Lives of the Ten Orators* 839f).

Demosthenes paid the actor Neoptolemus ten thousand drachmas for training him in voice control (Plutarch *Lives of the Ten Orators* 844f).

Demosthenes declined to pay the prostitute Lais ten thousand drachmas to sleep with him, *remarking as he turned away in shock at her exorbitant demand, "I don't buy regret at such a high price"* (Aulus Gellius *Attic Nights* 1.8).

Aristotle is credited with writing treatises on the constitution of 158 states. All the others are lost, but the *Athenian Constitution*, doubtfully ascribed to him, survives almost complete on a papyrus published in 1891. It lists the following duties of the city administrators:

- *Two drachmas is to be the maximum amount charged for the hire of a female musician. If two people wish to hire the same girl, they are to cast lots for her.*
- *They must ensure that waste collectors dump sewage at least one mile from the city walls.*
- *They must prevent the blocking of streets by houses that are built too far out or by balconies extending over them.*
- *They are responsible for the removal of the bodies of those who die in the streets, employing public slaves for the purpose.*
- *They must ensure that drains in the upper stories of buildings do not discharge straight into the street, and that house doors do not open outward.*

All Greek house doors used to open outward. This is an inference from comedy, where people knock on the door and make a noise when they are about to come out, so that people passing by or standing outside can hear them and not be surprised when the door opens out into the street (Plutarch *Life of Publicola* 20).

When Themistocles was exiled, much of his property was taken across to Asia by his friends. The amount discovered and put into the public treasury was one hundred talents according to Theopompus or eighty talents according to Theophrastus, even though Themistocles had property worth no more than three talents when he first entered politics (Plutarch *Life of Themistocles* 25).

There are about seven thousand surviving votes for the banishment of an individual from Athens for ten years, written mostly on broken pottery (*ostraca*). *Ostraca* usually contain just the name of the person, sometimes with his father's name, and perhaps also the name of his *deme* (village or parish). An *ostracon* against Pericles's father, Xanthippus, who was ostracized in 484 B.C., runs to a whole elegiac couplet: *This ostracon declares that Xanthippus, son of Ariphron, is the most unjust of the corrupt officials.* Other *ostraca* attempt to be witty:

- *Megacles, son of Hippocrates, and his horse as well.*
- *Cimon, get out, and take your sister with you.*
- *Themistocles, son of Neocles,* κατάπυγος [*catapygos*, bugger; the Athenians called the middle finger the buggery finger (*Pollux Onomasticon* 2.184)].
- *I ostracize Hunger, son of noble parents* may also be facetious, but it is reminiscent of the ritual cry at the ceremony known as "Driving out Famine": *people strike one of their household slaves with wands of agnus castus and drive him out the door while chanting "Out with Hunger, in with Wealth and Health!"* (Plutarch *Table Talk* 693f).

When the Athenians were intent on ostracizing him, Aristides was approached by an illiterate countryman, who asked him to write "Aristides" on his ostracon. "Do you know Aristides?" he asked. The man said

Three ostraca against Themistocles (all actually spelled "Themisthocles") and one against Hippocrates.

no, but explained that he was irritated at constantly hearing him called "The Just." Aristides said nothing; he merely wrote his name on the ostracon and gave it back (Plutarch *Sayings of Kings and Commanders* 186*b*). Despite his reputation for justice (he was left in charge of the spoils won from the Persians at Marathon, while the rest of the army rushed back to defend Athens), Aristides was ostracized in the 480s.

Despite the fame of the institution, it seems that only about ten men were ever ostracized from Athens. There were similar processes in other *poleis*. In Syracuse, it was known as *petalismus* (from πέταλον [*petalon*, "leaf"]), votes being written on olive leaves. The Athenian Council wrote preliminary ("straw") votes on leaves (Aeschines *Against Timarchus* 111).

When a man from the obscure island of Seriphos told Themistocles that he owed his fame not to his own merits but to his city, Themistocles replied, "What you say is true: if I had been from Seriphos, I'd not have become famous, but neither would you, if you had been an Athenian" (Plutarch *Life of Themistocles* 18). Seriphos was notoriously insignificant: *Stratonicus the lyre-player asked his host on Seriphos which crimes were punished with exile. When he was told that those found guilty of fraud were sent into exile, he said, "Well then, why don't you commit fraud, so as to escape from this confinement?"* (Plutarch *On Exile* 602a).

An owl armed like Athena.

A group of sixty joke-tellers used to meet in the temple of Heracles in the deme of Diomeia, and they were known in Athens as "The Sixty." . . . Such was their reputation for entertainment that Philip of Macedon sent them a talent so that they would write down their jokes and send them to him (Athenaeus *Wise Men at Dinner* 614*d*).

Alcibiades had a wonderfully fine big dog that he had bought for a very high price. He cut off its beautiful tail. When his friends protested and told him that the whole city was upset about the dog and was voicing its disgust at him, he laughed and said, "That's just what I intended. I want the Athenians to chatter about this, so that they don't say anything worse about me" (Plutarch *Life of Alcibiades* 9).

If anyone were to say that the Athenians were born neither to be at peace themselves nor to allow others to be at peace, he would only be speaking the truth (Thucydides *History* 1.70). This opinion is expressed by ambassadors from Corinth hoping to conclude an alliance with Sparta against Athens just before the outbreak of the Peloponnesian War.

· VII ·

SPARTA

*Whenever mention is made of the Spartans, none
of them can hide how much he relishes the prospect
of even eating them raw*

(Xenophon *Hellenica* 3.3, referring to the slaves
and others suppressed by the Spartans).

*Because they do not trust the helots, their slave population, the Spartans
confiscate the handles of their shields when they are not away on campaign. They have also devised locks for their doors that they think are
strong enough to withstand any attempt by the helots to break in* (Critias
frg. 37).

*The Spartans used to force the helots to drink large quantities of undiluted
wine, and then they brought them into the mess halls to show the young
men what drunkenness meant. They also made them sing and dance in a
demeaning and ridiculous fashion* (Plutarch *Life of Lycurgus* 28).

*To maintain control of the helots, the Spartans used to send specially
selected young warriors, the* crypteia [secret police], *out into the countryside to murder any of them that they found going about at night. Sometimes the* crypteia *went into the fields during the day and killed any helot
who was particularly sturdy and fit. Thucydides [History 4.80] records
that the Spartans picked out about two thousand helots whom they set free*

as a reward for their bravery and took them in procession around the sanctuaries with garlands on their heads; soon afterward, however, they all disappeared, and no one ever found out how they were done away with (Plutarch *Life of Lycurgus* 28).

An earthquake of unprecedented severity shook Laconia [in 464 B.C.], breaking off mountain peaks and destroying all but five houses in Sparta. King Archidamus understood the danger that was yet to come. He saw the citizens trying to salvage their valuables and had the trumpet give the signal for an enemy attack, to make them all rally to him immediately with their weapons. That and that alone saved Sparta in this crisis, for the helots came rushing from all over the countryside to put an end to the Spartan survivors (Plutarch *Life of Cimon* 16).

There was a law in Sparta against having an unmanly complexion or being overweight, since the one indicated effeminacy, the other laziness. It was required by law that the young men should stand naked in public before the Ephors every ten days. They were commended if their bodies looked solid and strong, well honed with exercise. But, if any of their limbs were soft and flabby, pudgy with fat accrued through sluggishness, they were beaten and censured. Cooks in Sparta were skilled exclusively in preparing meat. Any cook who had any further expertise was driven out of the city, as a rite of purification to ensure against sickness (Aelian *Miscellaneous History* 14.7).

When two brothers were quarreling, the Spartan Ephors fined their father for allowing his sons to wrangle (Plutarch *Sayings of the Spartans* 233f).

Every year in Sparta, boys are flogged with whips for a whole day on the altar of Artemis. They are frequently whipped to death, but they endure it cheerfully and proudly, competing with one another to see who can withstand the greatest number of strokes. The winner is held in particularly high regard (Plutarch *Spartan Customs* 239d).

It is said that a Spartan refused a lavish bribe to lose a wrestling match at the Olympic Games and defeated his opponent after a hard struggle. Someone asked him what good his victory was to him, and he replied with a laugh, "I shall be positioned in front of our king when I fight our enemies" (Plutarch *Lycurgus* 22).

In the other Greek states, a soldier who behaves as a coward is called a coward, but is not otherwise stigmatized. In Sparta, on the other hand:

- *Everyone is ashamed to have a coward share his mess-table.*
- *Everyone is ashamed to wrestle with him in the gymnasium.*
- *He is often left unpicked when teams are being chosen for ball games.*
- *In choral dances, he is driven out to the least commendable positions.*
- *He has to make way for others on the street.*
- *He has to give up his seat even to younger men.*
- *He has to maintain his female relatives at home, bearing the blame for their not finding a husband.*
- *He himself cannot find a wife and has to pay the fine for not marrying.*
- *If he goes about looking cheerful, like those who have not been convicted of cowardice, he has to bear the blows of his betters.*

(Xenophon *Constitution of Sparta* 9.4)

Plutarch adds to this list of sanctions against cowards that such men are required *to go around unkempt, wearing cloaks with patches of dyed cloth, and with one side of their beards shaved off* (*Life of Agesilaus* 30).

To ensure against greed in Sparta, Lycurgus completely devalued all gold and silver coinage, ruling that iron alone should be used instead. Moreover, he gave only a slight value to a great weight and volume of iron, so that an amount worth very little would require a large room to store it and a team of oxen to transport it. This currency law removed many injustices from Sparta, for who would steal, or take as a bribe, something that he could not hide or enjoy possessing? The iron bars could not even be chopped into smaller pieces, for they were made brittle and hard to work by being dipped in vinegar when red-hot (Plutarch *Life of Lycurgus* 9).

The coin at the beginning of this chapter is Spartan, but from the 1st century B.C., when the traditional way of life was entirely gone.

After the Battle of Plataea, the Spartan helots were ordered to collect the plunder from the Persian camp. They stole many items and sold them to the Aeginetans. This laid the foundation for Aegina's great prosperity, for they bought the gold from the unwitting helots as if it were merely brass (Herodotus *Histories* 9.80).

Bibasis *was a Spartan dancing contest, for girls as well as for boys. Dancers had to jump up and touch their buttocks with their feet. The jumps were counted. An inscription for one girl reads, "I managed one thousand jumps in the* bibasis, *more than any other girl"* (Pollux *Onomasticon* 4.102).

On the wedding night a Spartan bride's female attendant cropped her hair, dressed her in a man's clothes, and left her alone on a low couch in her dark bedroom. Her husband came stealthily to her from his military quarters, taking extreme care not to be caught with his wife. This would go on for a long time, and some Spartans even became fathers before seeing their wives in the daylight (Plutarch *Life of Lycurgus* 15).

King Aristodemus of Sparta died just after his wife, Argeia, had given birth to twin sons. It was customary for a king's eldest son to succeed him, but it was impossible to distinguish which was the elder, since they were so alike. The Spartans asked their mother, but she said that even she could not tell them apart—she actually knew perfectly well, but wanted both of the boys to be kings. . . . A Messenian called Panites suggested that they watch Argeia, to see which child she washed and fed first. If she followed the same routine every time, they would have the information they needed. But if she washed them and fed them in no set order, then it would be clear that she had no idea which was the elder. She did not know why she was being watched, and they found that she consistently favored one baby when she fed and washed them. So the child she favored was taken away and reared at public expense as being the elder twin (Herodotus *Histories* 6.52).

The Spartans, inhabiting Laconia, were famous for the laconic brevity with which they expressed themselves:

> *An Athenian was mocking the Spartan swords for being so short, saying that jugglers in the theaters could swallow them easily. The Spartan king, Agis, replied, "Yes, but we can reach our enemies with these daggers of ours." Likewise, what Spartans say may be brief, but it goes straight to the point and catches the listener's attention* (Plutarch *Life of Lycurgus* 19).

> *Exiles from Samos came to Sparta and asked the officials for help. Since they were in desperate need, they made a long speech. When they had finished, the Spartans said they had forgotten the first part of what they said and could not understand the rest. The Samians tried again, bringing in a sack and saying simply, "the sack needs flour." The Spartans said that saying "the sack" was superfluous, but they did agree to help them* (Herodotus *Histories* 3.46).

> *When someone was looking at a picture of Spartans being slaughtered by Athenians and said, "How brave the Athenians are," a Spartan retorted, "In the picture"* (Plutarch *Sayings of the Spartans* 232f).

> *Philip of Macedon wrote to the Spartans: "If I invade Laconia, I'll drive you out." The Spartans wrote back: "If"* (Plutarch *On Talkativeness* 511a).

> *When Philip entered their territory and wrote asking whether they wanted him to come as a friend or as an enemy, the Spartans replied, "Neither"* (Plutarch *Sayings of the Spartans* 233e).

> *He had a field smaller than a letter sent from Sparta* (a line from a lost comedy quoted at Ps.-Longinus *On the Sublime* 38).

· VIII ·

ALEXANDER THE GREAT

When asked how he was able to achieve so much in
such a short time, Alexander replied, "By not
procrastinating about anything"
(*Gnomologium Vaticanum* 74).

Because he had only one eye, King Philip of Macedon, the father of Alex-
ander, used to become angry if anyone mentioned the Cyclops or referred
to eyes at all. And Hermias, the ruler of Atarneus, for all that he was
otherwise easygoing, could not tolerate anyone referring to knives, or cut-
ting, or surgery, since he was a eunuch (Ps.-Demetrius *On Style* 293).
Philip was struck in the right eye by an arrow or a spear at the siege of
Methone in 355/354 B.C. *Through the will of some divinity, at a music*
festival just before he suffered this misfortune, each of the three musicians
in a flute contest chose to play a different version of the Cyclops story
(Didymus *Commentary on Demosthenes* 12).

Three pieces of good news were reported to King Philip at the same time:
the first was that his team had won the four-horse chariot race at the
Olympic Games; the second that his general, Parmenion, had defeated the
Dardanians in battle; the third that his wife Olympias had borne him a
son. Stretching his hands up to heaven, he said, "Oh God, grant me some
minor misfortune to offset these good things!" For he was well aware that

Fortune tends to begrudge us great prosperity (Ps.-Plutarch *Condolences to Apollonius* 105*a*).

Alexander gained possession of the whole of Asia in fewer years than it took Isocrates to write his Panegyric *urging war against the Persians* (Ps.-Longinus *On the Sublime* 4.2).

When someone asked Alexander whether he would rather be Achilles or Homer, he replied, "What do you think yourself? Would you rather be an Olympic victor or the herald who announces other people's victories?" (Plutarch *Sayings of Kings and Commanders* 185*a*).

Alexander once saw a messenger running joyfully toward him, stretching out his right hand. He asked him, "What news have you for me, my friend? Has Homer come back to life?" For Alexander thought that the only thing his achievements still needed was someone to give them lasting fame (Plutarch *How to Assess One's Progress in Virtue* 85*c*).

Alexander went to Troy and sacrificed to Trojan Athena. He dedicated his own armor in her temple and took instead of it some armor that had been set up during the Trojan War. They say that his attendants used to carry these weapons into battle in front of him. There is a story that he also sacrificed to Priam at the altar of Zeus of the Hearth, as a way to avert Priam's anger from the family of Neoptolemus, from whom he was descended (Arrian *Anabasis of Alexander* 1.11). Neoptolemus, the son of Achilles, had butchered Priam at this altar.

The people of Lampsacus erected a statue of Anaximenes at Olympia for averting the wrath of Alexander from them in the following way. Lampsacus supported the Persian king, or was at least suspected of doing so, and Alexander seethed with anger and threatened the citizens with the direst punishment. Fearing for their wives, their children, and their state itself, they sent Anaximenes to intercede, since he was acquainted with both Alexander and Philip before him. They say that when Alexander found out why Anaximenes was coming, he swore by the Greeks' gods, whom he

called by name, that he would do the opposite of whatever it was that Anaximenes asked him to do. Anaximenes said, "Grant me this favor, your majesty: enslave the women and children of Lampsacus, raze the whole city to the ground, and burn their temples." Alexander could find no way to counter this trick; constrained by his oath, he reluctantly pardoned the people of Lampsacus (Pausanias *Guide to Greece* 6.18). For Anaximenes's deviousness, see also p. ~~154~~. *152*

Most of Alexander's officers were afraid of the depth of the river Granicus and of the rough and uneven terrain on the far bank, which they would not be able to occupy without a fight. Some of them also thought they should adhere to the usual observations for the month—the Macedonian kings were not accustomed to lead out the army in the month of Daesius [May–June]. *But Alexander bolstered their morale by ordering them to repeat the month of Artemisius* [April–May] (Plutarch *Life of Alexander* 16).

To flatter Alexander, the architect Dinocrates planned to carve Mt. Athos as the statue of a man, with the walls of a very large city in his left hand and a huge cup in his right hand to collect the water of all the rivers on the mountain, and then to pour them out of the cup into the sea (Vitruvius *On Architecture* 2 Preface).

Choerilus was a bad poet who followed Alexander and described his wars. Alexander is said to have commented that he would rather be Homer's Thersites [the ugliest and most worthless Greek soldier] *than Choerilus's Achilles. He agreed with Choerilus that he would be given a gold coin for every good verse he wrote, but a punch for every bad one. Because his poetry was far more often bad than good, Choerilus was punched to death* (Scholion to Horace *Art of Poetry* 357).

Callisthenes, the great-nephew of Aristotle, accompanied Alexander on his march to the east, writing an account of the campaign. He recorded how the sea did obeisance to Alexander by retreating to allow him to pass (Eustathius on Homer *Iliad* 13.29).

Since the philosopher Callisthenes opposed the Persian custom of obeisance, Alexander trumped up a charge of conspiracy against him: he had all his limbs chopped off, along with his ears, his nose, and his lips, and then he had him paraded around, shut up in a cage with a dog, as a wretched and sorry sight to intimidate everyone else (Justin *Epitome* 15.3).

When Alexander was besieging Tyre, many of the citizens dreamed that Apollo told them that he was going over to Alexander. They reacted as if the god were a mortal whom they had caught in the act of deserting. They put ropes around his colossal statue and nailed it to its base, calling him an Alexandrist (Plutarch *Life of Alexander* 24). *The statue had originally stood outside the Sicilian city of Gela and was taken as plunder by the Carthaginians, who sent it to Tyre* [their mother city]. . . . *Alexander captured Tyre at the same hour of the same day of the year as the Carthaginians had seized the statue* (Diodorus Siculus *The Library* 13.108).

Alexander's anger afforded the victors a gruesome sight: when his madness was exhausted in butchering the Tyrians, two thousand more were hung up, fixed to crosses, all along the shore (Quintus Curtius *History of Alexander the Great* 4.4, describing the aftermath of Alexander's seven-month siege of Tyre).

Alexander was clearly distressed by King Darius's assassination. He took off his own cloak and covered his corpse with it. When he subsequently caught Bessus [Darius's killer], *he had him ripped apart. Two straight trees were bent over toward each other, and part of Bessus's body was tied to each of them; when they were released and sprang forcefully up, the part of Bessus's body that was attached to each tree went with it* (Plutarch *Life of Alexander* 43).

Alexander was angry with one of his bodyguards, a Macedonian named Lysimachus, and locked him in a room with a lion. When he found that Lysimachus had overpowered the beast, he admired him greatly and honored

him as much as any of the Macedonian nobles (Pausanias *Guide to Greece* 1.9). After Alexander's death, Lysimachus ruled vast territories in Europe and Asia Minor, but failed to found a dynasty. *Lysimachus frightened one of his own courtiers by throwing a wooden scorpion into his lap. His victim jumped up in a panic, but when he realized it was a joke, he said, "Your majesty, now it's my turn to frighten you: give me a talent of silver!"* (Plutarch *Table Talk* 633b).

Alexander captured an Indian archer who was said to be so skilled that he could shoot an arrow through a finger-ring. He told him to demonstrate his ability, but the archer refused. Alexander became angry and ordered him to be executed. The Indian told those who were leading him away that he had not practiced for many days and was afraid he might not succeed. When Alexander heard this, he was amazed and had the man released, sending him off with a reward, because he preferred death to seeming to be unworthy of his reputation (Plutarch *Sayings of Kings and Commanders* 181b).

Alexander's camp in India was attacked by

- *White lions, bigger than bulls;*
- *Huge pigs of various colors;*
- *Bats as big as doves with teeth like those of humans;*
- *An Odontotyrannus, with three horns and bigger than an elephant;*
- *Poisonous shrews, bigger than foxes.*

(Alexander's Letter to Aristotle about India 7)

When the Indian king Porus unleashed huge lions against his troops, Alexander is said to have repulsed them by inducing them to attack heated statues set up in front of his battle line (*Life of Alexander, King of the Macedonians* 36). We are not told precisely how he heated the statues.

Some say that Alexander did not drink much, even though he did spend a lot of his time in discussion with his friends over wine. But Philinus demonstrates by reference to the royal diaries that this is nonsense: there are very

frequent entries recording that he spent a whole day sleeping off his drinking, and sometimes the day after that as well (Plutarch *Table Talk* 623d).

Alexander saw that his companions had become altogether decadent, with a vulgar and expensive lifestyle. Hagnon had silver nails in his boots, Leonnatus had sand brought from Egypt by a troupe of camels for his gymnastic exercises, Philotas had hunting-nets twelve miles long, and they used more myrrh for their massages and bathing than previously they had used olive oil (Plutarch *Life of Alexander* 40).

Alexander is said to have exuded very fragrant sweat that gave his clothing a sweet aroma (Plutarch *Table Talk* 623e).

When his close friend Hephaestion died, Alexander not only sheared the manes of his horses and mules, but also removed the battlements from city walls, so that even cities would seem to be in mourning (Plutarch *Life of Pelopidas* 34).

The chance survival of a Babylonian oracle recording the ominous birth of a lamb with three heads, three necks, and three buttocks also informs us that it was cloudy in Babylon on the day that Alexander died there in 323 B.C.

Alexander had lain unburied in Babylon for thirty days when it was rumored that the land that received his body would enjoy great and long-lasting prosperity. Ptolemy stole the corpse and set off for Egypt. Only Perdiccas tried to stop him. Ptolemy had a dummy made to resemble Alexander and laid it out on a costly bier, but sent the actual body on to Egypt with no pomp along a secret and little-traversed route. Perdiccas got control of the decoy, and by the time he realized that he had been tricked, it was too late to continue the pursuit (Aelian *Miscellaneous History* 12.64).

The tomb of Alexander has not yet been located. Perhaps the most remarkable expedition to find it was undertaken by a team of psychic archaeologists, who scuba dived in sordid conditions in the harbor of Alexandria in 1979. The year before, the tomb of Alexander IV, the son of Alexander the Great and the Bactrian princess Roxane, was discovered without psychic aid at Vergina in Macedonia. Another tomb, discovered there in 1977, was long thought to be that of Philip II, Alexander the Great's father, but some archaeologists now reject this view. Philip's tomb would have been easy to find if Alexander had lived long enough to carry out his alleged plan to build a pyramid for him as big as the biggest pyramid in Egypt (Diodorus Siculus *The Library* 18.4). Cleopatra and Mark Antony were also buried in Alexandria; their tomb has likewise eluded detection.

> *When people addressed him as a god, Alexander said*
> *that there were two things that made him skeptical*
> *about that, his need for sleep and his need for sex*
>
> (**Plutarch** *How to Tell a Flatterer from a Friend* 65f).

· IX ·

GREEKS AT SEA

When Anacharsis the Scythian wise man was asked
whether the living or the dead were more
numerous, he asked, "In which group do you count
sailors?"

(Diogenes Laertius *Lives of the Philosophers*
1.104).

Why is it that fishermen, collectors of purple shells, and indeed all those
who gain their livelihood from the sea have red hair? (Ps.-Aristotle *Problems* 966*b*).

The thirty-oared ship in which Theseus and his companions sailed to Crete
to fight the Minotaur was preserved for many centuries by the Athenians.
They used to replace the old timbers with sound new ones, and the ship
was an example for the philosophers of the paradox of change, with some
of them saying that it was still the same ship, others that it was not
(Plutarch *Life of Theseus* 23).

Anyone who arrives later than the appointed time to prepare for the com-
petition must explain his lateness to the organizers of the games. Valid
reasons for being late are illness, capture by pirates, shipwreck (*Olympia*
Inscriptions 56).

Letting down an inverted cauldron gives divers a chance to breathe, for it remains full of air and does not fill up with water (Ps.-Aristotle *Problems* 960*b*).

Divers are sometimes provided with devices that enable them to stay underwater for a long time, drawing air from above the water, just as nature has endowed elephants with a huge nostril that they raise out of the water and breathe through whenever they are crossing water (Aristotle *Parts of Animals* 659*a*). Elephants do actually breathe this way when crossing rivers.

I ordered a big iron cage to be made, with a glass jar just over two feet wide inside it. . . . The third time I submerged, I went down almost five hundred feet and saw fish of very many sorts swimming around me. Then a very big fish took the cage in its mouth and pulled me to shore a mile away. There were 360 men in the four boats that let me down into the water, and it dragged them all along. When it reached the shore, it crushed the cage with its teeth and hurled it up onto the dry land. I was panting and practically dead with fright, and I fell down and gave thanks to heavenly Providence for saving me from the awesome beast. I said to myself, "Alexander, stop trying to do the impossible, in case you lose your life in exploring the depths" (*The Greek Alexander Romance* 2.38).

A dolphin does not panic if caught in a net. It eats its fill of the fish trapped with it and then bites its way out through the meshes. If the fishermen catch it, they sew rushes to its dorsal fin and let it go. If it gets caught again, they recognize the stitching and give it a beating. But this rarely happens, for the dolphins are grateful for the pardon they receive on the first occasion (Plutarch *The Cleverness of Animals* 977*f*).

Ship owners protect their vessels from lightning by wrapping the hides of seals or hyenas around the mast (Plutarch *Table Talk* 664*c*).

These are some names of ships in the Athenian fleet in the mid-4th century B.C.:

Actis	*Sunbeam*
Charis	*Grace*
Comoedia	*Comedy*
Democratia	*Democracy*
Eirene	*Peace*
Eleutheria	*Freedom*
Halcyon	*Kingfisher*
Hipparche	*Queen of the Horses* (a horse transport)
Leaena	*Lioness*
Lycaena	*She-wolf*
Nike	*Victory*
Salpinx	*Trumpet*
Sophia	*Wisdom*
Tragoedia	*Tragedy*

The largest ancient ship of which a wreck survives is the *Madrague de Giens*, a Roman freighter about 130 feet long with a capacity of almost forty tons, which went down in the 1st century B.C. off the French coast, about twenty miles east of Toulon. The Hellenistic Greek kings, however, had constructed very much larger vessels, as an expression of their wealth and power. Perhaps the largest of all ancient transport ships was the *Syracusia*, commissioned by King Hieron of Syracuse and designed by Archimedes. It is described in some detail by Athenaeus (*Wise Men at Dinner 206d*):

- *It had twenty banks of oars.*
- *Its construction required as much timber as sixty quadriremes.*
- *It could transport ninety thousand bushels of grain, ten thousand jars of pickled fish, six hundred tons of wool, and six hundred tons of other cargo.*
- *The officers' quarters were decorated with mosaic floors telling the whole story of the* Iliad.
- *It had a gymnasium, promenades with shady gardens, a shrine to Aphrodite, a library, baths, stalls for twenty horses, a seawater pond full of fish, a catapult designed by Archimedes that could throw stones of 180 pounds and spears eighteen feet long.*

Unfortunately, it was too big for most harbors, so Hieron renamed it the *Alexandris* and sent it as a gift to Ptolemy of Egypt, who hauled it ashore at Alexandria. It never sailed again.

Xerxes branded the sea and whipped it (Herodotus *Histories* 7.35; he gave the Hellespont three hundred lashes and branded it for destroying his first bridge of boats from Asia to Europe). *He also sent a letter to Mt. Athos: "Noble Athos, with your peaks reaching to Heaven, do not oppose my project* [to cut a canal across the peninsula] *with large and unmanageable boulders; otherwise, I shall cut you down and throw you into the sea"* (Plutarch *On Controlling Anger* 455e).

In Xerxes's camp there was a man named Scyllias, the best diver of the time. He had salvaged many of the Persians' possessions for them after a shipwreck and held onto many of them for himself. I cannot say for sure how he managed to desert to the Greeks, but I should be surprised if the report of the incident is true, namely that he dived into the sea at Aphetae and did not surface until he reached Artemisium, covering a distance of about ten miles underwater. I personally think he went across in a boat (Herodotus *Histories* 8.8).

It has always been the case that many things that have a basis in fact lose their credibility because the truth is covered over with falsehood . . . for those who enjoy listening to stories have a tendency to embellish them and corrupt the truth by tainting it with lies (Pausanias *Guide to Greece* 8.2). Pausanias seems rather more scrupulous than some authors in the stories he is willing to record, but it is difficult to endorse his addition to the story of Scyllias, that *he taught his daughter Hydna to dive, and then they, father and daughter, contributed to the destruction of the Persian fleet during the violent storm by dragging away the anchors and any other protection the triremes had* (*Guide to Greece* 10.19).

People often take Maltese lapdogs or monkeys to distract them on a voyage. A ship once capsized in a storm off Cape Sunium near Athens. A dolphin spotted a monkey swimming away from the wreck and took it on its back,

A soldier riding a dolphin.

thinking it was a human being. When they approached Piraeus, the port of Athens, it asked the monkey if it was an Athenian, and the monkey replied that it belonged to a distinguished Athenian family. Then the dolphin asked it if it knew Piraeus, and the monkey said they were close friends. The dolphin, irritated at the monkey's lies, dived and left it to drown (Aesop *Fable* 75). Aesop directed this tale *at those who, despite their own ignorance, think that they can trick other people.*

The rest of the crew were farmhands, who had never even touched an oar a year before, and every one of them had some physical defect. So long as we were sailing along in safety, they kept exchanging banter, calling each other, not by their real names, but according to their misfortunes—Limper, Ruptured, Lefty, Squinter—for each of them had some such distinguishing feature. This caused us no little amusement, but when danger came, it was no longer a laughing matter (Synesius *Letter* 4).

When the architect Sostratus had completed the lighthouse at Pharos [one of the Seven Wonders of the Ancient World], *he inscribed his own name on the stonework and then plastered it over. On the outer facing he inscribed the name of the ruling king* [Ptolemy I], *being well aware that the inscription on the plaster would soon fall off, revealing the words, "Dedicated to the Savior Gods by Sostratus, son of Dexiphanes, from Cnidus, on behalf of those who sail the sea"* (Lucian *How to Write History* 62).

There is a house in Acragas called "The Trireme" because some young men got very drunk there and thought they were sailing in a trireme that was caught in a storm. They were so out of their minds that they threw all the furniture and bedding out of the house as if they were jettisoning cargo into the sea (Timaeus *frg.* 149).

There are those who maintain that the people of Cyme are mocked for their stupidity because they imposed no harbor taxes for the first three hundred years after the foundation of their city, and hence they did not enjoy this revenue; it seemed as if it took them a long time to realize that they were living in a city by the sea (Strabo *Geography* 13.3.6; for the Cymaeans' stupidity, see also pp. 5, 248). Such revenue could be very lucrative: the tax on wine imported into Egypt in the Ptolemaic period was 33 percent.

In the military and financial crisis of 413 B.C., *instead of exacting tribute the Athenians imposed a 5 percent tax on their allies on all goods imported or exported by sea. They reckoned that this would bring in more revenue* [as well it might, nearly all the allies being island-*poleis*] (Thucydides *History* 7.28).

We grumble at customs inspectors, not when they examine goods that are being imported openly, but when they rummage through the baggage of

private individuals, looking for things that have been hidden (Plutarch
On Curiosity 518e).

*When someone was admiring the dedications made on the island of
Samothrace* [to the gods who protected seafarers], *Diogenes the Cynic
said, "There'd be far more if those who weren't saved had also set up dedications"* (Diogenes Laertius *Lives of the Philosophers* 6.59).

> I'm not astounded if someone goes to sea, but I am
> if he does it a second time
>
> (Philemon *frg.* 183).

· X ·

GREEKS AND BARBARIANS

*I am grateful to Fortune for three things; first, that
I was born a human being, not a beast; secondly,
that I was born a man, not a woman; thirdly, that
I was born a Greek, not a barbarian* (Hermippus
of Smyrna *frg.* 13). This sentiment is attributed
to both Thales and Socrates. Plutarch records
that, *on his deathbed, Plato thanked Fortune that
he was born a human being, not an irrational
animal, a Greek, not a barbarian, and that he
lived during the lifetime of Socrates*
(*Life of Marius* 46).

According to Aristotle:

- *Races living in cold places and in northern Europe are full of spirit, but rather lacking in intelligence and skill, and so they manage to stay free, but lack the political qualities needed to rule their neighbors.*
- *The races of Asia are intelligent and skillful, but lack spirit, and so they tend to suffer subjection and slavery.*
- *But just as Greece is situated between these types, so the Greeks share the characteristics of both. They are free and enjoy the best political institutions, and have the potential to rule the world, if only they could attain political unity.*

(*Politics* 1327*b*)

Capitoline Venus

ROMANS

Whereas the Greeks defined a barbarian as anyone who was not Greek, the Romans defined a barbarian as anyone who was not Greek or Roman.

Pompey never went into battle without first reading Iliad XI, *for he was a great admirer of Agamemnon* [whose most heroic deeds are recounted in that book], *and Cicero was reading Euripides's* Medea *as he was being carried along in a litter, until the murderers chopped off his head* (Ptolemy the Quail quoted by Photius at *The Library* 190.151a).

Some naked men would have been put to death as a result of a chance encounter with Livia, the wife of Augustus, if she had not saved them by observing that, to decent women, men in such a state are just like statues (Dio Cassius *History of Rome* 58.2). The Romans tended to be suspicious or contemptuous of the Greeks'

liberal attitude to nudity. But there are exceptions. The statue on the right is presumed to represent Marcia Furnilla, who was married briefly to the future emperor Titus in the 60s A.D. Whether or not the precise identification is correct, the blend of Roman verism with the Greek idealism of the Capitoline Venus on page 92 is rather startling.

Nero was keen to win the tragic competition at the Isthmian Games, but neither threats nor an enormous bribe would make a talented rival named Epirotes give way to him. So the emperor had his men pin Epirotes to a pillar in the theater and crush his throat with the straight edges of their ivory writing tablets (Philostratus *Nero* 9).

I have sent you an account of my consulship written in Greek. There may be things in it that might seem to an Athenian to be slightly less than polished Greek, but I won't repeat what I think Lucullus said about his His-tories, *that he had inserted barbaric expressions and solecisms here and there to make it easier to recognize as the work of a Roman* (Cicero *Letters to Atticus* 1.69).

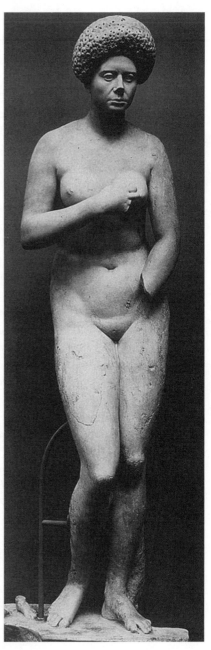

Marcia Furnilla

If you point your nose toward the sun and open your mouth wide, you'll be able to tell the time to passersby (*Greek Anthology* 11.418; i.e., you will be like a sundial). The word for "nose," ῥίνα (*rhina*) here has a short first vowel; this is incorrect, a surprising violation of the extremely strict Greek metrical practices. It is possibly significant, therefore, that the epigram was written by the emperor Trajan (ruled A.D. 98–117); when Tiberius (ruled A.D. 14–37) had queried the propriety of using a Greek term when speaking Latin, a court flatterer had told him that, because he was emperor, he could do as he wished (Suetonius *On Grammarians* 22).

The *Meditations* of Marcus Aurelius (ruled A.D. 161–180), the nearest Rome ever came to a "philosopher-king," are written in simple but fairly elegant Greek and may not have been intended for publication. Their content is wide ranging and varied; for example:

- *From my tutor, I have learned not to support either the Green or the Blue stable in the horse-races, nor to be a fan of either the light-shield or the heavy-shield fighters in the gladiatorial contests* (1.5).
- *From Diognetus, I have learned not to be preoccupied with trivial things, not to believe in what magicians say about incantations and driving away evil spirits, and not to tap quails* [see p. 52] (1.6).
- *You are a little soul, carrying around a corpse, as Epictetus used to say* (4.41).
- *Mankind's affairs are ephemeral and cheap; yesterday is a drop of semen, tomorrow is a pickled fish and ashes* (4.48).
- *Soon you will be ashes or a skeleton, a mere name or not even a name: a name is just a sound, a faint echo. What we value most in life is vain, rotten, and petty; we are like puppies snapping at each other, or quarrelsome children who laugh but soon start to cry* (5.33).
- *Consider anyone who is disgruntled or discontented with anything to be like a piglet kicking and squealing when it is being sacrificed* (10.28).

Sacrificing a piglet. The dish has an inscription, added before the cup was fired: ΕΠΙΔΡΟΜΟΣ ΚΑΛΟΣ (*EPIDROMOS KALOS*, "Epidromus [is] handsome."

OTHER FOREIGNERS

Children are not reared properly among the Germans. But this work of mine is not written for the benefit of the Germans or for any other wild and barbaric people, any more than for bears, or lions, or wild boar, or any savage beasts; rather it is meant for Greeks and those who, even if they are barbarians by birth, nevertheless aspire to Greek customs (Galen On Preserving Health 6.51).

If it is not actually true that King Sardanapallus of Assyria was killed while working wool with his womenfolk, it might well have happened to someone else (Aristotle *Politics* 1312a).

The Persians regard themselves as being in every respect by far the best race . . . and those who live furthest away from them to be the worst (Herodotus *Histories* 1.134).

The Egyptians regard as barbarians all those who do not speak the same language as they do (Herodotus *Histories* 2.158).

The Pharaoh Neco sent a Phoenician expedition south from the Red Sea to circumnavigate Africa. . . . They claimed something that I find incredible, but others may believe: that they had the sun on the right hand [i.e., to the north] *as they sailed around* (Herodotus *Histories* 6.64). Their claim is validated by precisely the detail that arouses Herodotus's disbelief.

While Rhodopis, a very beautiful prostitute, was bathing, and her attendants were guarding her clothes, an eagle swooped down, snatched one of her shoes, and flew off with it. It carried it to Memphis, where the Pharaoh Psammetichus was judging lawsuits, and dropped it into his lap. Psammetichus was amazed at the shapeliness and craftsmanship of the shoe and at what the eagle had done. He ordered a search to be made throughout Egypt for the woman whose shoe it was. When he found Rhodopis, he married her (Aelian *Miscellaneous History* 13.33). This tale may not be the direct ancestor of the Cinderella story, but *The Sorcerer's Apprentice* has a clear classical pedigree, being based, via a ballad by Goethe, on a story in Lucian's *Lover of Lies.*

Some Greeks maintain that the prostitute Rhodopis built the Pyramid of Mycerinus. But they are wrong. . . . They are unaware that she lived many generations after the kings who built the pyramids. . . . She was brought to

Egypt as a slave and had her freedom bought for her by Charaxus, the brother of Sappho the lyric poet. She stayed in Egypt and, because of her great beauty, earned a large amount of money for someone of her status, but not enough to finance such a pyramid (Herodotus *Histories* 2.134). Mycerinus ruled at the end of the 26th century B.C., two thousand years before Sappho. Psammetichus II, a pharaoh of the 26th dynasty, ruled from 595 till 589 B.C. and might at least have been Rhodopis's contemporary.

The Egyptian word for a pyramid is *mr*, the derivation of which is unknown, but that term cannot have produced *pyramis* in Greek. It may be that Greek mercenaries in Egypt in the 6th or 5th centuries B.C. compared them to the *pyramous*, a type of cake made with honey and wheat, or possibly with cheese.

The pyramids were built on a foundation of heaps of salt. When the work was complete, the Nile was diverted through them, completely dissolving the salt (Diodorus Siculus *The Library* 1.63).

We are astounded when we see the soaring summits of the pyramids, even if we are unaware that (as I have heard from the priests) they extend just as far underground (Aristides *The Egyptian Speech* 122).

The Nile, unlike all other rivers that empty into the Mediterranean, floods in summer rather than in winter. The Greeks did hit on the true explanation for this phenomenon, the monsoon rains in the Ethiopian highlands, but it seemed improbable, and many other theories were suggested. For example:

- It rises from an immeasurably deep spring between two mountains called Crophi and Mophi (according to an Egyptian priest, as reported skeptically by Herodotus at *Histories* 2.28).
- It comes from Oceanus, the stream that surrounds the inhabited world.
- It comes from somewhere far to the west, or to the east, or from the antipodes, where it would be winter during the northern summer.

- North winds keep it back in the winter.
- The ground soaks up water like a sponge in the cooler months and sweats it out in the hotter months.
- Alexander the Great thought he had discovered the source of the Nile when he reached the River Indus, for there were crocodiles there and a type of bean that grew also in Egypt (Arrian *Alexander* 6.1).
- There was also a theory that the Euphrates disappears into a marsh and rises again south of Ethiopia to become the Nile (Pausanias *Guide to Greece* 2.5).

Cats and ibises were so venerated in Egypt that to kill one even accidentally was punishable by death. Diodorus Siculus records how, in about 60 B.C., he witnessed a crowd in Alexandria lynching a Roman official who had inadvertently caused a cat's death (*The Library* 1.83). Neither their fear of Rome nor the officials sent by King Ptolemy could restrain them. Diodorus goes on to say that this extreme reaction is not so surprising when one considers that the Egyptians had once resorted to cannibalism during a famine rather than eat any sacred animal.

There are no guards on the frankincense trees in Arabia, for the owners do not steal from each other. But, by Heracles! at Alexandria, where the perfume is processed, it is just not possible to guard the factories well enough. The workers' aprons have a seal put on them, they have to wear a mask or a close-meshed net, and they are strip-searched before they leave work (Pliny *Natural History* 12.59).

There was an island, full of savage people. The women far outnumbered the men and had hairy bodies. The interpreters called them Γόριλλαι (*Gorillae*). *When we pursued them, we could not catch any of the males, for they clambered up the crags and defended themselves with rocks. But we did catch three females, who bit and scratched those who were bringing them reluctantly along. We killed and flayed them and brought the skins back to Carthage* (Hanno *Voyage Around Africa* 18).

In Libya there is a city called Dionysopolis that can never be located twice by the same person (Strabo *Geography* 7.3.6).

Herodotus is wrong to maintain that the semen of Ethiopians is black [*Histories* 3.101, where he says the same also of some Indians], *as if every part of a person with black skin should be black; he said this even though he could see that a black-skinned person's teeth are white* (Aristotle *On the Generation of Animals* 736a).

Amitrochates, the king of the Indians, wrote to King Antiochus, asking him to buy and send to him some sweet wine, some dried figs, and a sophist. Antiochus wrote back: "We shall send you the figs and the wine, but it is against the law in Greece for sophists to be put up for sale" (Athenaeus *Wise Men at Dinner* 14.652f).

Perhaps referring to the distant and mysterious island of Sri Lanka, Diodorus Siculus reports:

> *The tongues of the inhabitants have an odd quality, occurring by nature and deliberately accentuated. Their tongue is split along part of its length, and they divide it even further, so that it is double all the way to the root. This gives them the ability to imitate not only any articulate human utterance but also the various chatterings of birds and any type of sound. The strangest thing of all is that, if they meet two people, they can converse perfectly well with both of them, answering questions and discussing appositely whatever the topics of conversation may be: they talk to one person with one half of their tongue, and to the other with the other half* (*The Library* 2.56).

> *Each community rears a very large bird of a unique type, which they use to test the temperament of their infant children. They place the children on the bird's back, and it takes flight. Those that tolerate being carried through the air, they rear, but those that become nauseous and are filled with fear, they reject, believing that they would not live long and that they are of inferior temperament* (*The Library* 2.58).

The Scythians take the seed of the hemp plant and go into their tent, where they throw the seed on to red-hot stones. It burns like incense and produces a vapor such as no Greek steam bath could surpass. The Scythians revel in the steam and howl like wolves. They do this instead of bathing. They never wash their bodies with water at all (Herodotus *Histories* 4.75).

When the Greeks were marching through friendly territory on the Black Sea coast, the natives showed off to them the wealthy people's children, who had been fattened on boiled nuts, and were soft and very pale, and almost as broad as they were tall, with flowers tattooed all over them, back and front (Xenophon *Anabasis* 5.4). Nuts or not, it may be significant that the Greeks found jars full of slices of dolphin, preserved in salt, and others full of dolphin blubber, used by the natives as Greeks used olive oil. Perhaps surprisingly, dolphins still thrive in some parts of the Black Sea, though not in Turkish waters.

The Persians discuss their most serious issues while drunk, and the owner of the house invites them to reconsider their decision the next day when they are sober. If their decision still pleases them, they adopt it; if not, they let it go. Likewise, whatever they discuss while sober they reconsider when they are drunk (Herodotus *Histories* 1.133).

The Gauls have a strange and incredible custom that they observe especially when they are considering important affairs. They devote a human being to death and stab him with a dagger just above the diaphragm. They determine the future from the way he falls, from the way his limbs twitch, and also from the way his blood gushes out (Posidonius *frg.* 169).

The Gauls accept the Pythagorean doctrine that the human soul is immortal and that, after a fixed number of years, it enters a new body and begins a new life. At funerals, some people throw onto the pyre letters addressed to the deceased, in the belief that they will read them (Diodorus Siculus *The Library* 5.28).

There are people in Thrace who make a game of hanging themselves during their drinking parties. They tie a noose at a certain height, and directly under it they place a stone that is easily overturned by anyone who stands on it. They then draw lots, and the person who is chosen gets up on the stone, equipped with only a little knife, and puts his neck in the noose. Some one else comes up and moves the stone. If he is not quick enough to cut himself free with the knife, the man left hanging dies as the stone rolls away from under him, and the others laugh, regarding his death as a source of amusement (Athenaeus *Wise Men at Dinner* 155e).

I have heard that there is a tribe in Ethiopia that is ruled by a dog (Aelian *On Animals* 7.40).

Among the Bactrians, when people became feeble, whether through old age or disease, they used to be thrown to dogs that ate them. The dogs were reared specifically for this purpose and were called "undertakers." The land outside the Bactrians' main city looked clean, but inside the walls it was mostly full of human bones. Alexander put a stop to this custom (Strabo *Geography* 11.11). Athens was not so very different: *Leontius was coming up from Piraeus, outside the north wall, when he noticed some corpses lying on the ground at the place of public execution. He wanted to look at them, but at the same time he also felt uneasy and turned away. For a while he resisted the impulse and covered his eyes, but then he was overwhelmed by the urge to look at them, so he opened his eyes wide and ran over to the corpses, saying to his eyes, "You wretches, take your fill of this lovely sight!"* (Plato *Republic* 439e).

When Xerxes invaded Greece, the Thracian king took refuge on Mt. Rhodope and advised his six sons not to join the invasion—he was obviously a philhellene. They disobeyed, and when they returned, he blinded them all—not a very Hellenic thing to do (Aelian *Miscellaneous History* 5.11).

Ctesias, the Greek physician to Artaxerxes, the king of Persia, gives an appallingly detailed description of the execution inflicted on a soldier named Mithridates, who was misguided enough to claim the credit for killing the king's brother, Cyrus, when he attempted to seize the throne in 401 B.C. Artaxerxes, who claimed to have killed Cyrus personally, had Mithridates sunk in a trough with only his head and limbs protruding. He was force-fed, with a mixture of milk and honey poured into his mouth and over his face, which was completely covered with flies, while maggots and worms engendered by his feces and urine ate his body, penetrating into his entrails. Mithridates died after seventeen days (*Persian History frg.* 26).

The Tauri are a Scythian people. When their king dies, they bury his closest friends with him. When one of his friends dies, the king cuts off a small piece of one of his own earlobes, a larger piece if it is a closer friend. But if the dearest of all his friends dies, he cuts off the whole ear (The Vatican Paradoxographer *Wonders* 60).

There are Scythians who cut up and salt the flesh of their dead and then dry it in the sun. After that they string the pieces of meat together and wear them around their necks. Whenever they happen to meet a friend, they cut off a slice of meat with a knife and give it to him to eat. They keep doing this until there is no meat left (The Vatican Paradoxographer *Wonders* 61).

The Issedonians [a tribe on the Russian steppes] *have the following custom. When a man's father dies, his kinsmen drive sheep to his house. They sacrifice the sheep and cut up the meat, and they also cut up their host's dead father. Then they mix all the meat together and serve it up as a banquet. They strip the flesh from his skull, clean it out, and gild it. They regard it as a sacred object and perform great sacrifices annually in honor of the dead man. The son arranges this for his father, just as the Greeks observe the festival in honor of their ancestors. In other respects, they are said to be just, and their women have equal rights with the men* (Herodotus *Histories* 4.26).

There are ways in which no one is differentiated from other people as being either a barbarian or a Greek:

- *We all breathe through our mouths and noses.*
- *And laugh when we are happy.*
- *And weep when we are sad.*
- *And hear sounds through our ears.*
- *And see with our eyes in the sunlight.*
- *And work with our hands.*
- *And walk with our feet.*

(*Oxyrhynchus Papyri* 1364 and 3647, from Antiphon's *On Truth*)

The king of Parthia, Orodes, was familiar with the Greek language and with Greek literature, and the king of Armenia, Artavasdes, actually composed tragedies, speeches, and works of history in Greek. They were listening to a performance of Euripides's Bacchae, *when the head of the Roman general, Crassus, was brought in, directly from the massacre at Carrhae [53 B.C.]. A tragic actor, Jason of Tralles, used it as a stage prop, as the head of Pentheus, while he performed the role of Agave, Pentheus's mother, who was one of the Bacchantes who dismembered him, imagining him to be a lion. When the chorus asked Agave who killed him, Jason/*

Orodes II of Parthia (ruled 57–38 B.C.). Despite their oriental appearance, the Parthian kings were thoroughly Hellenized. The inscription on the reverse of this drachma, a Greek unit of coinage, is in Greek: "King of Kings, Arsaces [all Parthian rulers adopted this official name], benefactor, glorious, philhellene, just."

Agave replied, "The glory is mine," but Pomaxathres, who had decapitated Crassus, jumped up and seized his head, claiming that he had a better right to say this than Jason did (Plutarch *Life of Crassus* 33).

In the far north, there is no longer any land, or sea, or air, but a mixture of all three, like a jellyfish . . . so that it is impossible to travel through it either on foot or in a boat. Pytheas claims to have seen the jellyfish-like substance personally (Pytheas *frg.* 7).

> *Anything that the Greeks take over from*
> *barbarians they eventually improve*
>
> (**Plato** [?] *Epinomis* 987*d*).

· XI ·

ATHLETICS

Success in competition gives release from sorrows
(Pindar *Olympian Odes* 2.51).

Although the date of the first Olympic Games was usually fixed at 776 B.C., other views persisted: *there is a tradition that Atreus* [the father of Agamemnon and Menelaus] *instituted the Olympic Games about 1,250 years ago, when he held funeral games for his father, Pelops, and that Hercules won every event at those games* (Velleius Paterculus *History of Rome* 1.8).

There were far fewer events in the ancient Olympics than there are now and many more states from which competitors might be drawn than there are countries competing in the modern Games (even though only Greeks were eligible to take part; we should not of course suppose that all the more than one thousand known Greek *poleis* were always represented). Moreover, there was only a single winner in each event, not the three medal winners of today. Olympic success was therefore an even more notable distinction than it is now. Most states will have had to wait for many Olympiads to achieve a victory in any event.

According to Julius Africanus *Chronographiae frg.* 65, the sprint (ca. two hundred meters) was the only competitive event in the first thirteen Olympic Games. It is also the only event for which he preserves an almost complete list of winners in the first 249 Olympic Games (i.e., for almost a thousand years). Athenian cultural dominance is not paralleled in athletics; Athenians won the sprint a mere eight times, the last occasion being the 110th games, in 336 B.C.

Theocritus of Chios, a 4th-century B.C. orator (not to be confused with the Syracusan pastoral poet), *was refused permission by the people of Chios to erect a statue of himself in the portico, since that honor was reserved for Olympic victors. He retorted, "If one of you wins at Olympia, move my statue to the fishmarket"* (*Gnomologium Vaticanum* 340). If any inference can be drawn from records for the sprint, his statue may have avoided the fish market for a long time; that event was won by Chians only twice, in consecutive games by Demetrius and Eras in the mid-2nd century A.D.

If you place heavy weights on a plank of palm wood, pressing it until it can no longer bear the load, it does not give way downward, bending in a concave manner. Instead it rises up to counter the weight, with a convex curve. This is why, according to Plutarch [*Table Talk* 724e], *the palm has been chosen to represent victory in athletic competitions; the nature of the wood is such that it does not yield to pressure* (Aulus Gellius *Attic Nights* 3.6).

The people of Sybaris wanted to eclipse the glory of the Olympic Games, so they waited till the festival was being held and then tried to entice the athletes away to Sybaris with highly inflated prizes (Athenaeus *Wise Men at Dinner* 521f).

At an unspecified Olympic Games, the first seven runners to finish in the sprint, the oldest and most prestigious event, were all from Croton (Strabo *Geography* 6.1.12).

Astylus of Croton won the sprint and the double race in three consecutive Olympic Games. At the second and third festivals, he had himself proclaimed as a Syracusan, to ingratiate himself with Hieron, the tyrant of

Syracuse. The people of Croton therefore turned his house into a prison and pulled down his statue that stood beside the temple of Hera (Pausanias *Guide to Greece* 6.13).

Sotades won the long race at the ninety-ninth Olympic Games [384 B.C.] *and was proclaimed victor as a Cretan, which is what he was. He styled himself an Ephesian at the next Olympic festival, after receiving a bribe from the Ephesians. The Cretans punished him for this by exiling him* (Pausanias *Guide to Greece* 6.18). Generally speaking, there was little mobility in citizenship between *poleis*. A remarkable proportion of grants of Athenian citizenship, recorded mostly in inscriptions on stone, were made to bankers.

When someone was daunted by the journey to Olympia, Socrates asked him why. "Don't you walk around nearly all day long at home? Don't you walk home for lunch? And for dinner? And to sleep? Don't you know that if you join up all the walking about you do in five or six days you'd easily reach Olympia from Athens?" (Xenophon *Memorabilia* 3.13). Olympia is just over two hundred miles from Athens.

A Chian was angry with his slave and said to him, "I'm not going to send you to the mill, I'm going to take you to Olympia." He apparently considered it a far more bitter punishment to be a spectator at the Olympic Games, roasting in the rays of the sun, than to be put to work grinding flour in a mill (Aelian *Miscellaneous History* 14.18).

Nasty and difficult things happen in life. Don't they happen at the Olympic Games? Don't you suffer in the heat? Don't you get crushed by the crowds? Isn't the bathing of poor quality? Don't you get soaked when it rains? Don't you get your fill of noise and shouting and other such unpleasant things? And yet I suppose you balance all this against the wonderful spectacle and put up with it (Epictetus *Discourses* 1.6).

Around the temple of Poseidon at Corinth during the Isthmian Games, you could hear:

- *Lots of wretched sophists exchanging noisy insults, while their so-called pupils brawl with one another;*
- *Lots of writers reading their stupid works;*
- *Lots of poets singing their poems to an approving audience;*
- *Lots of jugglers doing tricks;*
- *Lots of fortunetellers telling fortunes;*
- *Countless lawyers overturning justice;*
- *Not a few peddlers peddling whatever they happen to have.*

(Dio Chrysostom *On Virtue* 9)

During the Olympic Games the flies at Pisa observe a truce, as it were, with visitors and locals alike. Even though so many sacrifices are made, with so much blood shed and so much meat hung up, they willingly disappear, crossing to the other bank of the river Alpheus. They are just like the women there, except that they are more restrained. For women are excluded by the rules of the competition and the propriety attendant on it, whereas the flies withdraw from the rituals of their own accord, keeping away from the ceremonies throughout the whole time allotted to the Games. Once the Games are over, they come home, pouring into Elis again, like exiles granted permission to return (Aelian *On Animals* 5.17).

Berenice of Rhodes was the only woman to be the daughter, sister, and mother of Olympic victors (Pliny *Natural History* 7.133). Other writers describe her status as even more exceptional: her three brothers were Olympic victors, the youngest winning the pancratium at three successive festivals, and she also had a nephew who won at Olympia. Both the Rhodian soccer team and the island's airport are named after her father, Diagoras, who twice won the boxing event at Olympia. His victory in 464 B.C. is commemorated in Pindar's seventh *Olympian Ode*, ninety-five lines long, which was attached in golden letters to the wall of the temple of Athena at Lindos on Rhodes.

On the road to Olympia, before it crosses the river Alpheus, there is a mountain with high and sheer cliffs, called Typaeum. There is a law that any woman caught either at the Olympic Games or even across the Alpheus on the days when women are excluded should be pushed off these cliffs.

They say that no woman has ever been caught, with the single exception of Callipateira. (Some people say her name was Pherenice.) Since her husband was dead, she dressed herself like a trainer and took her son to Olympia to compete. Her son was victorious, and her clothes fell off as she jumped the fence of the trainers' pen to congratulate him. She was released unpunished, out of respect for her father, her brothers, and her son, all of whom were Olympic victors. A law was passed, however, that in the future trainers were to come naked to the Games (Pausanias *Guide to Greece* 5.6).

I do not absolve trainers from blame in bribery scandals. They come to training sessions with plenty of money, which they lend to the athletes at a higher rate of interest than is paid even by merchants who invest in risky overseas trade. They do not care about the reputation of the athletes; they give them advice about buying and selling victory, while keeping a sharp eye on their own profits (Philostratus *The Gymnast* 45).

The least successful athletes, those who have never won any victories, suddenly call themselves trainers and start shouting in harsh and barbarous tones, just like pigs (Galen *Thrasybulus* 5.894).

In early times, it was the custom for athletes to compete with their clothing tucked up, but Coroebus ran naked when he won the short footrace at Olympia [in 720 B.C.]. *I think he deliberately allowed his belt to fall off, realizing that a naked man runs more easily than does a man with his clothing tucked up* (Pausanias *Guide to Greece* 1.44).

Athletes sometimes had their penis tied up to assist freedom of movement. The foreskin was pulled forward and tied up with a string called the *cynodesme*, which means literally "dog leash."

When Herodorus of Megara blew his trumpet, it was difficult to come near him, on account of the loudness of the blast. He won the trumpet event at all four great festivals [the Olympic, Pythian, Isthmian, and Nemean Games] *seventeen times* (Pollux *Onomasticon* 4.89). If his victories were consecutive, this would have taken sixty-eight years.

Theagenes of Thasos was a phenomenally successful athlete in several events, winning fourteen hundred crowns at the various festivals. According to Pausanias (*Guide to Greece* 6.11), his father was said to have been Heracles, who visited his mother in the guise of her husband. After Theagenes died one of his enemies used to whip his statue every night. It eventually fell on him, and the dead man's sons prosecuted it for murder. The statue was thrown into the sea. But then the crops on Thasos failed. The Delphic oracle told the Thasians to take back their exiles. They did so, but the crops still failed. The oracle told them they had forgotten Theagenes. Some fishermen caught the statue in their net, it was restored to its original position, and the famine ended. Statues of him were set up in many parts of Greece and among the barbarians, and he was thought to have the power to cure illnesses. The base of the statue on Thasos still survives, and the island's soccer team is named in his honor.

Polydamas of Scotussa was not only a great athlete:

- He killed a lion on Mt. Olympus with his bare hands.
- He fought a bull, which only escaped by leaving one of its hooves in his grasp.
- He stopped a chariot that was being driven at full speed.
- When Darius of Persia invited him to his court at Susa, he challenged three of the elite royal guard, the Immortals, to fight him three against one, and he killed them all.
- When he and his friends were picnicking in a cave, the roof began to crack. Everyone else ran out, but Polydamas thought he could hold the roof up. And so he died.

(Pausanias *Guide to Greece* 6.5)

Diodorus Siculus notes that *when Polydamas was crushed by the rocks it was obvious to all that it is of dubious benefit to have great strength but little sense* (*The Library* 9.14).

Milon of Croton was one of the most famous ancient athletes, winning the wrestling contest six times (once in the boys' category) at

Olympia and seven times at Delphi in the Pythian Games (again, once in the boys' category):

- No one could wrest a pomegranate from his fist, even when he did not squeeze the pomegranate enough to bruise it.
- He could stand on a discus that had been greased and defy all attempts to knock him off it.
- He could tie a cord around his forehead, then hold his breath until the veins stood out and broke the cord.
- He came across a dried tree trunk with wedges driven into it to split it. Unfortunately he was arrogant enough to think he could split it by himself. He put his hands into it, the wedges slipped, and his hands were trapped. He was stuck there until wolves devoured him.

(Pausanias *Guide to Greece* 6.14)

It is said that Taurosthenes's victory at Olympia [in 444 B.C.] *was reported to his father on Aegina that very same day by a figure in a vision. But it is also said that Taurosthenes took with him a pigeon that had a nest of chicks still moist and unfledged; as soon as he had won, he released it, with a piece of purple cloth attached to it, and it flew back to its chicks* (Aelian *Miscellaneous History* 9.2).

Athletes live a dozy sort of existence that is risky for their health. Don't you see how they sleep their way through life and suffer severe illnesses if they deviate even slightly from the diet prescribed for them? (Plato *Republic* 404a).

- *Dust from clay is good for cleansing and encourages moderation in sweating.*
- *Dust from terra-cotta opens the pores to induce sweating.*
- *Dust from bitumen gives warmth.*
- *Dust from black and yellow earth softens and nourishes the body.*

Wrestling with a bull.

- *Yellow dust also makes the body glisten, a delight to look at when the athlete is well built and in good training.*
- *Dust should be sprinkled gently with a free movement of the wrist and with the fingers widely spread, and it should cover the athlete like a fine down.*

(Philostratus *The Gymnast* 56)

Arrhachion, who had won the pancratium twice before, was wrestling in the final at Olympia [in 564 B.C.]. While his opponent was squeezing his neck, he broke one of his opponent's toes. Arrhachion died of suffocation just as his opponent gave in because of the pain in his toe. His corpse was crowned and proclaimed victor (Pausanias *Guide to Greece* 8.40).

Evening was approaching when Creugas of Epidamnus and Damoxenus of Syracuse were boxing at the Nemean Games, so they agreed that each should allow the other to inflict one free punch. Boxers at that time were still wearing soft gloves that left the fingers uncovered. Creugas punched

A graffito from Perge in Asia Minor.

Damoxenus on the head. Then Damoxenus told Creugas to raise his arm.
As soon as he did so, Damoxenus struck him with straight fingers under
the ribcage. The sharpness of his nails and the force of the blow were such
that he drove his hand right into Creugas's body. He grabbed his intestines
and tore them as he pulled them out (Pausanias *Guide to Greece* 8.40).
Damoxenus was adjudged to be cheating, because the blow from each
finger was regarded as a separate punch, and a boxer was in any case
only allowed to strike his opponent on the head, not on the body, so
Creugas was posthumously declared victor.

Eurydamas of Cyrene won the boxing event. He had his teeth knocked out,
but he swallowed them to prevent his opponent from realizing what had
happened (Aelian *Miscellaneous History* 10.19).

This man, who now looks so battered, used to have a nose, a chin, eye-
brows, ears, and eyes. Then he entered a boxing competition and lost them
all, so he did not receive his share in the inheritance from his father. For
his brother showed a little picture of him to the judge, who ruled that he
was someone different, since he had none of the same features (Lucillius
Greek Anthology 11.5, a fictitious inscription for a statue).

When a humble and very inferior boxer is matched against a famous op-
ponent who has never been defeated, the spectators immediately side with
the weaker fighter, shouting encouragement to him and punching when he
does. If he manages to hit his opponent on the face, leaving a mark, this
really sets them off. They shout insults at the champion, not because
they hate him or have no respect for him, but simply because they feel cu-
riously sympathetic to the underdog and give him their support (Polybius
Histories 27.9).

Melancomas of Caria was a boxer, but he was as healthy as any runner.
He trained so rigorously that he was able to stand with his guard up for
two days in succession, and no one could catch him taking a rest, as usu-
ally happens. He forced his opponents to give up, not just before he received
a punch, but also before he himself dealt a punch. He did not think

courage consisted in hitting and being hit; he thought that such a style of boxing indicated a lack of stamina and a desire to end the match (Dio Chrysostom *Melancomas II* 7).

It is best if a boxer has a small belly, for this allows him to move quickly and breathe easily. On the other hand, a big belly has the advantage that it impedes an opponent who is trying to punch your face (Philostratus *The Gymnast* 34).

Apollas, who wrote On Olympic Victors, *tells how Demaenetus of Parrhasia took part in the human sacrifice that the Arcadians were still making every year in honor of Zeus the Wolf God. On tasting the entrails of the boy who had been sacrificed, he turned into a wolf. But after ten years he changed back into a human being, trained as a boxer, and came home as a winner from the Olympic Games* (Pliny *Natural History* 8.82). Pliny offers this story as an example of the extent of Greek gullibility, noting that "no lie is so barefaced that it lacks support from someone."

According to Thucydides, to promote his case for being appointed to command the Sicilian expedition, Alcibiades boasted: *I entered seven teams in the chariot-race at Olympia, more than any private individual ever did before, and I not only won the victory but came second and fourth as well, and it was all done in a style worthy of a victor* (*History* 6.16). Euripides credited him with first, second, and third places.

Dionysius I, the tyrant of Syracuse, sent several four-horse chariots to compete in the Olympic Games, along with professional declaimers to recite his poetry. His chariots crashed into each other, his poetry was mocked, and the ship bringing his delegation back to Sicily was wrecked. The sailors who managed to get back to Syracuse put the blame for the disasters on Dionysius's bad poetry, but his flatterers persuaded him that every brilliant accomplishment is envied before it is admired, so he did not give up his enthusiasm for poetry (Diodorus Siculus *The Library* 14.109).

When Exaenetus of Acragas won the foot race at the ninety-second Olym-
pic Games [in 412 B.C.], *he was led back into the city in a chariot. Quite*
apart from the splendor of the rest of the parade, he was escorted by three
hundred chariots, each drawn by two white horses and all belonging to
citizens of Acragas (Timaeus *frg. 26a*).

Empedocles [the pre-Socratic philosopher] *is said to have won the single*
horse race in the same Olympic Games in which his son was victorious
either in wrestling or in one of the running races (Diogenes Laertius
Lives of the Philosophers 8.53).

In his short treatise *On Exercise with the Small Ball*, Galen sets out his
reasons why such exercise is superior to all other types of gymnastic
activity:

- *It exercises the body and gives pleasure to the soul.*
- *It requires little equipment or investment of time.*
- *It exercises all parts of the body, at an intensity of the participants'*
  choosing.
- *Catching the ball develops good hand-eye coordination.*
- *Most other exercises encourage lethargy. Even wrestlers at the Olympic*
  Games tend to put on weight and develop breathing difficulties. People
  like that are useless as leaders in war or politics; one would sooner entrust
  such duties to pigs.
- *Running causes excessive weight loss. Being able to run did not give the*
  Spartans supremacy in war. Running exercises some parts of the body too
  much, others too little, and this nourishes the seeds of disease.
- *Ball playing is risk-free, whereas sprinting has caused many people to*
  burst vital blood vessels; horseback riding can damage the kidneys, or the
  chest, or the testicles; and there is no need to mention wrestlers: they all
  end up disabled in some way or other.

In the old days, there were many types of ball games, and they were
taken very seriously. Among whole communities, Sparta was most in-
terested in ball games, among kings, Alexander the Great, among
private individuals, the tragedian Sophocles, who was highly
acclaimed when he acted the role of Nausicaa playing with a ball in

A game like field hockey on a late 6th-century B.C. funerary bas relief found in Athens.

his production of The Washerwomen *(Suetonius* On Children's Games *2).*

The following are debarred from stripping off to exercise in the gymnasium: slaves and freedmen and their sons, male prostitutes, those with no training in gymnastics, those who conduct business in the marketplace, drunks, madmen (Select Greek Inscriptions 27.261).

Charmus ran in the long distance event with five other competitors. Amazing as it may seem, he actually came seventh. "How," you may ask, "could he come seventh when there were only six runners?" A friend of his had run onto the track shouting, "Come on, Charmus!" That's why he came seventh. If he'd had five more friends, he'd have come twelfth (Nicarchus Greek Anthology 11.82).

Marcus once ran in the race in armor. He was still running at midnight, and the stadium authorities locked up, for they thought he was one of the stone statues. When they opened up again, he had finished the first lap (Nicarchus Greek Anthology 11.85).

Bind, bind down, restrain Antiochus, and Hierax, and Castor (also known as Dioscorus). Bind their feet, sinews, legs, spirit, strength, the 355

limbs of their bodies and souls, so that they may not make progress in the sprint, but remain like stones, unmoving, without running. With force, with force, with force, bind, bind the aforementioned as I requested, with force! (*Zeitschrift für Papyrologie und Epigraphik* 160 [2007] 163, part of a curse against athletes, written on a sheet of lead).

There are countless things wrong with Greece, but nothing so bad as athletes. . . . When they're young, they strut around as shining ornaments for their city, but when bitter old age befalls them, they're like threadbare cloaks with holes. I blame the Greeks for their custom of coming together to watch athletes, honoring useless pastimes as an excuse for feasting. For who has ever defended his country by winning a crown for wrestling well, or running fast, or throwing a discus, or punching someone on the jaw? (Euripides *frg.* 282). Aulus Gellius reports, however, that Euripides *competed as a boxer at the Isthmian and Nemean Games and was crowned as victor* (*Attic Nights* 15.20).

· XII ·

HOMER

*Who would listen to any other poet? Homer is
enough for everyone*
(Theocritus *Idyll* 16.20).

*I have done a lot of detailed research into the dating of Hesiod and Homer,
but I would not care to write about it, for I am only too aware just how
quarrelsome scholars of epic poetry are nowadays* (Pausanias *Guide to
Greece* 9.30). Nearly two thousand years later, *odium philologicum*, a
sad condition that can only afflict scholars with an unduly rigid com-
mitment to their own opinions, is not entirely extinct in Homeric
studies.

*A woman from Memphis, Phantasia, the daughter of Nicarchus, com-
posed the story of the Trojan War and the* Odyssey *before Homer did. It
is said that she deposited her books in Memphis, and that Homer went
there later and obtained copies from Phanites, the temple scribe, and composed his poetry in imitation of them* (Photius *The Library* 151b).

*After the conquest of Thebes, Daphne, the daughter of Tiresias, was taken
as a war captive to Delphi, where she made prophecies, changing her
name to Sibyl. Homer adopted many of her verses as ornaments for his
own poetry* (Diodorus Siculus *The Library* 4.66).

Corinnus was one of the pre-Homeric epic poets. He was the first to write an Iliad, *while the Trojan War was still in progress* (Suda s.v. Corinnus).

They say that Helen came and stood beside Homer in the night and ordered him to compose a poem about those who went on the expedition to Troy. She wished their death to seem more enviable than the life of all other people. It is also said that the charm and universal fame of Homer's poetry is partly due to his own artistry, but far more to Helen (Isocrates Praise of Helen 65).

According to Philostratus, Homer's father was the river Meles, a small stream flowing into the Aegean near Smyrna (*Lives of the Sophists* Preface).

Meleager claimed that Homer was a Syrian and that it was in accord with his ancestral customs that he represented the Greeks as abstaining from fish, even though there is a great abundance of fish at the Helles-pont (Athenaeus *Wise Men at Dinner* 157b). It is not coincidental that Meleager, an important literary figure in the early 1st century B.C., was himself a Syrian, from Gadara (home of the Gadarine swine).

Most people think Homer is Egyptian (St. Clement of Alexandria Stromata 1.66).

In a temple dedicated to Homer in Alexandria by Ptolemy Philopator, Galaton painted a picture of him vomiting, with all the other poets collecting what he threw up (Aelian *Miscellaneous History* 13.22). Keats and the other romantic poets might not have found this image very inspiring, but it is perhaps less alarming than its Roman equivalent: *When Virgil was reading Ennius* [the "Roman Homer"] *and someone asked him what he was doing, he replied, "I'm looking for gold on a dung-hill"* (Cassiodorus *Institutes* 1.1.8).

When Cleisthenes, the tyrant of Sicyon, was at war with Argos, he canceled the contests in the recital of poetry because the Homeric poems are so full of praise for the Argives and Argos (Herodotus *Histories* 5.67).

At the Great Panathenaea held in Athens every four years, relays of singers recited the complete Homeric epics without a break (Ps.-Plato *Hipparchus* 228*b*).

Alcibiades went into a school and asked for a copy of the Iliad. *When the teacher told him he didn't have any of Homer's poetry, he punched him and went away* (Plutarch *Sayings of Kings and Commanders* 186*d*).

To ensure that I grew up to be a good man, my father made me learn all of Homer's poetry. Even to this day, I could still recite the whole Iliad *and* Odyssey *from memory* (Xenophon *Symposium* 3.5).

Almost everyone in Borysthenes [on the north coast of the Black Sea] *is very keen on Homer, perhaps because they are still a warlike people. . . . They don't even want to hear about any poet except Homer. Most of them no longer speak an intelligible form of Greek, living as they do among barbarians; even so, nearly all of them know at least the* Iliad *by heart* (Dio Chrysostom *About Borysthenes* 9).

They say that Homer's poetry is sung among the Indians, translated into their language (Dio Chrysostom *On Homer* 6).

When the onlookers realized how closely the young Spartan resembled Hector, they trampled him to death (Plutarch *Life of Aratus* 3). We may wonder how Greeks in the historical period could agree on what a Homeric hero looked like. In the 6th century A.D., however, Johannes Malalas felt able to describe Hector as *swarthy, tall, well built, strong, with a fine nose and beard, curly haired, suffering from a squint and a stutter, noble in his bearing, an awesome warrior, with a deep voice* (*Chronographia* 105). His description of Hector's cousin, Aeneas, the founder of the Roman race, seems particularly surprising: *Aeneas was short and fat, with a strong chest; he was burly, with a ruddy complexion, a broad face, a shapely nose, light skin, a receding hairline, and a fine beard* (*Chronographia* 106).

Cicero mentions a copy of Homer's Iliad *written on parchment inside a nutshell* (Pliny *Natural History* 7.85). Pierre-Daniel Huet, a 17th-century French bishop, copied out eighty verses of the *Iliad* on a single line of a sheet of paper; at that rate, he could have included nineteen thousand verses on the page, over three thousand more than the *Iliad* actually contains.

The poems of Homer were lost through fire, flood, and earthquake, with the books all scattered and destroyed in different ways. Eventually, one man might have one hundred lines of Homer, another a thousand, another two hundred, and so on. That wonderful poetry was on the brink of oblivion. But then Pisistratus, an Athenian general, thought of a plan that would bring him glory and rescue the Homeric poems. He proclaimed throughout Greece that anyone who had lines of Homer should turn them in to him for a fixed price per line. Everyone with verses brought them in and was paid the fixed price without a quibble; even those who brought him verses that he had already received from someone else were paid just the same. . . . When all the verses had been collected, he summoned seventy-two scholars and asked them each individually to arrange the poems as he thought fit (Scholion to Dionysius Thrax *Art of Grammar* 26).

Scholars led by Aristarchus, and later by Zenodotus, arranged the Iliad *in accordance with the instructions of Pisistratus, the tyrant of Athens, and corrected it as they saw fit. Since the poem is so long and hard to read the whole way through, and therefore boring, they divided it into many books* (Eustathius *Commentary on the* Iliad Vol. 1, p. 9). In fact, whereas Pisistratus ruled Athens in the 6th century B.C., Zenodotus was head of the Library at Alexandria in the 3rd century, and Aristarchus in the 2nd.

Zenodotus excised *Iliad* 3.423–426 because they describe Aphrodite carrying a chair for Helen, a humble task he considered beneath the dignity of the great goddess. Decorum mattered to the scholars. Another critic, Aristonicus, was offended by *Odyssey* 11.525, in which Odysseus tells the ghost of Achilles how he had been given the responsibility of opening and shutting the door of the Trojan Horse: *this line should be excised as being undignified, for that is the task of a slave doorkeeper.*

Just as a man turns a sausage full of fat and blood now on one side, now on the other over a big hot fire, eager to have it cooked as soon as possible, just so did Odysseus toss and turn, plotting how he, alone against many, could get his hands on the shameless suitors (Homer *Odyssey* 20.25–30). Many Homeric similes are reworked by later epic poets, but not this one: it seems that only Homer himself could get away with such a splendidly vivid image. But perhaps he comes perilously close to crossing the line into bad taste when he describes the Trojan chariots rattling back home empty while their drivers "lie on the ground, much dearer to vultures than to their wives" (*Iliad* 11.162).

Some people are quite obviously insane, such as those who claim that Homer's two poems are about the elements of the universe and about the laws and customs of mankind. They make out, for example, that:

> *Agamemnon is the upper air.*
> *Achilles is the sun.*
> *Helen is the earth.*
> *Paris is the lower air.*
> *Hector is the moon.*
> *Demeter is the liver.*
> *Dionysus is the spleen.*
> *Apollo is bile.*
> (Philodemus *On Poems* 2)

Demetrius of Scepsis wrote thirty books of commentary on a little more than sixty lines of Homer, that is, on the Catalogue of the Trojans [*Iliad* 2.816–877] (Strabo *Geography* 13.1.45).

Eratosthenes declared that it will be possible to trace the route of Odysseus's wanderings when the cobbler is found who stitched up the bag of winds [given to Odysseus by Aeolus to assist him on his voyage home] (Strabo *Geography* 1.2.15).

Zoilus gained a reputation by whipping the statue of Homer (Galen *On the Method of Curing* 10.18). Hence he was known as Homeromastix ("Homer Whipper"). *He read his attacks on the* Iliad *and* Odyssey *to Ptolemy Philadelphus, but the king saw that he was merely abusing the father of poetry and the founder of philology, who was not there to defend himself, so he was angry and made no reply* (Vitruvius *On Architecture* 7 Preface 8).

Zoilus and others like him have made no useful contribution. They just barked pointlessly at Homer, sneering at his poetry and disparaging it (Tzetzes *Iliad* p. 3). When Zeus balances the destinies of Achilles and Hector in his golden scales, Zoilus asks if the destinies were made to sit or stand in the weighing-pans (*Iliad* 22.210), and when Patroclus's ghost disappears under the earth like a wisp of smoke, he points out that smoke dissipates upward (*Iliad* 23.100), crass and distracting inanities at two supreme moments in the poem. When Circe changes Odysseus's men into pigs, Zoilus describes them as "weeping wee piggies" (Ps.-Longinus *On the Sublime* 9.14).

Zoilus's death has been variously reported: either he was crucified by Philadelphus, or he was crucified on Chios after being stoned, or he was thrown alive onto a pyre at Smyrna. However he died, he thoroughly deserved it (Vitruvius *On Architecture* 7 Preface 8). Chios and Smyrna were two of the *poleis* that made particularly insistent claims to being Homer's birthplace.

Among the lesser poems attributed to Homer are *The Battle of the Frogs*, *The Battle of the Spiders*, and *The Battle of the Cranes*. These

Odysseus's men as pigs.

have perished, but *The Battle of the Frogs and the Mice*, a rather disappointing parody of martial epic, survives complete. Fragments of *The Battle of the Weasels and the Mice* have also been found (*Michigan Papyrus* 6946), but it is not actually attributed to Homer.

Pigres of Halicarnassus added a pentameter after every line of the Iliad, *making it an elegiac poem. He was the author of the* Margites *and* The Battle of Frogs and Mice, *which are attributed to Homer* (Suda s.v. *Pigres*).

Sotades of Maroneia wrote a version of the *Iliad* in a meter largely of his own devising, the Sotadean. Only six lines of his poetry survive, and all but one of them are doubtfully attributed. By far his most notorious line is a criticism of Ptolemy Philadelphus for marrying Arsinoe, his full sister: *He is pushing his prick into an unholy hole* (*frg.* 1). His second, and longest, fragment is no more edifying: *Uncovering the hole in his back passage, he pushed out through the wooded gorge an idly resounding thunderclap, the sort that an old plowing ox releases.* He is said to have been punished for his attacks on royalty by being thrown into the sea in a leaden jar (Athenaeus *Wise Men at Dinner* 621a).

Timolaus of Larissa was a rhetorician and a pupil of the philosopher Anaximenes of Lampsacus, but he also had an interest in poetry. He added another line after every line in the Iliad *and called his composition* Troicus (Suda s.v. *Timolaus*; the Suda attributes the same tour de force to Idaeus of Rhodes).

Nestor of Laranda rewrote the *Iliad*, omitting alpha from the first book, beta from the second, etc. Triphiodorus of Sicily perhaps did the same with the *Odyssey*, but Eustathius reports that he may have omitted only sigma, to ensure that his speech defect did not inhibit his pronunciation (*Commentary on the* Odyssey Vol. 1, p. 2). The Greeks had a word for such omissions: "lipogrammatic," literally "leaving out writing."

Almost nothing has survived from these reworkings and adaptations of Homer, but the loss to literature is probably not great. In the 1st century A.D., Attius Labeo translated both the *Iliad* and the *Odyssey* into Latin word for word. That in itself is a curious achievement, but "his translation was so atrocious that not even Labeo himself could understand it unless he had been purged with hellebore [to treat his insanity]" (Cornutus on Persius *Satires* 1.50).

· XIII ·

DRAMA

*It was customary in Athens to release
prisoners on bail for the duration of the Dionysiac
and Panathenaic festivals*
(Scholion to Demosthenes 22.170*b*).

Over a period of three consecutive days at the city Dionysia in Athens, there were twenty performances by dithyrambic choruses, nine tragedies, three satyr plays, and at least three comedies. It is difficult for the modern theatergoer to imagine, in particular, the cathartic pity and terror of a tragic trilogy, followed by a mood-altering satyr play. Neither Wagner's *Ring Cycle* nor even the Sturm und Drang of an international cricket match (thirty hours' play over five days) requires anything like so much stamina from the spectators.

Decamnichus led the conspiracy against Archelaus [the king of Macedonia], *who had once handed him over to Euripides the poet for a whipping. Euripides was offended when Decamnichus said something about him having bad breath* (Aristotle *Politics* 1311*b*).

I think my accuser could demonstrate the extent of my poverty more clearly than anyone else: if I were appointed to finance a tragic performance and challenged him to an exchange of property, he would prefer to put up the funding for a theatrical performance ten times rather than exchange property

once (Lysias *On the Refusal of a Pension* 9). Might Lysias be echoing Medea's famous utterance: "I would rather stand three times in the battleline than give birth once" (Euripides *Medea* 250)? If an exchange took place, the person originally called upon would then finance the undertaking. It is not clear precisely how, or how often, such transfers of property took place.

Dionysius I, the tyrant of Syracuse, received an oracle that he would die when he had defeated his betters. He assumed that this referred to his war with Carthage, so he withdrew his forces whenever victory seemed assured. He had delusions of being a great poet, but his poems were mocked both at the Olympic Games (see p. 116) and in his own court. He was, however, victorious in one of the Athenian dramatic competitions and died of drinking too much wine in celebration. This was interpreted as a vindication of the oracle, the other poets in the contest being better than he was (Diodorus Siculus *The Library* 14.109, 15.74).

At the festivals in honor of Dionysus, there was keen competition for the seats, involving some of the citizens in violence and injury. So the people decided that admission should no longer be free. A charge for seating was imposed, but the poor were disadvantaged because the rich could easily afford to pay this, and so a decree was passed limiting the charge to one drachma, and they called it "the price for the plays" (Photius *Lexicon* s.v. *Theorica*, "For the Plays"). The scholion to Lucian *Timon* 49 says that people even occupied seats during the night before a performance to be sure of seeing the plays.

Anaxandrides was rather sour tempered. If ever his comedies failed to win, he did not revise them as most dramatists do; instead, he let them be cut up and used as wrappers in the perfume market. He destroyed many painstakingly written plays, because old age had made him disgruntled with the spectators (Athenaeus *Wise Men at Dinner* 374a). Anaxandrides's plays are almost entirely lost. He seems to have been quite a character; Athenaeus reports in the same passage that he once rode on horseback into the theater at Athens and recited part of one of his own dithyrambs.

At his last banquet, Alexander the Great recited from memory a scene from Euripides's Andromeda *(Athenaeus* Wise Men at Dinner *537d).*

If you strip a tragic actor of his mask and his gold embroidered robe, all that is left is a funny little man hired for seven drachmas to perform at the festival (Lucian *Icaromenippus* 29).

A 3rd-century B.C. inscription records an actor-athlete's victories in plays by Euripides and other tragedians at various festivals throughout

A tragic actor.

Greece and also in the men's boxing at the Ptolemaic Festival in Alexandria (Stephanis [1988] *Dionysiakoi Technitai* No. 3003). The combination seems the more incongruous because of the particularly bloody nature of Greek boxing (see p. 115).

THEATRICAL WORDS

- *Theater*: "a place for watching" (from *theasthai*, "to look at"). "Theory" is related, being something looked at, contemplated, and therefore thought about.
- *Thespian*: this rather pretentious term for "actor" refers to Thespis, traditionally thought of as the founder of Greek tragedy in the 6th century B.C.
- *Drama*: "a thing done" (from *dran*, "to do"), a specialized sense for a very ordinary term; *poiema* (from *poiein*, another verb meaning "to do") has the same literal sense, but means "poem."
- *Tragedy*: the original meaning is generally agreed to be "goat song" (from *tragos* and *ode*), either because the actors originally dressed up as goats, or because the prize for victory in dramatic competitions was a goat (goats gnawed the roots of vines, which were sacred to Dionysus, the god of the festival).
- *Comedy*: a song (*ode*) sung either in a drunken procession (*komos*) or in a village (*kome*).
- *Scene*: the basic meaning is "tent"; in theatrical terms it is the stage on which the play was performed. In most Greek tragedies, the whole play is performed without a change of setting.
- *Chorus*: the original meaning is "dance" or "group of dancers." Their role in 5th-century B.C. tragedy was not restricted to dancing (and singing); they also conversed with the actors.
- *Orchestra*: the area in front of the stage where the chorus danced (*orcheisthai*).
- *Actor*: a Latin term, meaning literally "a person who does things." The Greek word is *hypocrites*; the basic meaning is "interpreter," but the modern sense of the word was already used in antiquity.
- *Protagonist*: it is strictly speaking incorrect to refer in the plural to the "protagonists" in a play, novel, or movie. Tragedy in the 5th century B.C. never allowed more than three performers with speaking roles, other

than the chorus, to be on stage at any one time; they were known as the protagonist, deuteragonist, and tritagonist (*protos, deuteros, tritos* ("first," "second," "third") and *agonistes* ("performer").

- *Catharsis*: literally "cleaning." By exciting feelings of pity and terror, tragedy cleanses us of such emotions (Aristotle *Poetics* 1449*b*).

Large bronze vessels used to enhance the acoustics in the theater at Corinth were taken as plunder when the Romans sacked the city in 146 B.C. (Vitruvius *On Architecture* 5.3), even though Rome itself would not have a permanent theater for another eighty-nine years.

Alexander wanted to have a stage made of bronze for his theater in Pella, but the architect refused to follow his instructions since that would ruin the actors' voices (Plutarch *A Pleasant Life Is Impossible on Epicurean Principles* 1096*b*).

Sophocles used to criticize Aeschylus for writing his plays while drunk, saying that "Even though he composes as he should, he does so without being aware of what he's doing" (Plutarch *frg.* 130).

The status of Aeschylus, Sophocles, and Euripides as the supreme Athenian tragedians has never been challenged. We tend to ignore the other tragedians who competed with them every year at the dramatic festivals in Athens, whose works survive mostly in occasional quotations by later authors and in scrappy papyrus fragments. The same tendency prevailed in antiquity:

> *In the year of the ninety-first Olympic Games, when Exaenetus of Acragas won the foot race* [i.e., 416 B.C.; a modern writer might have said, "In the year that the Athenians killed all the adult male inhabitants of Melos and enslaved all the women and children"], *Xenocles and Euripides competed against each other. Xenocles, whoever he was, won first prize. . . . This was ridiculous. Either those responsible for the vote were witless, ignorant, and incapable of reaching a sound decision, or they had been bribed. And yet both these explanations are strange and unworthy of Athens.* (Aelian *Miscellaneous History* 2.8)

Aeschylus first competed in 499 B.C., but did not win first prize until 484, and Euripides had almost as long to wait for his first success, from 455 until 441. Sophocles's career, however, is said to have started in 468 with a victory.

Sophocles's *Oedipus the King* is regarded by many as the greatest surviving tragedy, but the trilogy in which it appeared was beaten into second place by Aeschylus's nephew, Philocles, of whose hundred or so plays almost nothing survives. *Sophocles was defeated by Philocles—O Zeus and all the gods! And with his* Oedipus *of all plays, to which not even Aeschylus himself could have had any answer!* (Aelius Aristides *In Defence of the Four* 526).

In 431 B.C., perhaps two years before Philocles's astounding success, Aeschylus's son, Euphorion, won what may have been his only victory, beating Sophocles into second place, while Euripides came in third with a trilogy that included the *Medea*.

Some idiosyncrasies in tragedies:

- Aeschylus's *Persae* is the only extant tragedy on a historical theme.
- Aeschylus's *Prometheus Bound* is the only extant tragedy without human characters (except the priestess Io, in the form of a cow).
- Aeschylus's *Oresteia* is the only complete extant trilogy (it is, in fact, the only trilogy from which more than a single play survives).
- Sophocles's *Philoctetes* is the only extant tragedy with no female roles.
- Euripides's *Andromache* is the only extant tragedy not written for performance in Athens.
- Euripides's *Bacchae* is probably the only extant tragedy not written in Athens.
- Euripides's *Cyclops* is the only complete extant satyr play.
- Ps.-Euripides's *Rhesus* is the only extant tragedy by someone other than the three great tragedians (if *Prometheus Bound* is by Aeschylus).
- Avenging the murder of Agamemnon is the only story treated by all three great tragedians in extant plays.
- All three great tragedians wrote plays entitled *Iphigenia, Ixion, Philoctetes, Sisyphus,* and *Telephus.*

Sophocles was handsome as a young man, and even while he was still a boy he was an expert dancer and musician. After the Battle of Salamis, he danced around the trophy playing his lyre, naked and anointed with oil. (Some people say he wore a cloak.) When he put on his Thamyris, *he personally played the lyre, and he was a skillful ball player in the production of his* Nausicaa (Athenaeus *Wise Men at Dinner* 20e).

The Athenians allowed Pothinus the puppeteer to perform on the very stage on which Euripides and the other tragedians put on their inspiring plays (Athenaeus *Wise Men at Dinner* 19e).

After the disaster in Sicily, some Athenians owed their lives to Euripides. For none of the Greeks overseas yearned for his poetry more than did those in Sicily. Every time they heard a little sample of his poetry from a traveler, they learned it by heart and took great pleasure in passing it on. Many members of the expedition embraced Euripides affectionately when they reached home, since some had been released from slavery for teaching their captors whatever they could remember of his poetry, and others had been given food and drink when they were wandering about after the battle, in return for singing choral passages from his plays (Plutarch *Life of Nicias* 29).

After the death of Euripides, Dionysius, the Sicilian tyrant, sent a large sum of money to his heirs and acquired his lyre, his writing tablet, and his stylus (Hermippus of Smyrna *frg.* 94). He also bought Aeschylus's writing tablet (Lucian *Against the Ignorant Book Buyer* 15).

The *Hypothesis* to Euripides's *Medea* records a tradition that it is a reworking of a play by Neophron that Euripides passed off as his own. The surviving fragments of Neophron's play do have some affinities to that by Euripides.

Rejecting lines 1366–68 of Euripides's *Orestes* as spurious, an ancient commentator remarks: *No one could readily accept that these three lines are by Euripides. It is more likely that the actors wrote them, so that they could simply open the door of the palace to come on stage, and not hurt*

themselves by jumping off the roof. They inserted these verses so that their entrance through the door would seem logical. But what they say subsequently contradicts their coming through the door.

Euripides is said to have had a very strong dislike for almost all women, either from an innate aversion to their company, or because he had had two wives at the same time (the Athenians had passed a decree making that legal [because of the high number of casualties in the Peloponnesian War]*), and he was thoroughly put off by his marriage to them* (Aulus Gellius *Attic Nights* 15.20).

The unusual nature of Aeschylus's death makes it worth recording. He went outside the walls of the Sicilian city in which he was staying and sat down in a sunny spot. An eagle flying over with a tortoise in its talons mistook his shiny bald head for a stone. It dropped the tortoise on Aeschylus's head, so that it could break its shell and eat its flesh. By that blow the source and beginning of tragedy in its more powerful form was extinguished (Valerius Maximus *Memorable Deeds and Sayings* 9.12 ext. 2). Pliny refines this tale by adding that Aeschylus stayed out in open places in the hope of cheating a prophecy that he would be killed by a falling object (*Natural History* 10.7).

This tale of Aeschylus's bizarre demise may be inspired by one of his plays. A fragment of the mostly lost *Necromancers* reads:

> *A heron flying overhead will strike you with dung emptied from its belly. Your aged scalp from which the hair has fallen out will be made to fester by a spine from its food gathered in the sea.*
> (Aeschylus *frg.* 478a, where Tiresias prophesies Odysseus's death)

Similarly, the story of Euripides's death has tragic overtones. *Euripides was returning from dinner with King Archelaus of Macedon, when he was torn to pieces by dogs set on him by some jealous rival* (Aulus Gellius *Attic Nights* 15.20) In the *Bacchae*, one of the plays in Euripides's final trilogy, Pentheus is torn apart by his female kinsfolk.

Sophocles is also said to have died in a remarkable way. The *Life of Sophocles* records that

- *he choked on an unripe grape,*
- *he died of joy when told that his last play had been victorious, or*
- *reading aloud a long section near the end of his* Antigone *with no commas or other punctuation that would allow him to pause to take a breath put too much of a strain on his aged body.*

· XIV ·

SPECTATORS
AND CRITICS

*Theocritus of Chios heard a recital by a mediocre
poet, who then asked him which bits he thought
were good. Theocritus replied, "The bits you left out"*
(*Gnomologium Vaticanum* 338).

*The poet Timocreon of Rhodes was exceedingly arrogant. When he came
forward to compete in a musical contest, someone asked him where he was
from, and he replied, "You will hear where I am from in a little while,
when the herald announces my victory." This response offended the audience so much that the judge almost had to interrupt his song. . . . When he
left the stage in defeat, the same person asked him again where he was
from, and he replied, "From Seriphos"* (Philodemus *On Vices* 10). For
Seriphos as a nondescript and undistinguished island, unlike Rhodes,
see p. 67.

*There were officials in the theater who carried canes to ensure good order
among the spectators* (Scholion to Aristophanes *Peace* 734).

*The spectators used to hoot and whistle and drum their heels against their
seats whenever they wanted to clear an actor off the stage* (Pollux
Onomasticon 4.122).

When we are really enjoying something, we ignore everything else. People who eat snacks during theatrical performances do so mostly when the acting is poor (Aristotle *Nicomachean Ethics* 1175*b*).

When power was transferred from the people to just a few men and the oligarchy was in control, fear fell upon the poets. It was not possible to mock anyone openly, since those who were insulted could take the dramatists to court. Alcibiades drowned Eupolis in the sea for criticizing him in the Baptae (Platonius *On Differences in Comedies frg.* 1). The manner of Eupolis's death alleged here is appropriate, because *Baptae* means "Bathers."

The Athenians do not allow the populace as a whole to be the target of criticism in comedy, whereas they encourage attacks on individuals. They are well aware that a person made fun of by comedians is rarely someone in the lower orders of society, but is usually someone who is rich, well born, or influential. The few poor people from the lower classes who are attacked are either busybodies or have ideas above their station, and criticism of them in comedy is not objectionable (Ps.-Xenophon *The Athenian Constitution* 2.18).

The Athenians used to flock to the theater to hear abuse and criticism hurled at them, and gave prizes to the dramatists who did this best. Aristophanes and the other comedians suffered no harm for it. But when Socrates did the same thing without the obscene dances and silly songs, they did not tolerate it (Dio Chrysostom *To the People of Tarsus* I 9).

Just before Heraclides took part in a dramatic competition, he dreamed that he was cutting the throats of the audience and the judges. He was unsuccessful. They were not likely to give him their votes when he had cut their throats (Artemidorus *Interpretation of Dreams* 4.33).

There are men who entertain crowds by showing that their bald heads can withstand anything: boiling pitch being poured over their heads, a ram trained to charge fiercely from a distance to head-butt them, pottery being broken over

them, lots of things that make the spectators shudder. . . . Watching such a performance, I counted my blessings (Synesius *In Praise of Baldness* 13).

⚱

In the Painted Porch at Athens, I recently saw with my own two eyes a street entertainer swallowing a cavalry sabre with a sharp point and a vicious blade. After that, induced by a few small coins, he also inserted a hunting spear, point downward, all the way into his entrails. And then a wonderfully supple boy, whose movements were so snakelike that he seemed to have no bones or sinews, clambered along the haft of the spear as it projected over the other performer's head (Apuleius *Metamorphoses* 1.4).

⚱

The Ascolia was a festival in honor of Dionysus, in which inflated skins were placed in the middle of the theater and people tried to jump on them, either hopping on one foot or using both. They made the spectators laugh by the way they fell about on the skins (Scholion to Aristophanes *Wealth* 1129). Such inflated skins might be greased to make people slip about on them all the more (Pollux *Onomasticon* 9.121).

⚱

When Simonides was dining with the rich Thessalian aristocrat Scopas, he sang a song that he had composed in his host's honor, in which he had included many details about Castor and Pollux as a standard poetic ornament. But Scopas very meanly told Simonides that he would pay him for only half of the song; he could ask Castor and Pollux for the rest if he liked, since he had praised them just as much. Moments later, Simonides was called away to meet two young men, who wanted to see him urgently. When he went to the door, he could not see anyone, but at just that instant the ceiling of the dining room collapsed, crushing Scopas and his kinsmen (Cicero *On the Orator* 2.352). The young men were, of course, Castor and Pollux. Cicero goes on to relate that *the corpses were so mangled that they could not be identified for burial, but Simonides distinguished them by recalling where each person had been reclining,* and he records how this gruesome incident inspired Simonides to invent a system of mnemonics based on visualization.

⚱

Socrates was frequently portrayed or referred to in plays, and I would not be surprised if he was easy to recognize among the characters, for the mask-makers obviously made a very good likeness of him. But on one occasion foreigners in the audience did not know who was being made fun of, so they began to murmur, asking who this man Socrates was. Socrates was in the theater—not by chance, but because he knew the play was about him—and he was sitting in a prominent place. He put an end to the foreigners' confusion by standing up and staying on his feet throughout the performance (Aelian *Miscellaneous History* 2.13).

When Aristophanes made so much fun of him in the Clouds, *someone asked Socrates if he was not upset at being the butt of comedy, but Socrates replied, "Not at all, for being teased in the theater is just like being teased at an oversized symposium"* (Plutarch *On the Education of Children* 10*d*).

A proposal is said to have been made to the Spartans and their allies [after their final victory in the Peloponnesian War] *that the population of Athens should be sold into slavery, and Erianthus of Thebes suggested that Athens should be razed to the ground and the land given over to sheep grazing. But when the leaders gathered for a symposium and a Phocian sang the first chorus of Euripides's* Electra, *they were all moved to pity, and it seemed a harsh act to destroy and obliterate such a famous city, one that produced such poets* (Plutarch *Life of Lysander* 15).

During a dramatic festival at Athens, the actor who was to perform the role of queen asked the producer Melanthius for a large number of expensively costumed attendants. When he did not get them, he was upset and held up the performance by refusing to appear. But Melanthius shoved him out on stage, shouting, "Don't you see Phocion's wife always going around with just a single slave-girl, whereas you give yourself airs and are the ruin of our women?" His words were clearly audible, and the spectators welcomed them with great applause and cheering (Plutarch *Life of Phocion* 19). Phocion is largely forgotten now, but he was one of the foremost Athenian politicians of the 4th century B.C., famous and exceptional for his simple and honest lifestyle.

Jason, the tyrant of Pherae, used to bury people alive, or dress them in the hides of wild boar or bears and then set his hunting dogs on them, tearing them to pieces or shooting them for sport; he had the whole adult population of two allied and friendly cities surrounded by his bodyguards and massacred while they were holding an assembly; he sanctified and garlanded the spear with which he had murdered his uncle, and sacrificed to it, addressing it as "Lucky." But once, when he was watching an actor performing scenes from Euripides's Trojan Women, *he rushed out of the theater. He sent the actor a message, telling him not to be upset or allow his departure to affect his performance; he said he had not left because he thought little of his acting, but rather because he was ashamed to let the people see him weeping at the sufferings of Hecuba and Andromache when he had never shown pity to any of those he had murdered* (Plutarch *Life of Pelopidas* 29).

Some say that, when Aeschylus brought the chorus members onto the stage one at a time in the performance of the Eumenides, *it caused such a shock that children fainted and women had miscarriages* (Life of Aeschylus 9).

Even while he was still standing in silence on the stage, a tragic actor frightened the people of Ipola, a small town in Spain. When they saw him striding across the stage wearing his high tragic boots and his awesome garments, and with the mouth of his mask gaping open, they were terrified; then, when he raised his voice and shouted out loud, most of them ran off as if a demon had put them to flight (Philostratus *Life of Apollonius* 5.9).

It is undignified if the producers of plays force a laugh by having the actors throw little figs and other dried fruit to the audience (Aristophanes *Wealth* 797–99).

When a character in one of Euripides's tragedies argued that wealth mattered more than morality, *the whole people rose up together to throw both the actor and the play out of the theater, but Euripides leaped out*

into the middle of the stage, begging them to wait and see the evil end in store for the character who admired gold so much (Seneca *Epistles* 115.15).

When the audience demanded that he should remove a particular thought from one of his plays, Euripides reacted by coming forward on stage and saying that it was his practice to write plays to instruct the people, not to learn from them. This did not, however, earn him a reputation for arrogance (Valerius Maximus *Memorable Deeds and Sayings* 3.7 ext. 1).

Theodorus, the tragic actor, may have had a point in not allowing any other actor, even a mediocre one, to come on stage before he did, in the belief that the audience comes to appreciate the voices it hears first. The same applies to all aspects of life: we always like best what we get to know first (Aristotle *Politics* 1336b).

Judges, don't let our play suffer because the lottery made it the first to be performed. . . . Don't be like evil prostitutes who remember only their latest customers (Aristophanes *Assembly Women* 1158).

A lyre-player was giving a performance in Iasus, and all the people listened to him for a while. But when the fish market bell rang, everyone went off to buy fish, except for one man who was hard of hearing. The musician went up to him and said, "Thank you, sir, for the compliment you have paid me and for your appreciation of music. Everyone else went away when they heard the bell." The deaf man replied, "What's that? Has the bell rung already?" When the lyre-player told him that it had, he said good-bye, and even he stood up and went away (Strabo *Geography* 14.2).

When Plato read his treatise On the Soul *[i.e., the* Phaedo*], Aristotle was the only member of the audience who stayed until the end* (Diogenes Laertius *Lives of the Philosophers* 3.37).

They say that, when the distinguished poet Antimachus was reading his well known poem to an invited audience, and everyone except Plato had got up and left, he remarked, "I'll keep reading all the same, for Plato

alone is worth an audience of a hundred thousand" (Cicero *Brutus* 191). *Antimachus salivated freely and was called "The Drizzler," because he used to spray those with whom he was conversing* (Diogenianus *Proverbs* 8.71).

A pompous sophist named Philagrus asked his audience in Athens to suggest a topic, on which he would then make an extempore speech. He did not know that the audience members were in possession of copies of a speech he had already delivered in Asia. They suggested that same topic, and as he began to deliver an allegedly spontaneous speech, they read it along with him (Philostratus *Lives of the Sophists* 579). It is not unknown for professors nowadays to deliver lectures that repeat all but verbatim their already published research.

When he was asked which of Demosthenes's speeches he thought the best, Cicero replied, "The longest one" (Plutarch *Life of Cicero* 24).

> *When a mediocre lyre-player repeatedly asked him*
> *which part of his performance he particularly*
> *enjoyed, Stratonicus replied, "The bits before the*
> *opening passage"*
> (***Gnomologium Vaticanum*** 523).

· XV ·

BOOKS AND PAPYRI

*When Socrates was asked why he did not write
anything, he replied, "Because I see that material
to write on is much more valuable than anything
I might write"*
(**Stobaeus** *Anthology* 3.21).

Pronapides of Athens [Homer's teacher, according to Diodorus Siculus
The Library 3.67] *instituted the practice of writing in lines that we still
use nowadays. In early times, people wrote either in coils, or in rectangles,
or in columns, or* boustrophedon ("as oxen turn [when plowing]", i.e.,
right to left and left to right alternately) (Scholion to Dionysius Thrax
Art of Grammar 183).

*Ptolemy was so enthusiastic about books that he even ordered every book on
every ship that came to Egypt to be brought to him. He had them copied onto
new papyrus, and the copies were given to the owners of the books, whereas
the originals were deposited in the libraries with the ascription "From the
Ships"* (Galen *Commentary on Hippocrates's* Epidemics 17a.606).

*The way Ptolemy negotiated with the Athenians demonstrates very clearly
his enthusiasm for acquiring old texts. He gave them a security deposit of
fifteen talents of silver for the authorized texts of Sophocles, Euripides, and
Aeschylus, on the understanding that he would make copies and return*

the originals safely. He made expensive copies on papyrus of the highest quality, then kept the originals and sent the Athenians the new texts, telling them to keep the fifteen talents (Galen *Commentary on Hippocrates's* Epidemics 17a.607).

❦

When he was contending with Eumenes, the king of Pergamum, in the acquisition of a library, Ptolemy cut off supplies of papyrus. This led to the invention of parchment at Pergamum and the subsequent widespread use of that material in guaranteeing the immortality of human accomplishments (Pliny *Natural History* 13.70). Parchment was originally finely scraped animal skins, and the term "parchment" is derived from *charta pergamena*, "writing material from Pergamum."

♈

Before the kings in Alexandria and Pergamum became such zealous collectors of old books, authorship was never falsified. But as soon as bounties were paid to the people employed in collecting books written by a particular ancient writer, they started to bring in many books that they falsely attributed to that author (Galen *On Hippocrates's* Nature of Man 15.105).

⚱

Ptolemy Philadelphus (ruled 283–246 B.C.) summoned seventy-two Israelite elders to Alexandria and placed them in separate chambers. He then instructed each of them separately to prepare a Greek translation of the Hebrew Torah (i.e., the first five books of the Old Testament). Thanks to divine intervention, the translations the elders produced were all identical (*The Talmud* Megillah 9).

⚱

The complete Greek translation of the Old Testament is known as the *Septuagint*, from the Latin *septuaginta*, "seventy." However, because there were seventy-two elders involved (six from each of the twelve tribes of Israel, according to, e.g., St. Cyril *Catacheseis* 4.34), and since, according to other sources, they completed their task in seventy-two days, it might more accurately be called the *Septuaginta Duo*.

♈

To enhance Alexandria's reputation as a center for learning, Ptolemy Euergetes (ruled 246–221 B.C.) instituted games in honor of Apollo and the Muses, with prizes awarded to the winners in musical and literary contests. The spectators unanimously signaled to the judges the contestant that they thought should win the poetry prize. Six of the judges agreed, but the seventh, Aristophanes of Byzantium, said the prize should go to the poet who had pleased the audience least. The king and the crowd were highly indignant, but Aristophanes stood up and accused all the other poets of plagiarism, citing from memory from an infinite number of volumes stored on particular shelves in the Library. The poets confessed, and Aristophanes was given a generous reward and appointed head of the Library (Vitruvius *On Architecture* 7 Preface).

Aristophanes of Byzantium was one of Alexandria's greatest scholars. He wrote influential studies on the text of Homer and other poets, on the Greek language, and on many other topics. He was also at least partially responsible for the development of the system of written accents used to denote the pronunciation of Greek, a rather fearsome convention still in force in the modern language until 1982, when the Greek Ministry of Education introduced a much simpler system. Like Henry Higgins in *My Fair Lady*, Aristophanes fell in love with a flower girl. But he had a rival:

> *Some animals experience wild and frenzied erotic passions, but in others such feelings are refined, delicate, and almost human. For example, the elephant that loved the same flower girl as did the scholar Aristophanes in Alexandria declared its love no less clearly than he did. For it would always bring her fruit as it went through the market and stand beside her for a long time, putting its trunk like a hand inside her clothing and gently fondling her lovely breasts.*
> (Plutarch *Whether Land or Sea Animals Are Cleverer* 972d)

Didymus, who wrote more than anyone else has ever done, once objected to some story as being absurd, but then one of his own books was brought forward as the authority for it (Quintilian *Education of the Orator* 1.8.18). As a reflection on his stamina and perhaps also his lack of sensitivity in writing almost four thousand works, mainly, it seems, digests of other scholars' writings, Didymus was nicknamed Χαλκέντερος (*Chalcenterus*, "Bronze Guts"). The incident related by Quintilian earned him a second nickname, βιβλιολάθας (*Bibliolathas*, "Book Forgetter").

What is the point of having countless books, if the owner scarcely reads through their titles in his whole lifetime? Their sheer number is an impediment to learning: it is far better to give oneself over to a few authors than to browse through many. Forty thousand books were burned in the fire at the Library in Alexandria. Others may praise that library as the most splendid monument to royal wealth, as Livy did, when he said that it was the outstanding achievement of the good taste and care of the kings. But it was not good taste or care; it was learned decadence—indeed, not even learned, since they had bought the books not for study but for show, just as many people who know less about literature than a child does have books not as tools for study but just to decorate their dining room. So buy books you need, don't buy them just for show (Seneca *On Tranquility of Mind* 9.4).

No book will be taken out, for we have sworn it. The Library will be open from the first hour to the sixth (notice in the public library built in the Athenian agora during the Roman period).

When the barbarians captured Athens [in A.D. 267], *they gathered all the books in the city together, intending to burn them. But one of them, who was apparently wiser than the rest, persuaded them not to do so, arguing that if the Greeks wasted their time on books, they would neglect military matters and be that much easier to subdue* (Zonaras *Annals* 3.150).

When he was away from home, a friend wrote to a teacher asking him to buy him some books. The teacher neglected the request, and when he met his friend on his return home, he said, "That letter you sent me about the books, I didn't get it" (Philogelos *Joke Book* 17).

A snake's intestine, measuring 120 feet, with both the *Iliad* and the *Odyssey* inscribed on it in letters of gold, perished in a fire that destroyed a library of 120,000 books in Constantinople in the late 5th century (Zonaras *Annals* 14.2).

In order to write in letters of gold without using gold, you need:

> *One part celandine*
> *One part pure resin*
> *One part gold-colored arsenic*
> *One part pure gum*
> *One part tortoise bile*
> *Five parts egg white.*

To twenty measures of these ingredients, dried, add four measures of Cilician saffron.

You can write with it not only on papyrus and parchment, but also on polished marble, and it will have the appearance of gold should you wish to draw a design on any other surface (Leiden Papyrus 10.74).

Thucydides's *History* runs to 153,260 words. Demosthenes is said to have copied out the whole work eight times (Lucian *Against the Ignorant Book Buyer* 4). A 5th-century A.D. orator named Marcellus learned all of Thucydides by heart, but was unable to say anything worth listening to (Damascius *Life of Isidore* frg. 138).

Dionysius wrote a tragedy, which he called Parthenopaeus, *and he attributed it to Sophocles. Heraclides quoted from it in one of his own works as if it really was by Sophocles. Dionysius then told him what he had done. But Heraclides refused to believe him, so Dionysius told him to look at the first letters of the opening eight lines. They spelled "Pancalus," which was the name of Dionysius's lover. Heraclides still refused to believe him, saying that it might be mere coincidence, so Dionysius sent him another message telling him that he would also find as acrostics, "An old monkey does not get caught in a trap—actually, it does, but only after a long time" and "Heraclides doesn't understand writing and yet he's not ashamed" (Diogenes Laertius Lives of the Philosophers 5.92).* Heraclides was more perceptive in proposing that the earth revolves on its axis from east to west every twenty-four hours.

Epicharmus left behind him treatises in which he discusses natural philoso-
phy, collects maxims, and writes about medicine. He added acrostics to
most of them to prove that he was the author (Diogenes Laertius *Lives of*
the Philosophers 8.78).

Anaximenes retaliated against a personal enemy in a way that was both
very clever and very nasty. He had a talent for rhetoric and for imi-
tating the style of rhetoricians. He had fallen out with Theopompus, the
son of Damasistratus, so he wrote an abusive tract attacking the Athe-
nians, the Spartans, and the Thebans in the style of Theopompus, whose
name he inscribed on it as the author. He had copies sent to the various
cities, and so Theopompus came to be hated throughout all Greece
(Pausanias *Guide to Greece* 6.18). For Anaximenes's deviousness, see
also p. 77.

The smallest surviving book from antiquity is the Cologne *Mani*
Codex, written on parchment in Egypt in the early 5th century A.D. It
consists of 192 pages, each measuring only 3.5 x 4.5 cms, and each with
23 beautifully written lines of Greek. For excellent pictures, visit the
Papyrus Collection of the University of Cologne at http://www.uni-
koeln.de/phil-fak/ifa/NRWakademie/papyrologie/index.html. It is
important not simply as an artifact, but also for its content, because it
provides much valuable information about Mani, the founder of
Manichaeism.

PAPYRI

Nearly all newly discovered papyrus texts are published in academic
journals. In recent times, however, there has been a famous exception.
In 1992 an Italian bank gave the University of Milan funds to purchase
mummy-wrappings, which turned out to contain some 122 epigrams,
almost all previously unknown, by the Hellenistic poet Posidippus. A
photograph of the papyrus, too small to read, and a translation of four
poems appeared in the bank's glossy report in 1993, followed in the

same year by a deluxe gift edition of twenty-five poems (including the four already known). This was intended for the bank's investors, but full and authoritative publication did not take place until 2001. The frustration endured by scholars during the long wait was considerable.

Greetings from Theon to his father Theon. You did a fine thing in not taking me with you to the city. If you refuse to take me with you to Alexandria, I won't write you a letter, or speak to you, or say good-bye to you. When you go to Alexandria, I won't take your hand, or greet you ever again. That's what will happen if you won't take me. It was nice of you to send me presents. Please send me a lyre. If you don't send me one, I won't eat, I won't drink. So there! I hope you stay well (*Oxyrhynchus Papyrus* 119).

I, Horion, send greetings to my lord brother Macarius. Deliver to the men working on my behalf six jars of local wine. That is, six jars only. I, Horion, have signed for only six jars (*Oxyrhynchus Papyrus* 3875). The last sentence is a rather anxious countersignature by Horion himself.

I've written to you a thousand times telling you to cut down the vines. And yet today I received another letter from you asking what I wish should happen. My reply is: cut them down, cut them down, cut them down, cut them down, cut them down! So there, I'm telling you over and over again (*Oxyrhynchus Papyrus* 3063).

Senpamonthes greets her brother Pamonthes. I have sent you the embalmed body of Senyris, my mother, with a label around her neck. I paid the shipping costs in full and sent it on the boat belonging to Gales, the father of Hierax. The mummy is marked for identification, with a pink linen shroud and her name written over the stomach. I pray that you are well, my brother (*Paris Papyrus* 18*b*). The sender, the addressee, and their mummy all have Egyptian names, but this 2nd- or 3rd-century A.D. letter is written in Greek.

Oxyrhynchus Papyrus 1121 (written in A.D. 295) bears the rather uninformative indication of the date, "Written in the consulship of the present consuls." The Roman method of signifying the year was by the names of the consuls in office, and hence the document would more properly have been dated, "In the consulship of Nummius Tuscus and Annius Anullinus," but their appointment may not yet have been known in Oxyrhynchus, a hundred miles upstream from Cairo.

To Apion from Dionysius, greetings. Our divinely fortunate rulers have decreed that the value of the Italian coinage should be halved. So make haste to spend on my behalf all the Italian money you have, buying goods of any sort, whatever the asking price may be. I'll be sending a clerk to help you. Don't try to cheat me, for I'll find out. May you have a long and healthy life, my brother (Rylands Papyrus 4.607, from the early 4th century A.D.). Inflation was a severe problem at many periods, and nervous letters such as this must have been commonplace.

Right in the middle of a 1st-century A.D. papyrus document from Crocodilopolis (*London Papyrus* 3.604), consisting almost entirely of a relentlessly monotonous list of personal names, someone who is not the original copyist has added the marginal comment ψωλοκοπῶ τὸν ἀναγιγνώσκοντα (*psolokopo ton anagignoskonta*, "[I do something to?] the reader"). The verb is not known from other sources. Since, however, it is a compound of ψωλός, explained in ancient scholia as either "with an erection" or "circumcised," and -κοπῶ, which is related to κόπτω "I strike," it is an easy assumption that the scribe is expressing his exasperation at the tedium of the document's contents.

Calliorhoe to her ladyship, Sarapias, greetings. I have been doing obeisance to lord Sarapis every day on your behalf. Ever since you have been away, ἐπιζητοῦμέν σου τὰ κόπρια (*epizetoumen sou ta kopria*), *in our longing to see you* (Oxyrhynchus Papyrus 1761). So begins a letter from one Egyptian lady to another in the 2nd or 3rd century A.D. Here again the translation is not quite certain, but the power of the sentiment is unmistakable, whether the difficult phrase means "we have been missing your turds" or "we have been looking for your turds."

· XVI ·

PHILOSOPHERS

*Most people fear Greek philosophy the way children
fear bogeymen*
(St. Clement of Alexandria *Stromata* 6.10.80).

*The priest of Apollo gave Pythagoras an arrow that he had brought with
him from the god's shrine. This arrow would prove useful in helping
Pythagoras overcome the difficulties that befell him on his long wanderings. Riding on it, he could traverse trackless regions, such as rivers, lakes,
marshes, and mountains, and he used it also to perform purifications and
to cause winds and plagues to abate in cities that asked for his help* (Iamblichus *On the Pythagorean Way of Life* 91).

When a deadly snake bit Pythagoras, he bit it in return and killed it
(Aristotle *frg.* 191).

*They say that Pythagoras once had pity on a dog that was being beaten,
and said, "Stop, don't strike him, for that is the soul of a dear friend of
mine; I recognized him when I heard his voice"* (Xenophanes *frg.* 7,
mocking Pythagoras's belief in the transmigration of souls). Xenophanes and his followers were criticized for *making philosophers' heads
very dizzy with their contentious discussions, without adding anything
constructive to philosophical enquiry* (Aristocles of Messene *frg.* 1).

A Pythagorean did not get out of bed until he had gone over in his mind everything that had happened to him the day before. This was how he did it: he tried to recall the first thing he said or heard, then the first, second, and third orders he had given to his slave after getting up, and so on for the rest of the day. He also tried to recall who the first person was that he met on going out, and who the second, and then the first, second, and third things that were said, and so on. He tried to recall everything that happened to him during the day, in the order in which each incident occurred. If he had time enough when he woke up, he would go over the events of two days earlier as well. The Pythagoreans exercised their memory because they thought that nothing is as vital for understanding, for science, and for wisdom as is the ability to remember (Iamblichus *On the Pythagorean Way of Life* 29).

Some people reproached Thales of Miletus for his poverty, as if that were proof that philosophy is useless. But he noticed from his study of the stars while it was still winter that there was going to be a bumper olive harvest. So he took a cheap lease on all the olive-presses in Miletus and on Chios, getting them at a bargain rate since no one bid against him. When harvest-time came and many farmers suddenly needed presses all at the same time, he hired them out on whatever terms he pleased. By making a great deal of money this way, he demonstrated that philosophers can easily become rich if they want to, but that this is not what they are keen to do (Aristotle *Politics* 1259a).

When Heraclitus realized that he was dying, he lay down in the sun and ordered his slaves to cover him with cow dung. Stretched out in this way, he died on the second day and was buried in the marketplace (Diogenes Laertius *Lives of the Philosophers* 9.3).

Empedocles the philosopher went off to Mt. Etna, and when he reached the crater he jumped in and disappeared, wishing to foster the belief that he had become a god. But the truth became known later, when the volcano threw up one of his sandals. For he used to wear sandals with soles of bronze (Diogenes Laertius *Lives of the Philosophers* 8.69).

Pythagoras required his new students to observe a five-year period of silence (Plutarch *On Curiosity* 519c).

Greek accounts record that the philosopher Democritus deliberately deprived himself of his eyesight, because he thought that his musings and meditations about nature would be that much sharper and more focused if he freed them from the distractions and obstacles that eyesight entails (Aulus Gellius *Attic Nights* 10.17).

Democritus was very old and close to death. His sister was upset that he might die during the Thesmophoria, for that would bar her from carrying out her duty to the goddess. He said she should cheer up and told her to bring him warm bread every day. By putting the bread under his nostrils he kept himself alive for the three days of the festival, and as soon as it was over, he passed painlessly away, having lived for one hundred and nine years (Diogenes Laertius *Lives of the Philosophers* 9.43).

Socrates was exceptional in that he did not discuss the nature of the universe, speculating on the state of what the sophists call the cosmos and on the forces that cause celestial phenomena; on the contrary, he used to point out the foolishness of those who concern themselves about such things (Xenophon *Memoirs of Socrates* 1.1.11).

When Socrates was asked if the earth was spherical, he replied, "I haven't popped my head up to look" (*Gnomologium Vaticanum* 489).

During the Potidaea campaign [432 B.C.], Socrates defended Alcibiades when he fell wounded. In the retreat after the Battle of Delium [424], Alcibiades, who was on horseback, stayed with Socrates and a small group of infantry, to keep them covered when the enemy were pressing hard and killing many of the Athenian soldiers (Plutarch *Alcibiades* 7).

When a nasty and arrogant young man kicked Socrates, everyone with him was roused to such indignation that they wanted to prosecute him.

Socrates merely said, "If a donkey had kicked me, would you have thought that I should kick it back?" But the young man did not get away with what he had done: everyone mocked him and nicknamed him "Kicker," and so he hanged himself (Plutarch *On Educating Children* 10c).

When someone punched Socrates, his only reaction was to observe that it was a pity people didn't know when they should wear a helmet when they went out (Seneca *On Anger* 3.11).

Socratic enquiry, based on question and answer, requires a degree of cooperation from the person with whom Socrates is debating. It is not always forthcoming:

> *When we had reached this point in the discussion, and it was obvious to everyone that the definition of justice had been completely reversed, Thrasymachus, instead of answering my question, said, "Tell me, Socrates, do you have a nurse?"*
>
> *"What do you mean?" I said. "Shouldn't you be answering my question, rather than asking me things like that?"*
>
> *"I ask because she's leaving you with a runny nose, instead of wiping the snot away."*
>
> (Plato *Republic* 343a)

Socrates began to study lyre-playing at an advanced age, for he thought it better to learn that skill late rather than never (Valerius Maximus *Memorable Deeds and Sayings* 8.7 ext. 8).

Some people say that Plato's conception was particularly distinguished, since an image of Apollo had intercourse with his mother, Perictione. He was born on the same day of the month that the Athenians call Thargelion as Latona is said to have given birth to Apollo and Artemis on the island of Delos (Apuleius *On Plato's Teaching* 1.1). For a slightly earlier dating for Artemis's birthday, see p. 251.

Plato was originally called Aristocles, but his name was changed by his trainer, the wrestler Ariston of Argos, on account of his stocky physique

[πλατύς *(platys)* means "broad"]. *But there are also those who attribute the nickname to the breadth of his style or to the breadth of his forehead. Some people also say that he wrestled at the Isthmian Games* (Diogenes Laertius *Lives of the Philosophers* 3.4).

I do not know if it is true, but here is a story that I have heard. They say that Plato, because he was so poor, was intending to go off to serve as a mercenary. But Socrates came upon him when he was buying weapons and dissuaded him from going by arguing with him about what was right and making him yearn for philosophy (Aelian *Miscellaneous History* 3.27).

Antiphanes used to say as a joke that there is a city where it is so cold that words freeze as soon as they are spoken, and conversations that take place in winter can only be heard when the spring thaw comes. He said that likewise most people do not understand until old age what Plato tells them when they are young (Plutarch *How to Assess One's Progress in Virtue* 79a).

When Plato arrived in Syracuse, the tyrant Dionysius was gripped by a mad enthusiasm for philosophy, and the palace was full of people doing geometric calculations in the dust. But when Plato fell from favor, and Dionysius relapsed from philosophy into drinking and womanizing, all the geometers, as if transformed by some Circe, became ignorant, idle, and stupid (Plutarch *On Flattery* 52d).

Although he had been so keen that Plato should visit him, Dionysius soon fell out with him, calling his arguments senile, and he sent him to Aegina to be sold as a slave. Anniceris of Cyrene bought him and sent him home to Athens. Plato's friends there immediately tried to reimburse Anniceris, but he would not take their money, saying that it was not only the Athenians who were entitled to look after Plato. When Dionysius found out what happened to Plato, he wrote asking him not to speak ill of him, but Plato wrote back that he was too busy to think about him at all (Diogenes Laertius *Lives of the Philosophers* 3.19).

It is said that Plato was very prosperous, for he received more than eighty talents from Dionysius of Syracuse (Diogenes Laertius *Lives of the Philosophers* 3.9).

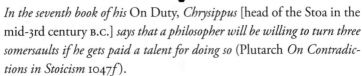

It is said that Aristotle received eight hundred talents from Alexander to support his research on animals (Athenaeus *Wise Men at Dinner* 398c).

In the seventh book of his On Duty, *Chrysippus* [head of the Stoa in the mid-3rd century B.C.] *says that a philosopher will be willing to turn three somersaults if he gets paid a talent for doing so* (Plutarch *On Contradictions in Stoicism* 1047f).

Plato criticized the Socratic philosopher Aristippus for buying a large number of fish. When Aristippus told him that they had cost only two obols, Plato said he would have bought them for that price. "So you see, Plato,"replied Aristippus, "it's not that I'm a gourmet, but that you're a miser" (Athenaeus *Wise Men at Dinner* 343d).

Two of Aristippus's now lost dialogues were entitled "A Response to Those Who Criticize Me for Spending Money on Old Wine and Prostitutes" and "A Response to Those Who Criticize Me for Spending Money on Gourmet Food" (Diogenes Laertius *Lives of the Philosophers* 2.84).

Antisthenes, another of the followers of Socrates, fell out with Plato and wrote a dialogue attacking him, in which he changed Plato's name to Sathon, a masculine proper name based on the rather coarse word σάθη (*sathe*), meaning "penis" (Diogenes Laertius *Lives of the Philosophers* 3.35).

Philosophers say that, if Jupiter spoke Greek, he would speak like Plato (Cicero *Brutus* 121). Plato's reputation as a stylist is enhanced by the contrast with Aristotle, whose Greek tends to be very unattractive.

Even at the age of eighty, Plato did not stop combing, curling, and braiding his dialogues. Every philosopher knows about the loving care he took with them. The story about his writing tablet is especially familiar: *after his death, the opening words of the* Republic, *"Yesterday I went down to Piraeus with Glaucon, the son of Ariston," were found on it with all sorts of changes* (Dionysius of Halicarnassus *On Literary Composition* 25). As befits their dialogue form, most of Plato's works begin in this low-key manner; as Quintilian notes (*Education of the Orator* 8.6.64), it is the rhythm, not the content, of the sentence that he was aiming to perfect.

When Diogenes the Cynic asked him for some wine, Plato sent him a whole jar full. Diogenes then said, "If someone asks you what two and two make, will you say twenty?" He also made fun of Plato for being an endless talker (Diogenes Laertius *Lives of the Philosophers* 6.26).

When Diogenes asked him for a drachma, Alexander the Great replied, "Such a gift is unworthy of a king." When Diogenes said, "Give me a talent then," Alexander replied, "Such a request is unworthy of a Cynic philosopher" (*Gnomologium Vaticanum* 102).

Diogenes used to go around the Ceramicus begging from the statues, and he'd tell those who wondered what he was doing that he was in training for meeting with refusals (Plutarch *On Compliancy* 531f).

Diogenes used to say that most people are just a finger's breadth away from insanity: if someone goes around with his middle finger stuck out, he is regarded as mad, but not if it is his little finger (Diogenes Laertius *Lives of the Philosophers* 6.35). For the middle finger as the "buggery" finger, see p. 65.

Plato's definition of man as "a two-footed creature without feathers" won great approval, so Diogenes plucked a rooster and brought it into the

school, saying, "This is Plato's man." "With flat nails" was added to the definition (Diogenes Laertius *Lives of the Philosophers* 6.40).

When Diogenes heard that Didymon the adulterer had been caught, he said, "He deserves to be hung by his name" (Diogenes Laertius *Lives of the Philosophers* 6.51; a pun on δίδυμοι [*didymoi*], literally "twins," but playing here with the sense "testicles").

When Diogenes came to Myndus and saw that the gates were huge, though the city itself was very small, he cried out, "Myndians, close the gates, or your city will get away!" (Diogenes Laertius *Lives of the Philosophers* 6.57).

Diogenes frequently masturbated in public and used to say, "How I wish I could relieve my hunger by rubbing my belly." There are other stories told about him, but it would take a long time to record them, for there are a lot of them (Diogenes Laertius *Lives of the Philosophers* 6.69).

The man from Stagira [i.e., Aristotle] was short and bald, a stammerer, lecherous, pot-bellied, and addicted to prostitutes (Anonymous *Planudes's Anthology* 11).

Aristotle was Plato's most outstanding pupil. He had a lisp, scrawny legs, and small eyes. He used to wear flashy clothes and rings and tended his hair very carefully (Diogenes Laertius *Lives of the Philosophers* 5.1).

After wasting his inheritance, Aristotle went off to serve as a soldier. This did not work out well for him, so he turned to selling medicines. It was only when he overheard the arguments of philosophers, many of whom had less aptitude than he did, that he adopted the habits that he later displayed (Aelian *Miscellaneous History* 5.9).

Here are the reasons for the first disagreement between Plato and Aristotle. Plato did not approve of Aristotle's lifestyle, nor of the way he dressed. For Aristotle wore elaborate clothes and shoes, and he used to have his hair cut in a style that Plato found off-putting; he wore many rings and showed them off proudly; he had a sneering expression, and the inappropriately garrulous way he talked created a bad impression of his character. These traits are all unsuited to a philosopher—of course they are (Aelian *Miscellaneous History* 3.19).

Plato used to call Aristotle "Colt." What did he mean by that name? As everyone knows, a colt kicks its mother as soon as it has had enough milk. So Plato was hinting at a degree of ingratitude in Aristotle. When Aristotle had received from Plato the greatest seeds of philosophy and the greatest introduction to the discipline and was full up with the best things he had to offer, he pulled against the reins; taking his friends with him, he set up a different school and declared himself Plato's rival (Aelian *Miscellaneous History* 4.9).

Zeno does away with motion, declaring that "a thing that moves does not move either in the place where it is or in the place where it is not" (Diogenes Laertius *Lives of the Philosophers* 9.72).

- *At every instant during its flight an arrow occupies a space equal to itself.*
- *If it occupies a space equal to itself, it must be motionless.*
- *Therefore it is motionless at every instant during its flight.*
- *Therefore it is at rest throughout the entire time of its flight.*

(Zeno's *Third Paradox*)

Here is an amusing story about Herophilus the physician. He was a contemporary of Diodorus, who was always expounding sophistic arguments, especially about movement. Diodorus dislocated his shoulder and came to Herophilus to have it seen to. Herophilus teased him very wittily: "Your shoulder was dislocated either in the place where it was or in the place where it wasn't, but it can't have been dislocated either in the place where it was or in the place where it wasn't; therefore, it wasn't dislocated." Diodorus implored him to drop such arguments and give him the appropriate medical treatment (Sextus Empiricus *Outlines of Pyrrhonism* 245).

When all his fellow-passengers had turned pale in a storm, Pyrrho, the founder of Skepticism, stayed calm and strengthened their spirits by pointing to a piglet on board that kept on eating steadily. "The wise man," he said, "ought to be in such a serene state" (Diogenes Laertius *Lives of the Philosophers* 9.68).

Pyrrho was chased up a tree by a dog. The bystanders laughed at him, and he said it was hard to lay aside one's human nature (Aristocles of Messene *frg.* 4.26). He might have done better if he had just sat down; Aristotle claims that dogs do not bite those who act in that humble manner (*Rhetoric* 1380*a*).

I congratulate you on coming to philosophy untainted by any education (Epicurus *Letters frg.* 43).

Epicurus wrote: "I think that the 'Heavy Groaners' will even claim that I was a pupil of the 'Jellyfish,' and that I listened to his lectures along with young men suffering from a hangover." In calling his teacher Nausiphanes a jellyfish, he implies that he was dull (Sextus Empiricus *Against the Professors of Liberal Studies* Preface).

A law had been passed at Lyctus on Crete banishing anyone who adopted the effeminate, unworthy, and disgusting philosophical beliefs of the Epicureans and was hostile to the gods. If any such person was foolish enough to go there in contempt of the law's provisions, he was to be bound in a pillory at the town hall for twenty days, with honey and milk poured over his naked body, to make him a feast for bees and flies. After the allotted time he was to be released and, if he was still alive, he was to be pushed over a cliff, dressed in women's clothing (Aelian *On Animals frg.* 39).

How powerful are we to imagine was the eloquence of the Cyrenaic philosopher Hegesias? He used to portray life's ills so vividly that he sowed in the hearts of his audience a desire to commit suicide. That is why King Ptolemy banned him from lecturing on that subject anymore (Valerius Maximus *Memorable Deeds and Sayings* 8.9 ext. 3).

Four men being stung by bees or hornets.

Crates the Cynic was called "The Door-Opener" because he used to go into people's houses at random and start giving advice. He also gave his daughter in marriage on a thirty-day trial (Diogenes Laertius *Lives of the Philosophers* 6.86, 6.95).

We tend to think of philosophers strolling along engrossed in calm and quiet debate, but the manager of a nearby gymnasium once felt compelled to ask Carneades, the head of the Academy, to keep his voice down (Diogenes Laertius *Lives of the Philosophers* 4.63).

How can a man find time to be a philosopher if he is tied to domestic duties? Doesn't he have to provide little cloaks for his children, and send them off to their teacher with their little writing tablets, their writing instruments, and their notebooks, and prepare their beds for them as well? (Epictetus *Discourses* 3.22.74).

Some of the philosophers in the Academy are so keen to puzzle those who discuss the comprehensible and the incomprehensible with them that they resort to such strange topics as whether it is possible for someone in Athens to smell eggs being cooked in Ephesus, and they debate whether they really are in the Academy discussing such things, and not actually lying at home in bed laying out their arguments in a dream (Polybius *Histories* 12.26).

Aulus Gellius (*Attic Nights* 7.13) lists the following topics for discussion at the philosopher Taurus's symposium:

> *When does a dying person die? Is it when he is already in a state of death or when he is still alive?*

> *When does a person who gets to his feet get to his feet? Is it when he is already standing or when he is still sitting?*

> *When does a person learning an art become an artist? Is it when he already is one or when he is not yet one?*

He goes on to observe: *Whichever of these two answers you give, what you say will be absurd and ridiculous, and it will be even more absurd if you say that both answers are correct or that neither of them is correct.*

If you really want to be a philosopher, brace yourself from the very start to endure mockery
(**Epictetus** *Enchiridion* 22).

MATHEMATICS

It has often happened that people have talked
happily with me, because of my work among the
sick, but when they discover that I am also an
expert mathematician, they avoid me

(Galen *On the Uses of the Parts of the Body*
10.14).

"Geometry" is a quite ridiculous name for the discipline it denotes (Plato
[?] *Epinomis* 990d).

*The flooding of the Nile repeatedly takes away and adds soil, altering the
configuration of the landscape and hiding the markers that separate one
person's land from that of someone else. Measurements have to be made
over and over again, and they say that this was the origin of geometry*
[literally "land measuring"], *just as accounting and arithmetic started
with the Phoenicians, through their interest in trading* (Strabo *Geography*
17.1.3).

*Pythagoras was not vulgarly lavish when he sacrificed to the gods. He
propitiated them with barley bread, cakes, frankincense, and myrrh. He
scarcely ever offered an animal sacrifice, just the occasional rooster or a
little pig. He did, however, sacrifice an ox when he discovered that the
square on the hypotenuse of a right-angled triangle is equal to the squares*

on the other two sides—but those who record this more accurately say that the ox was made of dough (Porphyry *Life of Pythagoras* 36).

Hippocrates of Chios [one of the most important mathematicians of the 5th century B.C., not to be confused with his contemporary, Hippocrates of Cos, the great physician] *was a merchant. He fell foul of a pirate ship and lost everything. He prosecuted the pirates in Athens and, since the case required him to stay there for a long time, he went to listen to philosophers. He showed such a gift for geometry that he tried to find a formula for squaring the circle* (Philoponus *Commentaries on Aristotle's Physics* 16.31). Squaring the circle was a famous geometrical problem. It was not until 1882 that it was shown to be impossible to solve.

The oracle of Apollo told the people of Delos that, to be freed from a plague, they should build him an altar twice the size of the existing one. The architects were at a loss how to construct a solid figure twice as big as another solid figure, so they went to Athens to consult Plato. He told them that the god did not really want an altar double in size; the purpose of the oracle was to censure the Greeks for neglecting mathematics and undervaluing geometry (Theon of Smyrna *On the Usefulness of Mathematics in Reading Plato* 2).

We'll study astronomy just as we study geometry, as a set of problems to solve, but we'll ignore things that are actually in the sky if we mean really to get to grips with astronomy and to turn our natural intelligence to good use (Plato *Republic* 530b).

Plato was once shipwrecked by a storm on the desolate shore of an unknown region. Everyone else was terrified by the unfamiliarity of the place, but he is said to have noticed some geometrical figures drawn in the sand and to have shouted to his companions to be cheerful, for he could see signs of humanity (Cicero *Republic* 1.29).

Plato did not want mathematics to be part of philosophy, but a preliminary training for it, just like grammar and rhetoric. That is why he had inscribed over the door of his lecture room: "Let no one come in without an understanding of geometry" (Ps.-Galen *On the Divisions of Philosophy* 2).

Alexander the Great asked Menaechmus the geometrician to explain geometry to him in an abbreviated way, but Menaechmus replied, "My lord, throughout the country there are Royal Roads and roads for ordinary people, but in geometry there is only one road for everyone" (Stobaeus *Anthology* 2.31.115). The Royal Road, though established long before, was developed by Darius I to maintain rapid contact with the far-flung parts of the Persian empire. The same story is told of Ptolemy I and Euclid.

Someone who had begun to study geometry with Euclid asked him, when he had learned the first theorem, "What benefit do I get from learning this?" Euclid called his slave and said to him, "Give him half a drachma, for he has to make a profit from whatever he learns" (Stobaeus *Anthology* 2.31).

Skill in language has a small, but essential, role to play in education, no matter what the subject may be, for the manner in which something is explained affects its comprehensibility. But fine speaking is not so very important and is really just a show put on to appeal to the listener. After all, no one uses grand language when teaching geometry (Aristotle *Rhetoric* 1404a).

Archimedes deliberately wrote as briefly as seemed possible about the most complex geometrical and arithmetical concepts. He clearly had such love for those disciplines that he could not tolerate any extraneous material being mixed with them (Pappus *The Mathematical Collection* 8.1026).

The surviving corpus of Greek mathematics is fairly large, but it is almost entirely lacking in literary appeal of any sort. Archimedes seems particularly austere, for he wrote in a form of Doric (the broad dialect of his native Syracuse), which struck speakers of Attic as being somewhat uncouth.

When Archimedes was concentrating on his drawing board, his attendants had to drag him bodily away, so that they could undress him and anoint him; even then he would continue drawing diagrams in the oil on his skin (Plutarch *Old Men in Public Affairs* 786b).

Dionysiodorus, the well-known geometrician from Melos, was not reliable, but I cannot bring myself to omit this instance of Greek vanity. . . . When he died, a letter was said to have been found in his tomb, written to those above by Dionysiodorus himself. It stated that he had gone down from his tomb to the deepest region of the earth, a distance of 42,000 stades (Pliny *Natural History* 2.248). Despite this autopsy, and allowing for variations in the length of a stade, Dionysiodorus's figures for the diameter of the earth, and hence the circumference also, are about 25 percent too large.

Courtiers are like counters on an abacus. Just as the person doing the calculation can decide that a counter is worth a mere copper coin at one moment, but a whole talent at the next, so it depends on a single nod from a king whether his courtiers are prosperous or lie groveling at his feet (Polybius *Histories* 5.26).

Archimedes jumped out of his bath, yelling, "I have found it" [εὕρηκα, heureka] *as if divinely inspired or possessed, and off he went shouting that over and over again. But we've never heard of any such passionate cries of "I've eaten it" or "I've kissed her" from a glutton or a sex-addict, even though there are and always have been countless thousands of such decadent people. We are disgusted by those who reminisce too passionately about meals, for deriving too much enjoyment from petty and inconsequential pleasures. But we share the enthusiasm of scientists like Archimedes and agree with Plato's verdict on mathematics, that even though people may neglect it through ignorance and lack of experience, "it forces us to*

accept its importance because of the delight it brings" [*Republic* 528c]
(Plutarch *A Pleasant Life Is Impossible on Epicurean Principles* 1094c).

*Whereas time causes grief and other emotions to alter and cease, when has
the mere passage of time ever persuaded anyone that he has had enough of
"twice two are four" or "all radii of a circle are equal" and made him
change his mind about such beliefs and give them up?* (Galen *On the
Doctrines of Hippocrates and Plato* 4.7.43).

Archimedes's *Sand-Reckoner* calculated the number of grains of sand
that would fill up the entire universe. He fixed on a total of 8×10^{63}
grains. His calculation was based on the largest available unit of
numbers, the myriad (= 10,000).

*Xenocrates declared that the number of syllables that can be produced by com-
bining the letters of the alphabet is 1,002,000,000,000* (Xenocrates *frg.* 89).

*Odd numbers are more perfect than even ones, for they have a beginning,
an end, and a middle, but even numbers lack a middle* (Stobaeus
Anthology 1.5).

*Always ensure that there is an odd number of sheep in your flocks, for this
has some natural power to keep them safe and secure* (*Farm Work* 18.2).

*Theodorus of Samothrace said that Zeus laughed for seven days without a
pause after he was born, and that is why seven was considered a perfect
number* (Photius *Lexicon* 152b).

- *There are seven phases of the moon: twice crescent, twice half moon,
  twice gibbous, and once full.*
- *The Bear and the Pleiades have seven stars.*
- *The equinoxes are seven months apart* [by inclusive reckoning], *as are
  the solstices.*

- *The soul has seven parts: the five senses, the voice, and the reproductive part.*
- *The body has seven complete parts: the head, the neck, the chest, two feet, and two hands.*
- *There are seven internal organs: the stomach, the heart, the lung[s], the liver, the spleen, and the two kidneys.*
- *There are seven openings in the head: two eyes, two ears, two nostrils, and one mouth.*
- *We see seven things: body, distance, shape, size, color, movement, and position.*
- *There are seven variations in the voice: sharp, deep, circumflected, rough, smooth, long, and short.*
- *There are seven types of movement: up, down, forward, back, right, left, circular.*
- *There are seven vowels: α, ε, η, ι, ο, υ, ω.*
- *The lyre has seven strings.*
- *Plato composed the soul from seven numbers in the* Timaeus.

A seven-string lyre.

- *There are seven ages of life: infant, child, adolescent, young man, adult, elder, and old man, and the change from each age to the next takes place every seven years.*

(Anatolius *On the First Ten Numbers* 11; he comments that "all things are seven-loving," but gives similar, if rather shorter, lists for each of the other numbers from one to ten)

Why should numbers be equated with causes? There are seven vowels, a musical scale comprises seven chords, there are seven Pleiades, animals lose their teeth when they are seven years old (at least, some do, but others do not), there were seven heroes who fought against Thebes. So, is it the nature of the number seven that ensures that there were seven heroes, or that the Pleiades are made up of seven stars? Or could it be that there are seven heroes because Thebes had seven gates, or for some other reason? We count seven stars in the Pleiades, and twelve in the Bear, but people elsewhere count more stars in both (Aristotle *Metaphysics* 1093a, arguing against the Pythagoreans' tendency to see numbers as the origin of things).

The day was divided into twelve equal segments. The number twelve was chosen because it is the most useful. It can be divided into halves, thirds, quarters, sixths, and twelfths, a quality possessed by no lower number and by no higher number until twenty-four (Galen *On the Diagnosis and Cure of the Sins of the Mind* 5.83).

NUMBER GAMES

The twenty-four letters of the alphabet were used to denote numbers, with three additional characters, the archaic letters *digamma*, *koppa*, and *sampi*, used for 7, 90, and 900.

α	1
β	2
γ	3
δ	4
ϵ	5
ζ	6
F	7
η	8
θ	9
ι	10
κ	20
λ	30
μ	40
ν	50
ξ	60
ο	70
π	80
ϙ	90
ρ	100
σ	200
τ	300
υ	400
φ	500
χ	600
ψ	700
ω	800
ϡ	900

Hence, for example, the word ἄλφα (*alpha*) has a value of 532 (1 + 30 + 500 + 1), while the word βῆτα (*beta*) has a value of 311 (2 + 8 + 300 + 1). There was a certain fascination in matching words and phrases that had the same numerical equivalents. *Oxyrhynchus Papyrus* 3239 contains a list of such "isopsephic" pairs. For example:

Αἴγυπτος/ἱλαρὰ γεωργία	*Aigyptos/hilara georgia*	Egypt/fertile farming	1064
Ἀχιλλεύς/φιλεῖ Πάτροκλον	*Achilleus/philei Patroklon*	Achilles/ loves Patroclus	1276
ἄμπελος/αἰεὶ οἶνος	*ampelos/aiei oinos*	vine/always wine	426
βοῦς/ἄρουρα	*bous/aroura*	ox/plowland	672
Διόνυσος/ἡδονὴ θεῶν	*Dionysos/hedone theon*	Dionysus/ pleasure of the gods	1004
Διόνυσος/χάρμα μέθης	*Dionysos/charma methes*	Dionysus/ joy of drunkenness	1004
Ἔρως/ὁ πετάμενος θεός	*Eros/ho petamenos theos*	Eros/the winged god	1105

The principle was applied to prophecy:

> *Seeing a weasel in a dream signifies an evil and tricky woman and a law-suit, for "law-suit" (δίκη, dike) and "weasel" (γαλῆ, gale) are isopsephic (42).*
> (Artemidorus *Interpretation of Dreams* 3.28.20)

> *Seeing an old woman in a dream foretells death to a sick person, since γραῦς (graus, "old woman") adds up to 704 and ἡ ἐκφορά (he ekphora, "the funeral") adds up to 704. An old woman symbolizes a funeral in any case, since she is going to die in the not very distant future.*
> (Artemidorus *Interpretation of Dreams* 4.24.5)

Suetonius preserves the most famous isopsephism, current in Rome after Nero killed his mother, Agrippina (*Life of Nero* 39):

> Νέρων/ἰδίαν μητέρα ἀπέκτεινε *Neron/idian metera apekteine* Nero/ own mother killed

50 + 5 + 100 + 800 + 50 = 1,005

10 + 4 + 10 +1 + 50 + 40 +8 + 300 + 5+ 100 + 1 + 1+ 80 + 5 + 20+ 300
+ 5 + 10 + 50 + 5 = 1,005

There are a number of stylish isopsephic epigrams in the *Greek Anthology* by the mathematician and astronomer Leonides of Alexandria (6.321, 6.322, 6.324–29, and 9.344–56). In 6.329, addressed to Agrippina in celebration of her birthday, the letters in both couplets add up to 7,579: might Leonides have had something to do with the isopsephic charge of matricide?

Leonides's first sequence in Book Six of the *Greek Anthology* is interrupted by an epigram of a perhaps even more ingenious type, by the otherwise unknown Nicodemus of Heraclea. It is palindromic, making the same sense and preserving the same strict meter whether it is read forward or backward. Nicodemus's other epigrams, 6.314–20 and 9.53, are also all palindromic. I have never heard of anyone nowadays attempting such a poem, however brief.

Greek Anthology 12.6, one of many homosexual epigrams by Strato of Sardis, is a wittily forlorn and modestly isopsephic lament:

> πρωκτός (*proctos*, rectum) *and* χρυσός (*chrysos*, gold) *have the same numerical value* [1,570]. *I discovered this once when I did a simple calculation.*

Homer *Iliad* 7.264 and 7.265 both add up to 3,508:

> ἀλλ' ἀναχασσάμενος λίθον εἵλετο χειρὶ παχείῃ
> κείμενον ἐν πεδίῳ μέλανα τρηχύν τε μέγαν τε
> *all' anachassamenos lithon heileto cheiri pacheie*
> *keimenon en pedio melana trechun te megan te*
> *But giving ground he grasped a stone in his strong hand,*
> *a black one, both rough and big, lying on the plain.*

This monumentally useless discovery was made by an unknown scholar in the post-Renaissance period, and Aulus Gellius (*Attic Nights*

14.6) seems to imply that other such pairs of lines were known in antiquity. It has recently been determined, by computer search, that there are four more such pairs in the *Iliad* (1.490–91 = 3,833, 5.137–38 = 4,580, 6.162–63 = 3,221, 19.306–307 = 2,848) and three in the *Odyssey* (13.245–46 = 2,885, 18.388–89 = 3,511, 18.401–402 = 3,515) (J. L. Hilton *Classical Journal* 106 [2011] 386).

Plutarch's schoolteacher friend, Zopyrio, shows sound common sense when he says that *it is a mere coincidence that there is an equal number of syllables* (seventeen) *in the first lines of the* Iliad *and* Odyssey, *and likewise in their final lines* (sixteen) (Plutarch *Table Talk* 739a). As Quintilian says about compulsively detailed enquiries into the arcane aspects of mythological stories, "there are some things that it is to a teacher's credit not to know" (*Education of the Orator* 1.8).

· XVIII ·

SCIENCE AND TECHNOLOGY

Atomic theory goes back a long way, for it was
devised by Mochus of Sidon before the Trojan War

(Posidonius *frg.* 285).

NATURAL SCIENCE

We do not consider any of our senses as actually being wisdom, even
though they are our most authoritative sources of detailed information.
They do not tell us the "why" about anything. For example, they do not tell
us why fire is hot; they tell us simply that it is hot (Aristotle *Metaphysics*
981*b*).

Things burn more quickly in winter than in summer, for the summer
makes fire weaker, just as the sun also does, and just as fire itself makes
light weaker, whereas winter and the coldness of the surrounding air con-
centrate fire. Anything that is concentrated is strong—that is why light in
lamps carries farther (Theophrastus *On Fire frg.* 12).

To whiten a genuine pearl, the Indians use this method. They give it to a
rooster with its feed in the evening and search for it in its excrement in the
morning. The pearl has been cleaned in the bird's gizzard and is as bright
as it ever had been (Stockholm Papyrus 60).

Celandine root dyes fabric a gold color, by cold dyeing. But celandine is expensive, and the same result can be obtained with pomegranate root. If wolf's milk is boiled and then reduced to a powder, it dyes fabric yellow (*Stockholm Papyrus* 139). It seems reasonable to wonder how this particular quality of wolf's milk was discovered and how dyers obtained supplies.

A tunnel dug by Eupalinus of Megara on the island of Samos in the 6th century B.C. carried a water supply about half a mile through a mountain for over a thousand years. It was rediscovered in the 1880s and is regarded as one of the greatest feats of ancient Greek engineering.

The earth's core consists almost entirely of frost and ice (Plutarch *On the Principle of Cold* 953e).

[In the Red Sea] *the sun does not spread its light before it rises, as it does with us. They say that, when it is still pitch-dark night, the sun shines out suddenly and unexpectedly over the middle of the sea, like a very fiery lump of coal, shooting out huge sparks. . . . Quite opposite phenomena are said to occur in the evening: the sun seems to illuminate the world for not less than two hours, or even three, after it has set, and this is regarded by the natives of that region as the most pleasant time of the day, since the temperature goes down when the sun sets* (Diodorus Siculus *The Library* 3.48).

The Epicureans make the foolish claim that the sun consists of atoms, and that it is born with the day and dies when the day dies (Servius on Virgil *Aeneid* 4.584).

Heraclitus says, "The sun is as broad as a human foot, and does not grow bigger: for if it becomes broader, the Furies, allies of Justice, will find it out" (Column 4.5–9 of the 4th-century B.C. *Derveni Papyrus*, the oldest of all surviving Greek papyri, and one of the few substantial papyrus texts found outside Egypt).

If someone reached the limit of the sky and stretched out his hand, to where would he stretch it out? Surely not into nothing, for nothing that exists is in nothingness. But he will not be prevented from stretching out his hand, for it is not possible to be prevented by nothingness (Archytas of Tarentum, as cited at Eudemus *frg.* 65).

Now that all the richer, softer soil has been washed away, only the bare ground is left, like the bones of a diseased body. In former times . . . the plains were full of fertile soil and there was abundant timber in the mountains . . . in parts of which there is now only food enough for bees. . . . The annual rainfall used to make the land fruitful, for the water did not flow off the bare earth into the sea. . . . Where once there were springs, now the shrines [to the deities of the stream] *are all that is left* (Plato *Critias* 110e, on the deforestation of Attica).

We should not be too confident in dismissing as incredible the theory that India is connected to the region near the Pillars of Heracles, with the ocean forming a single unit. Those who support this opinion point out that the occurrence of elephants at both these extreme parts of the earth proves that they are connected (Aristotle *On the Heavens* 298a). At *Meteorology* 362b, Aristotle observes that *it is possible to travel right around the world, the only potential obstacle being the sheer extent of the ocean.*

In earlier times, all islands wandered about and had no foundations (Scholion to Apollonius of Rhodes *Argonautica* 3.42).

Why is it warmer when the sky is cloudy than when it is not? Is it because, as people said in antiquity, the stars are cold? (Ps.-Aristotle *Problems* 939b).

In the old days, the earth was drawn as a circle, with Greece in the center, and Delphi, as the navel of the earth, in the center of Greece. Democritus was the first to perceive it as being oblong, half as long again as it is wide (Agathemerus *Geography* 2.1).

Theophrastus records that Plato, when he grew older, regretted attributing to the earth the central position in the universe, as being a position it does not merit (Plutarch *Platonic Questions* 1006c).

The earth stays in the air without anything to hold it up, remaining fixed because it is equidistant from all other things. . . . We do not feel the heat of the stars because they are so far away. . . . The sun is bigger than the Peloponnese (Anaximander, quoted at Hippolytus *Refutation of All Heresies* 1.6, 1.8).

Aristarchus of Samos proposes that the fixed stars and the sun remain motionless, and that the earth goes around the sun on the circumference of a circle (a momentous suggestion recorded at Archimedes *The Sand Reckoner* 1), but the geocentric ideas of Aristotle and Claudius Ptolemy prevailed for two millennia. In the 16th century Copernicus revived the idea that the earth revolves around the sun, and astronomical proof was first obtained in 1727.

The moon resembles the earth in that its surface is inhabited. The animals and plants, however, are bigger and more attractive than those here; the animals there are fifteen times as big and do not void excrement (Philolaus *frg.* 20).

Anaximander maintains that human beings were originally created from animals that were of a different species. He reasons that the other animals are quickly able to find their own food, but humans alone need a long period of nursing, and if they had been like that from the beginning, they could not have survived (Plutarch *frg.* 179). More specifically, *Anaximander asserts that humans were first formed among fish, but having developed like dog sharks and become able to help themselves, they then came out of the sea and took possession of the land* (Plutarch *Table Talk* 730e).

According to Aristophanes, as recorded by Plato at *Symposium* 190c, there were originally three types of human beings, male, female, and androgynous. People were originally round, with their back and sides forming a circle. They had four hands, four feet, one head with two faces, four ears, two sets of private parts, and so on. They could move very quickly, forward or backward, rolling along on their eight limbs. The gods were afraid of their strength and considered annihilating them. But Zeus said:

> *"I think I have a plan that will allow humans to continue living, but will weaken them and make them less disorderly. I shall cut each of them in two, making them not only weaker, but also more useful to us because there will be more of them to offer sacrifices. But, if they are still insolent and refuse to live peacefully, I'll split them again, and they'll hop about on one leg."*

After saying this he cut humans in two, the way apples are split for pickling, or eggs are sliced with a hair.

When Zeus fashioned humans, he told Hermes to pour sense into them. Hermes made the same amount of sense for each person and started to pour it in. Smaller people were filled up by their allocation of sense and became intelligent, whereas tall people, since their allocation of sense reached only as far their knees, were less intelligent (Aesop *Fable* 110). Aesop may have derived personal satisfaction from the fable just cited: *Aesop, the writer of fables, was a great benefactor to mankind, but ill fortune made him a slave. He was disgusting to look at, rotten at his duties, potbellied, with a pointed head and a snub nose, swarthy, deformed, stunted, bandy-legged, with weasel* [i.e., short] *arms, a squint, and twisted lips* (*Life of Aesop* 1).

Why are humans the most thoughtful of all animals? Is it because they have very small heads in proportion to their body size? . . . People with small heads are more thoughtful than people with large heads (Ps.-Aristotle *Problems* 955*b*).

Why is it that no one can tickle himself? Is it for the same reason as that tickling by another person has more effect if done without warning? (Ps.-Aristotle *Problems* 965*a*).

It is an observable fact that human beings are, in general, getting smaller, and that very few people are taller than their parents. This is because the cycle of the ages is now approaching a period of great heat, and that exhausts the fertility of our semen. . . . Nearly a thousand years ago, the great poet Homer constantly lamented that people were physically smaller than in former times (Pliny *Natural History* 7.73).

Are we not to suppose that there have been all sorts of climate changes, during which it is likely that animals have changed in very many different ways? (Plato *Laws* 782a).

Xenophanes says that the land was once mixed with the sea. . . . As proof of this, he points out that shells are found far inland and on mountaintops (Xenophanes *frg.* 33).

The very troublesome problem about the egg and the bird was brought up for discussion. Which of them came first? My friend Sulla refused to take part in the debate, saying that with this little problem, as with a tool, we were opening up a serious and momentous controversy, namely the creation of the universe (Plutarch *Table Talk* 636a).

At Panopeus in central Greece there is a small building made of unbaked brick, and in it there is a statue of Pentelic marble, which some say represents Asclepius, others Prometheus. In support of their claim, the latter group point to two rocks lying in the ravine, each big enough to fill a cart. These rocks are the color of clay, not earthy clay, but rather such as is found in a gorge or a sandy stream. They smell just like human skin, and people say that they are the remnants of the clay from which Prometheus molded the whole human race (Pausanias *Guide to Greece* 10.4).

The Stoics maintained that, when the planets return to their original alignment, the universe will be destroyed in a great conflagration, and *then everything will happen again in exactly the same way as before. Socrates, Plato, every person will exist again, with the same*

friends and fellow citizens. The same things will happen to them . . . and every city, village, and field will appear again just as before. This restoration of the universe does not happen just once; it recurs ad infinitum (Nemesius *On Human Nature* 38). Chrysippus, the third head of the Stoa, concedes that there may be slight variations; birthmarks and freckles may not reappear the next time around (*Logic and Physics frg.* 624). The Peripatetic philosopher Sosigenes calculated that it takes 648,483,416,738,640,000 years for all the heavenly bodies to return to their original alignments, completing a "perfect year" (Proclus *On Plato's* Republic 2.23).

Some people think that everything has its origin in atoms and void. This idea is wrong, but it causes no actual wounds, or tumors, or distracting pain (Plutarch *On Superstition* 164 f).

INVENTIONS

I am Isis, the ruler of all lands. Hermes educated me, and with Hermes I invented letters, both hieroglyphic and demotic, so that the same script should not be used for writing everything (*Greek Inscriptions* 12.14, inscribed on a pillar in Memphis).

The god Theuth invented numbers, calculation, geometry, astronomy, checkers, dice playing, and also writing. He showed his inventions to Thamous, the god who ruled all of Egypt. . . . When he told him that writing would make the Egyptians wiser and give them better memories, since it is a drug that provides both memory and wisdom, Thamous replied: "Theuth, you are very ingenious, but the inventor of a skill is not the best person to judge the good or harm it may cause. As the indulgent father of writing, you have claimed the opposite of what it can actually do. Writing will make people forgetful, for they will neglect their memories. . . . They will hear a lot and seem to know a lot without learning anything, and will generally know nothing. They will be tedious to be with, seeming to be wise without actually being so" (Plato *Phaedrus* 274c).

186 · A CABINET OF GREEK CURIOSITIES

Palamedes invented dice playing and checkers as a way to console the Greek expeditionary force at Troy when it was suffering from starvation. A stone on which they played checkers used to be displayed there (Polemon *Periegesis frg.* 32).

The elder Pliny gives a very long list of inventors at the end of Book Seven of his *Natural History*, including these examples:

- *The Athenian brothers Euryalus and Hyperbius invented brick-kilns and houses. Before then people lived in caves.*
- *Inspired by swallows' nests, Toxius invented the technique of building with mud.*
- *Thread and nets were invented by Arachne.*
- *Laundering was invented by Nicias of Megara.*

Ajax and Achilles playing dice or a board game, with Athena looking on.

- *Shoemaking was invented by Tychius of Boeotia.*
- *The Spartans invented slavery.*
- *Aristaeus of Athens discovered honey.*
- *Anchors were invented by Eupalamus, masts and sail-ropes by his son Daedalus, sails by his grandson Icarus.*

In the 6th century B.C., Perillus of Athens constructed a metal bull for Phalaris, the tyrant of the Sicilian city of Acragas. *When you wish to punish anyone, shut him up in the bull, attach these tubes to its nostrils, and light a fire under it. Your victim will shriek and yell in unremitting pain, but his cries will reach you through the tubes as wonderfully sweet music, with poignant pipe-accompaniment and mournful mooing. He will be punished while you enjoy the music* (Lucian *Phalaris* 11). Phalaris made Perillus the bull's first victim. Epicurus maintained that *a virtuous person, even if shut up in the Bull of Phalaris, will declare, "How pleasant this is!"* (Cicero *Tusculan Disputations* 2.17).

When Queen Semiramis of Babylon was fighting the Indians, she realized that her forces were inferior, so she had model elephants made to terrorize the enemy, who thought elephants did not exist outside India. She had exact models made, filled with straw and covered with the hides of three hundred thousand black cattle. Inside each model there was a camel and a man to look after it, the idea being that, when the camel moved, it would look from a distance like a real elephant. Work on the dummies was carried out in a well-guarded stockade, so that the Indians would not hear about the scheme (Diodorus Siculus *The Library* 2.16).

Archytas the Pythagorean [who ruled Tarentum in the 4th century B.C.] *is said to have constructed a wooden dove that flew. It was balanced with weights and moved by means of a current of air hidden inside it* (Aulus Gellius *Attic Nights* 10.12).

A procession in Athens in honor of Demetrius of Phalerum was led by a mechanical snail that went along of its own volition, spitting out a trail

of slime (Polybius *Histories* 12.13). As well as ruling Athens from 317 until 307 B.C., Demetrius was a significant orator and philosopher, and in his later years he played an important role in the establishment of the Museum and Library at Alexandria. He deserves to be better known than he is today.

Nabis usurped power in Sparta at the end of the 3rd century B.C. When he was unable to extort money from the citizens, he resorted to a mechanical figure of a woman, splendidly dressed and made to look like his wife, Apege. *"Maybe I myself can't persuade you, but I think my Apege will." At this point, the device was brought in. The victim offered her his hand and embraced her when he had helped her rise from her chair. But her arms and hands, and her breasts as well, were covered in iron nails, concealed under her dress. Nabis then placed his hands on his wife's back, releasing springs that increased the pressure on the victim and gradually drew him closer to her breasts, making him agree to anything* (Polybius *Histories* 13.7).

The *Pneumatica* of Hero of Alexandria, written in the 1st century A.D., gives instructions (in varying degrees of detail) on how to construct seventy-eight mechanical devices, most of which are ingenious but with little practical application. They include a cup that fills with water when a five drachma coin is inserted (21), a bowl that dispenses different varieties of wine through the same tube depending on which of several lead balls is inserted (32), and two variations on a device that opens doors automatically (37, 38). Some are rather endearing. For example:

> At a fountain, or in a cave, or anywhere at all where there is running water, figures of several birds are set up, and near them there is an owl that turns automatically to look at them and then looks away again. When it looks away, the birds sing, but, when it looks at them, they stop. (14)
>
> In some place where there is running water, make an animal out of bronze or any other material. When a cup is offered to it, it drinks noisily, giving the impression of thirst. (29)

A little tree with a snake coiled around it is fixed on a stand. Heracles is standing nearby with his bow, and there is an apple lying on the stand. If anyone lifts the apple off the stand, Heracles shoots his arrow at the snake and it hisses. (41)

When a thief named Eurybatus was in prison, the guards started drinking with him. They untied his bonds and urged him to show them how he scaled up buildings. At first he refused, but eventually they persuaded him, and so he attached sponges [perhaps to deaden the noise during a burglary?] *and spikes to his feet and ran up the walls. While the guards were looking up in admiration of his skill, he made a hole in the thatched roof and jumped down, escaping before they could circle around and catch him* (Aristotle *frg.* 84). At a spectacle in 3rd-century A.D. Rome the crowd were entertained by a "wall-walker," who ran up a wall to escape from a bear (Historia Augusta *Lives of Carus, Carinus and Numerian* 19).

After losing a court case with his neighbor, Zeno, over the violation of a building permit, a Byzantine architect named Anthemius plotted revenge. He ran pipes up through the building's walls to the roof beams and paneling of Zeno's apartment. He then heated water in large cauldrons and forced steam under high pressure up the pipes, causing the beams and paneling to shake and creak. Zeno and his dinner guests ran headlong out into the street, terrified by what they thought was an earthquake (Agathias *Histories* 172).

Sophocles invented the bent walking stick
(**Satyrus** *Life of Sophocles* 5).

· XIX ·

ART

*When the art of painting was just starting out, still
as it were breastfeeding and in diapers, artists drew
such clumsy images of animals that they used to
write on them "this is a cow," "that's a horse," "this
is a tree"*

(**Aelian** *Miscellaneous History* 10.10).

*You go all the way to Olympia to see the works of Phidias and think it a
great misfortune to die before getting to know them* (Epictetus *Discourses*
1.6.23). The greatest of Phidias's sculptures at Olympia was the cult
statue in the temple of Zeus, regarded as one of the Wonders of the
World.

*The Athenian painter Parrhasius bought an old man when Philip was
selling the captives he had taken at Olynthus. He brought him to Athens,
where he tortured him and used him as his model for Prometheus* [who
had his liver eaten by an eagle every day]. *The Olynthian died under the
torture, and Parrhasius dedicated the painting in the temple of Athena*
(Seneca the Elder *Controversies* 10.5).

Zeuxis [Parrhasius's great rival] *flaunted the wealth he had acquired
through his paintings when he appeared at Olympia wearing a cloak
embroidered with his name in gold letters, and later he made a practice of*

giving his works away because he regarded them as beyond price (Pliny *Natural History* 35.62).

A man called Cleisophus fell in love with a statue of Parian marble on the island of Samos and locked himself up in the temple where it stood, thinking he could have sex with it. But he could not, because of the coldness and unyielding nature of the stone, so he gave up his desire and satisfied himself with a small piece of meat instead (Athenaeus *Wise Men at Dinner* 605f; the text and precise sense of the last few words are uncertain). Similar tales are told involving other temple statues, most notably Praxiteles's *Aphrodite of Cnidos*.

Phryne had asked Praxiteles to give her his most beautiful work. Being in love with her, he had agreed, but refused to say which work he thought the most beautiful. One day one of Phryne's slaves rushed in, declaring that fire had broken out in his studio and most, but not all, of his works were lost. Praxiteles ran out through the door at once, shouting that all his labor had gone for nothing if the flames had snatched his Satyr *and his* Eros. *Phryne told him to stay where he was and not to worry, for nothing bad had happened: he had simply been tricked into declaring which of his works were the most beautiful. That is how Phryne obtained Praxiteles's* Eros (Pausanias *Guide to Greece* 1.20).

Apelles was probably the most highly regarded artist in antiquity. Alexander the Great would allow no one else to paint his picture. Descriptions of some of his paintings have come down to us, but not a single one has actually survived. His *Aphrodite Rising from the Waves*, for which the model may have been Phryne (see above), was one of the most influential ancient paintings. It inspired, among many other works, Botticelli's *Birth of Venus*, for which the model is reputed to have been Simonetta Cattaneo de Vespucci, who was a distant relative by marriage of Amerigo Vespucci, after whom the Americas are named.

Piraeicus ranks as one of the most skillful of all artists. It may be that he owes his fame to his subject-matter, for he preferred to paint mundane things, and that gave him a very high reputation. He painted barber's shops, shoe factories, donkeys, dishes of food, and such like, and hence he earned the nickname Rhyparographos [Painter of Sordid Things]. *Some of his paintings are exquisite and fetch higher prices than the largest works of many other artists* (Pliny *Natural History* 35.112).

Myrmecides from Miletus and Callicrates the Spartan have created some amazing miniature works: a four-horse chariot hidden under a fly's wing, a couplet of poetry written in gold letters on a sesame seed. But I doubt if any serious person will approve of this, for what is it but a sheer waste of time? (Aelian *Miscellaneous History* 1.17). The name Myrmecides is highly suitable, for it means literally "son of an ant." The word for "ant," μύρμηξ [*myrmex*], is perhaps related to its Latin equivalent, *formica*, and the splendid regional English "pismire," thought to be inspired by the tendency of anthills to smell like urine.

Having incurred the wrath of Artemis, the goddess of hunting, Actaeon was torn to pieces by his own hounds. Here he seems to be making some headway against these rather runty dogs.

The artistry and cultural significance of 5th-century Athenian painted vases are out of all proportion to their original price, which is often scratched casually on the base. The highest known price for a vase was three drachmas, and one by the Achilles Painter, who ranks among the finest artists, cost a mere three and a half obols. The modest daily rate of pay for service on an Athenian jury was raised from two to three obols in the 420s, and six obols were worth one drachma.

STATUES

When a ghost was running about devastating their territory, the people of Orchomenus consulted the oracle at Delphi, and the god ordered them to find the remains of Actaeon and bury them in the earth. He also ordered them to make a bronze image of the ghost and fasten it to a rock with iron. I have myself seen this image (Pausanias *Guide to Greece* 9.38).

About seven miles from Marathon . . . not far from the sea, there is a little shrine of Nemesis, the deity most inexorably opposed to those who are presumptuous. It is thought that her anger fell upon the barbarians who landed at Marathon. They arrogantly supposed that nothing could stop them from taking Athens and, as if it were a fait accompli, *they brought a slab of Parian marble on which to sculpt a trophy. Phidias turned it into a statue of Nemesis* (Pausanias *Description of Greece* 1.32). Parts of the statue, which modern scholars attribute to Phidias's pupil Agoracritus, have been excavated. The Persians suffered again for their presumption ten years later: *the silver-footed throne of Xerxes, called the "war captive," sitting on which he watched the Battle of Salamis, was put on display in Athena's Parthenon* (Harpocration *Lexicon to the Ten Attic Orators* 56).

Socrates carved the statues of the Graces that stand in front of the entrance to the Acropolis (Pausanias *Guide to Greece* 9.35.7).

In a high-flown and dramatic passage at the beginning of Euripides's *Ion*, Ion grabs his bow and arrows to drive the swans of Parnassus away from Apollo's temple. It would be beneath the dignity of tragedy to spell out his motive for warding them off, but *Ion is seizing his bow and threatening the swan that is letting its droppings fall on the statues* (Ps.-Demetrius *On Style* 195).

An argument against pagan religion: *swallows and most other birds fly to the statues of the gods and void their droppings on them, with no respect for Olympian Zeus, or Epidaurian Asclepius, or Athena Polias, or Egyptian Serapis* (St. Clement of Alexandria *Protrepticus* 4.52).

In Aristophanes's *Birds*, the chorus of birds threatens the judges of the competing comedies: *If you don't award us the prize, you'd better have little hats made like the ones that statues wear. Any of you that doesn't have a hat, when you're wearing your white cloaks, that's when you'll pay, being pooped on by all the birds* (1114–17). A few lines later, the messenger bird comes on stage uttering perhaps the most exuberantly silly line in Aristophanes: ποῦ ποῦ 'στι, ποῦ ποῦ ποῦ 'στι, ποῦ ποῦ ποῦ 'στι, ποῦ; (*poo poo 'sti, poo poo poo 'sti, poo poo poo 'sti, poo?*, "Where, where's he, where, where, where's he, where, where, where's he, where?"

A statue with a meniscus.

Whenever you vote to honor someone with a statue . . . there he stands in no time at all, or rather, even before you have taken the vote. For the procedure is altogether ridiculous: your chief magistrate simply points to one of the statues conveniently to hand, the original inscription is removed, the new name is added, and the whole procedure for honoring the dedicatee is over (Dio Chrysostom *Rhodian Oration* 9).

Statues here on Rhodes are like actors. Just as actors perform different roles at different times, so your statues change their masks and stand there almost as if they were playing parts in a play. The same statue is sometimes a Greek, sometimes a Roman, or perhaps a Macedonian or a Persian. And sometimes the change is obvious straightaway, with clothing, shoes, and all such things exposing the trickery (Dio Chrysostom *Rhodian Oration* 155). Putting a new head on a statue was a quick, cheap, and widespread practice.

I really love Athens and want to have some memorial in my honor there, but I detest the practice of putting false inscriptions on statues of other people (Cicero *Letters to Atticus* 6.1).

In Athens, the colossal statues of King Eumenes and King Attalus, on which Antony's name had been inscribed, were toppled in a storm (Plutarch *Life of Antony* 60, a bad omen for the Battle of Actium).

At the temple of Hera outside Mycenae, there is a statue of Orestes with an inscription claiming it is the emperor Augustus (Pausanias *Guide to Greece* 2.17).

Augustus had two paintings by Apelles representing Alexander the Great set up in the busiest parts of the Forum. Claudius had Alexander's face cut out from them and Augustus's added instead (Pliny *Natural History* 35.94).

In the largest synagogue the Romans set up a bronze statue of Caligula riding in a four-horse chariot. They did this in such haste that, since they did not have a new chariot available, they brought a very old one from the gymnasium. It was covered in rust, and the ears and tails of the horses had been damaged, as had the pedestal and other parts of it. Some people say it was actually dedicated in honor of a woman long ago, the great-grandmother of the last Cleopatra (Philo of Alexandria *Embassy to Gaius* 134).

Finishing a statue.

Caligula planned to bring from Greece various statues of great religious and artistic significance, including that of Jupiter at Olympia, and to have their heads removed and replaced with his own head. . . . It had been decided to dismantle the statue of Jupiter at Olympia and take it to Rome, but it suddenly burst out with so loud a laugh that the scaffolding collapsed and the workmen fled (Suetonius *Life of Caligula* 22, 57).

Cleopatra gave herself the title "Queen of Kings," and her arrogance was so extreme that she tried to buy the statue of Zeus at Olympia by inundating the people of Elis with gold (Aelian *On Animals frg.* 55).

The route to the stadium at Olympia was lined with statues of Zeus commissioned from the fines imposed on athletes who broke the rules. They were intended *to make clear that an Olympic victory is to be won, not through bribery, but through swiftness of foot and strength of body* (Pausanias *Guide to Greece* 5.21).

Two statues of the boxer Euthymus, one in his hometown of Locri in Italy, the other at Olympia, were struck by lightning on the same day (Pliny *Natural History* 7.152).

The architect Timochares began work on a vaulted roof for the temple of Arsinoe at Alexandria, using the magnetic lodestone in its construction, his purpose being to make an iron statue of the queen seem to hang in midair. The project was halted by the death of the architect and also of King Ptolemy [Philadelphus], *who had commissioned the project in his sister's honor* (Pliny *Natural History* 34.14). There was just such a magnetically floating statue of Serapis in Alexandria (Nicephorus Callistus *Church History* 15.8). Claudian describes an otherwise unknown temple in which a statue of Venus, made of lodestone, attracts a statue of Mars, made of iron, so that the divine lovers are drawn together into each others' arms (*Minor Poems* 29); this statue may also have been in Alexandria, since Claudian was born there.

I hear that there is a law in Thebes that requires artists, whether painters or sculptors, to portray their subjects in a flattering manner. If the painting or statue is less attractive than the original, the law can impose a fine of one thousand drachmas on the artist (Aelian *Miscellaneous History* 4.4).

An eagle, the bird of Zeus, on a coin minted at Elis between the 91st and 94th Olympiads (416–404 B.C.).

There was possibly a similar law in Athens: Aristophanes teases Euripides for having warts on his eyelids (*Frogs* 1,247), but there is no hint of them in surviving sculptures of him. The famously and irredeemably ugly Socrates will have been a special case.

There used to be on show in Locri [in south Italy] *a statue of the lyre-player Eunomus, with a cicada perched on his lyre.* . . . . *He himself set up the statue after winning at the Pythian Games; while he was competing, one of the strings on his lyre broke, but a cicada settled on it and filled out the required sound* (Strabo *Geography* 6.1.9).

Two gigantic seated statues of Amenophis III of the 18th dynasty (ruled ca. 1387–1350 B.C.) are located on the west bank of the Nile at Thebes. After suffering earthquake damage in the early 20s B.C., one began to emit a "song" at dawn. Known as the "Colossi of Memnon," they became a tourist attraction. Strabo thought the "song" might be a hoax:

> *I was there with Aelius Gallus and his entourage of friends and soldiers* [in 26–25 B.C.] *and heard the sound at the first hour. I cannot state with certainty whether it came from the base or from the colossus or was made deliberately by one of the people standing round about the base.* (*Geography* 17.1.46)

Eight Roman prefects of Egypt, and one prefect's wife, commemorated their visits to Memnon with graffiti. A centurion, Lucius Tanicius, recorded the date and time of day when he heard the song on each of thirteen visits between November A.D. 80 and June 82. The last datable graffito is from A.D. 205. Septimius Severus (ruled A.D. 193–211), the last of several emperors to visit it, may have restored the statue and thus stopped the "song."

· XX ·

TOURISTS AND
TOURIST ATTRACTIONS

*Of the many artifacts purported to have been made by Hephaestus, the
only genuine one is the scepter that he fashioned for Zeus, and that was
passed down to Agamemnon, and is now venerated in Chaeronea, where
daily sacrifices are offered to it. There is a bronze bowl in the temple of
Apollo at Patara, which the Lycians say was made by Hephaestus and
dedicated by Telephus (who lived at the time of the Trojan War), but it
was constructed with a bronze casting technique invented later. The
Achaeans who live in Patras claim to have a chest made by Hephaestus
and brought from Troy by Eurypylus but, rather suspiciously, they do not
actually put it on display* (Pausanias *Guide to Greece* 9.40).

*At Delphi there is a moderate sized stone over which they pour olive oil
every day and on which they place unworked wool during every festival.
Some people believe that this is the stone that Cronus was given instead of
his child, and that he vomited it up again* (Pausanias *Guide to Greece*
10.24.6). Cronus ate his children at birth, for fear that one of them
would overthrow him, until Rhea saved Zeus with this trick.

*In Athens there is an opening in the ground about a foot and a half wide.
This is said to be where the water drained away after Deucalion's flood,*

and people throw a mixture of wheat flour and honey into it every year
(Pausanias *Guide to Greece* 1.18.7).

*In the marketplace at Corinth there are two statues of Dionysus, gilded all
over, except for their faces, which are painted red. . . . They say that the
Corinthians, advised by the Pythian oracle, looked for the tree on Mt.
Cithaeron from which Pentheus had spied on the Bacchantes and made
these statues from its wood* (Pausanias *Guide to Greece* 2.2.6).

*At Joppa there are huge rocks jutting out to sea, on which the indentations
left by the chains that bound Andromeda are still pointed out* (Josephus
The Jewish War 3.420). Andromeda was rescued from a sea monster by
Perseus.

At *Natural History* 16.238, Pliny reports that many trees still survive
from legendary times. For example, it is possible to see

Pentheus being torn apart by his mother and his aunt.

- *at Tibur* [mod. Tivoli] *three oak trees even older than its founder Tiburnus, who is said to have been the son of Amphiaraus, who died at Thebes a generation before the Trojan War;*
- *at Delphi, and also at Caphya in Arcadia, plane trees planted by Agamemnon;*
- *at the Hellespont, facing Troy, trees growing on the tomb of Protesilaus* [whose death on the shore fulfilled the oracle that the first Greek to land at Troy would die immediately]. *When they grow tall enough to see Troy, they wither, and then they grow again;*
- *at Argos the olive tree to which Argus tethered Io after she had been turned into a cow;*
- *on the road to Phrygia the plane tree from which Marsyas's skin was hung,* [that being the penalty he suffered] *after he lost his singing-contest with Apollo.* Aelian records that *if anyone plays a Phrygian tune to it, the skin moves, but if anyone plays in honor of Apollo, it stays still as if it were deaf* (*Miscellaneous Histories* 13.21);
- *on the coast of the Black Sea the laurel planted beside the tomb of King Bebryx, who was killed by Pollux in a boxing-match when the Argonauts landed there (it is known as the Laurel of Madness, because quarrels always break out on a ship if a sprig of it is brought on board.);*
- *at Athens the olive tree that Athena offered to the Athenians when she competed with Poseidon for patronage of the city.*

Heracles became nine-fingered when the Nemean lion bit off the other one. There is a tomb for the finger that was bitten off. Some people said that he lost the finger to the sting of a stingray, but there is a stone lion on view in Sparta, standing over the finger's tomb (Ptolemy the Quail in Photius *The Library* 190.147*a*). Bringing the Nemean lion to King Eurystheus was Heracles's first labor. His fingers were remarkably powerful: *Heracles struck Oeneus's cup-bearer dead with a single blow to the head from one finger because he did not like the drink he had served him* (Pausanias *Guide to Greece* 2.13.8).

Near the sanctuary of the Kindly Goddesses on the road from Megalopolis to Messene there is a small mound of earth surmounted by a finger made of stone. It is in fact known as the Memorial to the Finger, for it is said

that when Orestes was out of his mind, he bit off one of his fingers at this spot (Pausanias *Guide to Greece* 8.34).

In the marketplace at Elis I saw a rather squat building, like a temple, with no walls, but with a roof supported by oak columns. The local people all say that it is a memorial, but they do not remember who is being commemorated (Pausanias *Guide to Greece* 6.24).

Near the marketplace in Argos there is a mound of earth that is said to cover the head of Medusa, the Gorgon (Pausanias *Guide to Greece* 2.21.5). Pausanias later notes that some of Medusa's (snaky) hair was kept in the temple of Athena at Tegea, as a guarantee that the city would never be conquered (8.47.5).

Pausanias also notes that, in a different temple of Athena at Tegea, the hide of the Calydonian boar is on display. It had rotted with age and

Medusa's head, on an early 5th-century B.C. jar.

was entirely without bristles, and its tusks had been taken to Rome by Octavian, because the Tegeans had sided with Antony in the Actium campaign (8.46).

The following items are dedicated in the temple of Apollo at Sicyon:

- *Agamemnon's shield and sword*
- *Odysseus's cloak and breastplate*
- *Teucer's bow and arrows*
- *A box belonging to Adrastus (contents unknown)*
- *A bronze pot, dedicated by Medea, in which she cooked Pelias*
- *Palamedes's letters*
- *Marsyas's pipe and his skin*
- *Oars and rudders from the Argo*
- *The pebble with which Athena voted in the trial of Orestes*
- *Penelope's web*

(Ampelius *Book of Remarkable Things* 8)

Near the running track in Sparta there is a house that once belonged to Menelaus, but is now in private ownership (Pausanias *Guide to Greece* 3.14.6).

At Sparta there is an egg hung by ribbons from the ceiling of the temple of Hilaira and Phoebe, the daughters of Apollo; it is said to be the egg that, according to legend, Leda laid (Pausanias *Guide to Greece* 3.16.1). When Zeus, in the guise of a swan, raped Leda, in some versions of the myth she produced Polydeuces and Helen from an egg, but Castor and Clytemnestra by the normal mammalian birth process.

In the temple of Minerva at Lindos on the island of Rhodes there is a chalice dedicated by Helen. It is made of electrum [a naturally occurring alloy of gold and silver] *and is said to be the same size as her breasts* (Pliny *Natural History* 33.81).

There are two cities very close to each other in Cappadocia. They both have the same name, Comana, and they both make the same claims to fame. They share the same legends, and the artifacts they display are the same, most notably the sword of Iphigenia—both of them have it (Cassius Dio *History* 36.11).

Aeneas and his comrades consulted the oracle at Dodona about founding a colony. They dedicated to Zeus various objects from Troy, including bronze mixing bowls, some of which still survive, and the very ancient inscriptions on them prove who dedicated them (Dionysius of Halicarnassus *Roman Antiquities* 1.51).

The tourist guides at Argos know perfectly well that some of what they say is not entirely accurate, but they say it anyway, for it is not easy to get people to change their views (Pausanias *Guide to Greece* 2.23).

If Greece were deprived of its myths, there would be nothing to stop tourist guides from starving to death, for visitors don't want to be told facts, not even if they got them without paying (Lucian *Lover of Lies* 4).

May Jupiter save me from the guides at Olympia, and Minerva from those at Athens! (Varro *Menippean Satires* 35).

The guides were going through their usual patter, ignoring us when we begged them to cut their stories short and not to read out every single inscription (Plutarch *On the Pythian Oracle* 395a). Some guides at Delphi are still like this.

Herodotus seems to have suffered more than most tourists from such expositions. He claims to have been shown statues of 341 high priests in a temple of Hephaestus in Egypt, covering a period of more than eleven thousand years, and to have endured listening to the priests reciting to him a catalog of all their names (*Histories* 2.142).

There is a record on the pyramid in Egyptian writing of how much was spent on radishes, leeks, and garlic for the workmen. If I remember rightly, the guide who read the inscription to me said that this amounted to 1,600 talents of silver (Herodotus *Histories* 2.125). Because Greek tourists could not read hieroglyphs, the guides were free to say whatever they liked.

An early 4th-century B.C. drachma minted at Cnossus on Crete. As represented here, the Labyrinth is not complex, lacking the blind turns and bifurcations attributed to it in some of the literary sources.

I really must mention one of the strange things I saw at the pyramids. There are heaps of stone-chippings lying near them. Among these can be found chippings that are the size and shape of beans, along with what are apparently half-peeled ears of grain. The guides say that these are the petrified leftovers from the meals eaten by the workmen who built the pyramids, and this is not improbable (Strabo *Geography* 17.1.34).

When Himilcar took the Sicilian city of Acragas, he sent the most valuable items of plunder to Carthage. This booty included the Bull of Phalaris. In his Histories, *Timaeus maintained that this bull did not exist, but chance proved him wrong: nearly 260 years later, when Scipio sacked Carthage* [in 146 B.C.], *he restored the bull to the people of Acragas along with everything else of theirs that the Carthaginians still held. It is in Acragas even now as I write this history* (Diodorus Siculus *The Library* 13.90). For the Bull of Phalaris, see also p. 187.

On display in the temple of Athena of the City in Athens are a folding chair made by Daedalus [who constructed Minos's Labyrinth] *and the breastplate of Masistius* [the Persian cavalry commander who was killed just before the Battle of Plataea in 479 B.C.] (Pausanias *Guide to Greece* 1.27.1). This breastplate must have been a very special piece of work, for Masistius's armor was so comprehensive that the Athenians, when they unseated him from his horse, were unable to kill him until it occurred to someone to stab him in the eye (Herodotus *Histories* 9.22).

· XXI ·

RELIGION, SUPERSTITION, AND MAGIC

I am unable to know whether the gods exist or do not exist. There are many obstacles to knowing about this—the obscurity of the question and the brevity of human life

(**Protagoras** *frg.* 4).

At Sparta there are temples to Death, Laughter, and Fear (Plutarch *Life of Cleomenes* 9).

When Phoebus Apollo raised up in his arms the infant Hermes, [who would grow up to be] *the mighty slayer of Argus, the baby sent forth an omen, a wretched slave of the belly, an insolent messenger* [i.e., he passed gas], *and directly afterward he sneezed. Hearing this, Apollo dropped glorious Hermes on the ground* (*Homeric Hymn to Hermes* 293ff.).

Sitting on her father's knee when she was still just a little child, Artemis spoke like this to Zeus: "Let me keep my virginity for ever, Daddy, and give me many names [i.e., cult titles], *so that Phoebus* [Apollo, her twin brother] *can't match me"* (Callimachus *Hymn to Artemis* 4ff.).

Some odd cult-titles for pagan deities, collected for ridicule by St. Clement of Alexandria (*Protrepticus* 2.37):

> *Aphrodite the Gravedigger*
> *Aphrodite the Lovely Rumped*
> *Aphrodite the Prostitute*
> *Apollo the Glutton*
> *Apollo the Mouse God*
> *Apollo the Yawner*
> *Artemis the Choked*
> *Artemis the Cougher*
> *Artemis the Gouty*
> *Zeus the Averter of Flies*
> *Zeus the Bald*
> *Dionysus the Pig-Plucker* (χοιροψάλας; χοῖρος [*choiros*, "pig"] is
>   a slang term for the female genitalia, and ψάλλειν [*psallein*]
>   means to make the string of a musical instrument or of a bow
>   resound [a *psalm* being a song sung to the accompaniment of
>   a stringed instrument]; the scholion to Aeschylus *Persae* 1063
>   explains the phrase as "Dionysus the Depilator")

The box tree (πύξος [*pyxos*]) is sacred to Aphrodite, in honor of her buttocks (πυγαί [*pygae*]) (Cornutus *On the Nature of the Gods* 46, recalling the goddess's epithet καλλίπυγος [*callipygos*, "the Lovely Rumped"]).

♈

Hunting is a noble sport, but there is nothing glorious about fishing. None of the gods has deigned to be called "Conger Eel Slayer," as Apollo is called "Wolf Slayer," or "Mullet Shooter," as Artemis is called "Deer Shooter" (Plutarch *On the Cleverness of Animals* 965f).

⚱

We address as "Olympian" those deities who are responsible for the good things that happen to us, and both private individuals and whole communities build temples and altars in their honor. But we give less appealing names to those other deities who are responsible for disasters and punishments that befall us, and we do not honor them in our prayers or in sacrifices; instead, we perform rites intended to drive them away (Isocrates *Philippus* 117).

There was actually someone who wanted to set fire to the temple of Diana at Ephesus. His purpose in destroying such a beautiful building was to make his name famous throughout the whole world—he revealed this mad plan when he was being tortured on the rack. The Ephesians were quite right to decree that all record of this appalling person should be wiped out (Valerius Maximus *Memorable Deeds and Sayings* 8.14 ext. 5). His name is, in fact, known from several sources, but will not be repeated here.

A cliff on the island of Leucadia is called the "Lovers' Leap." It is reputed to put an end to the pangs of love, and Sappho is said to have been the first to jump off it. There was a tradition among the Leucadians that, at the festival of Apollo every year, a criminal should be thrown off the cliff as a way of averting evil from the community. He had feathers and birds of all sorts attached to him, to break his fall with their flapping, and there were numerous people waiting in a circle down below in small fishing boats, and they did their best to rescue him and take him away from Leucadia (Strabo *Geography* 10.2).

In olden times, the scapegoat was a means of purification. The ritual worked like this. If a city was struck by some disaster caused by divine wrath, whether famine, or plague, or some other harmful event, they se-lected the ugliest man in the city and led him off to be sacrificed, as a way of purifying and restoring the city. They set their victim in the appropriate place, with cheese, barley, and dried figs in his hand. Then they struck him seven times on the penis with squills, with branches of a wild fig tree, and with other such plants. Finally they burned him to death on a fire made from timber from wild trees and scattered his ashes on the sea and for the wind to carry off, in order to purify the ailing city, as I said (Tzetzes *Chiliads* 5.728).

The thing that most amazed me at Methana was the ritual to counter the wind called Lips, that blows from the Saronic Gulf and blights the vine-buds. When the wind blows, a rooster with completely white feathers is chopped in two, and two men run round the vines, each holding half of

the fowl. When they arrive back at their starting point, they bury it there (Pausanias *Guide to Greece* 2.34).

Take a tortoise of the sort found in marshes and turn it upside down in your right hand, and carry it all around your vineyard. After going around, go to the middle of the vineyard and place it on the ground, upside down but still alive, with a little bit of dirt heaped up round it so that it cannot turn itself over and go away. It will not be able to, so long as the earth under its feet is hollowed out, for without something to press against, it is stuck in the same place. If you follow this procedure, your farmland and all your property will be free from hail. Some people say that it is necessary to carry the tortoise around the farm and set it down at the sixth hour of either the day or the night (*Farm Work* 1.14).

Dogs were not considered entirely pure in olden times, for they were not sacrificed to any of the Olympian deities. When a dog is left at a crossroads as a meal for the earth goddess Hecate, it serves to avert and expiate evil. Puppies are sacrificed at Sparta to the war god Enyalius, the bloodiest of all deities. In Boeotia, there is a public ceremony of purification in which the populace files out of the city between the halves of a dog that has been split in two (Plutarch *Roman Questions* 290d).

Porphyry notes that all animals are worshipped somewhere in Egypt, and that it fits this pattern that, in the village of Anabis, a human being is worshipped and has sacrifices offered to him (*On Abstinence from Killing Animals* 4.9).

Some Egyptians have a tradition of worshipping a bull, the so-called Apis, while others worship goats, cats, snakes, onions, the breathings of the belly [i.e., farts, which St. Jerome specifies as being venerated at Pelusium (*Commentary on* Isiah 13.46)], *sewers, the limbs of irrational animals, and countless other very weird things* (Ps.-Clement *Recognitions* 5.20). This sentiment, attributed to St. Peter, is said to have made his hearers laugh, but he goes straight on to point out that the Egyptians find Greek religious practices just as absurd.

St. Clement of Alexandria himself (*Protrepticus* 2.39) also argues that the Greeks are no better than the Egyptians in their bizarre worship of animals. He notes, for example, the veneration of

- *storks and ants in Thessaly*
- *weasels in Thebes*
- *mice in the Troad*
- *flies at Actium*
- *sheep on Samos*

In the region of Daulis called Tronis, there is a shrine to the Founding Hero. The Phocians worship him with sacrifices every day. They pour the blood through a hole into the grave, but it is customary for the people themselves to eat the meat there (Pausanias *Guide to Greece* 10.4). Early Christians mocked this custom, but they themselves left holes in grave-slabs into which perfumes were poured.

At least in Athens, by the 5th century B.C. it was a common practice to carry small coins in one's mouth. The placing of coins in the mouth of a dead person to pay Charon for transport across the River Styx to the Underworld was therefore presumably regarded as the continuation of an everyday custom. Even in the 4th century, silver coins were minted worth as little as an eighth of an obol (= one forty-eighth of a drachma, which was the charge for admission to the theater in Athens). Such coins, so small that they were often thrown out unnoticed in archaeological digs, were replaced by bulkier bronze equivalents.

In Elysium, the fortunate dead enjoy horse riding, gymnastics, checkers, and playing the lyre (Pindar *frg.* 129).

Before the Battle of Marathon, the Athenians swore that they would sacrifice a goat to Artemis for every one of the enemy that they killed. After the battle, however, they could not find enough goats, so they decided to offer her an annual sacrifice of five hundred goats, a ritual that they still observe (Xenophon *Anabasis* 3.2.11). Herodotus says that about 6,400 barbarians were killed, as opposed to 192 Athenians (*Histories* 6.117).

It is often observed during a sacrifice that even when their hearts are already lying on the altar, animals not only continue breathing and bellowing loudly, but may actually run away, dying eventually through loss of blood (Galen *On the Doctrines of Hippocrates and Plato* 2.4.45).

SUPERSTITION

Superstition is a dreadful thing; like water, it always seeks the lowest level (Plutarch *Life of Alexander* 75).

The atheist thinks there are no gods; the superstitious man wishes there were none, but believes in them against his will, for he is afraid not to believe (Plutarch *On Superstition* 170f).

When people see wax images at their door, or at a crossroads, or at their parents' tomb, it is pointless trying to persuade them to make light of all such things, because they have no clear understanding of them (Plato *Laws* 933b).

Those who committed premeditated murder averted reprisals by cutting off parts of the victim's body and hanging them on a string around his neck. They passed the string through under his armpits, and hence the process is called "armpitting" (Aristophanes of Byzantium *frg.* 78). When Hesychius repeats this information, he helpfully specifies body parts as being "for example, ears and noses."

If a woman looks at a highly polished mirror during her menstrual period, a blood-colored cloudiness covers the surface of the mirror. It is particularly difficult to remove such stains from new mirrors (Aristotle *On Dreams* 459b).

On Cyprus, people cut copper into small pieces, which they then sow. When the rains come, the copper sprouts and shoots up, and they harvest it (Ps.-Aristotle *On Amazing Things Heard* 833a).

Since the olive tree is pure, it wants anyone who picks its fruit to be pure also and to swear that he has come from his own wife's bed, not from someone else's. If such conditions are met, it will bear more fruit the next season also. They say that innocent children tend the olive trees at Anazarbus in Cilicia, and that that is why olive production is so successful there (Farm Work 9.2).

How to make a barren tree produce fruit. Tighten your belt, tuck in your tunic, take up an axe or a hatchet, and rush up to the tree looking angry, as if you were going to chop it down. Someone should beg you not to chop it down, assuring you that it will produce fruit. Make a show of being persuaded to spare the tree. It will be very fruitful from then on. Empty bean pods scattered around the trunk also ensure that a tree bears fruit (Farm Work 10.83).

We should not credit the notion that Sirens exist in India that lull people to sleep and then shred them to pieces. Anyone who believes this would not hesitate to believe that, by licking his ears, snakes gave the prophet Melampus the power to understand the speech of birds. Such a person will also accept the story handed down by Democritus, that there are birds from the mixing of whose blood a snake is born, and that whoever eats the snake will understand conversations between birds (Pliny Natural History 10.137).

We avoid, especially in the morning, people who are lame in the right leg. And if anyone sees a eunuch or a monkey just as he is leaving home, he turns back, convinced that this means that everything is going to go badly for him that day (Lucian Pseudologistes 17).

It is said that a human being changes into a wolf during the festival in honor of Lycaean Zeus (i.e., Zeus the wolf-god). The change is not necessarily permanent; they say that, if he abstains from human flesh while he is a wolf, he becomes a human being again in the tenth year, but, if he has tasted human flesh, he remains a beast for ever (Pausanias Guide to Greece 8.2).

Odysseus and the Sirens.

Gello was a young girl who died prematurely. The people of Lesbos say that her ghost comes to visit children, and they blame her for their untimely deaths (Zenobius *Proverbs* 3.3).

Some people think that the bogey-woman Empousa is Hecate, others that she is a shape-shifting phantasm sent by Hecate. She often appears at midday, when sacrifices are being offered to the dead. Some say she has just one foot and derives her name from this [i.e., from εἷς (*heis*, "one") and πούς (*pous*, "foot"). *Others say that she has a donkey's leg* [deriving her variant name Ὀνοσκελίς (Onoscelis) from ὄνος (*onos*, "donkey") and σκέλος (*scelos*, "leg")] (Scholion to Aristophanes *Frogs* 293).

There is nothing remarkable if a mouse gnaws through a bag when it can't find anything to eat; it really would be remarkable if the bag were to

swallow the mouse (Bion of Borysthenes *frg*. 31, mocking the superstition that it is ominous if mice gnaw at man-made objects).

The astrologer Vettius Valens does not share his modern colleagues' tendency to accentuate the positive. His outlook for the other signs of the zodiac is no sunnier than in these examples:

- *People born under Capricorn are wicked and inconsistent, though they pretend to be good and sincere. They are oppressive, anxious, insomniac, partial to joking, full of big schemes, prone to making mistakes, fickle, criminal, dishonest, censorious, and disgusting.*
- *Taurus is a thieving and shameful sign. It causes fits, excision of the uvula, carbuncles, swollen glands, choking, pain in the nostrils through injury and disease, falls from a height or from animals, broken limbs, throat tumors, mutilation, sciatica, abscesses.*
- *People born under Scorpio die from sword wounds to the genitals or buttocks, retention of the urine, putrefaction, choking, snakes, violence, battle, attacks by robbers or pirates, political activity, fire, impaling, creeping creatures.*

(*The Astrological Anthologies* II, 110, 127)

MAGIC

Practitioners of the magic arts enhanced the mystery of their profession by claiming to use rather intimidating or exotic ingredients in their potions and other charms. A papyrus (*Greek Magical Papyri* 12.401) reveals the quite ordinary substances that are actually meant. For example:

baboon's tears	dill juice
blood of Hephaestus	wormwood
blood of Hestia	chamomile
blood of an eagle	wild garlic
blood of a Titan	wild lettuce
bone of a doctor	sandstone

crocodile dung	Egyptian earth
head of a snake	leech
seeds of a bull	dung-beetle's eggs
seeds of Ares	clover

Those who bet heavily on chariot races will have considered investment in curses a sound business practice. The following is part of the procedure involved in such an imprecation:

> *After drowning the cat, insert three thin metal sheets, one into its anus, one into its mouth, and one into its throat. Write what you have to say on a sheet of papyrus that has been wiped clean with cinnabar. Add the chariots, the charioteers, and the horses, then wrap the papyrus around the cat's body and bury it.* (Greek Magical Papyri 3.15)

A victory charm for a runner. While also inscribing the appropriate magical symbols, write this on his big toes: "grant me good fortune, sex-appeal, glory, grace" and as many of the usual things as you want (Greek Magical Papyri 7.390).

To make people drinking at a symposium look as if they have donkey snouts: at night take the wick from a lamp and dip it in donkey's blood, then make a new lamp with it and light it for the drinkers (Greek Magical Papyri 11b.1).

Burn the head of a hare under a drawing of a pair of gladiators, and they will seem to [come alive and] fight (Greek Magical Papyri 7.176).

To induce a sleeping woman to confess the name of the man she loves: put a bird's tongue under her lips or on her heart and ask the question—she will say his name three times (Greek Magical Papyri 63.8).

To find out by means of a die if a person is alive or has died: have your client throw a die in a bowl, and then have him fill the bowl with water. Add to the number on the die 612, which is the numerical value

A drunken deity, perhaps Dionysus, being carried along on a mule.

of the name of the god Zeus, and then subtract from the total 353, which is the numerical value of Hermes. If the sum remaining is an even number, he is alive, but if it is not, death has him (*Greek Magical Papyri* 62.47). Perhaps the ambience in which this ritual was conducted was sufficiently imposing to distract the customer from the simplicity of the mathematics. For the numerical value of words, see p. 175.

Engrave a quail on an onyx stone with a sea perch at its feet. Put under the stone some of the concoction used in lamps, and no one will see you, even if you take something away. Smear your face with the concoction and wear the ring. No one will see either who you are or what you are doing (*Cyranides* 1.15).

If you take some hairs from a donkey's rump, burn them and grind them up, and then give them to a woman in a drink, she will not stop farting (*Cyranides* 2.31).

> *If you want to play a joke on someone and cause him sleeplessness, remove the head from a living bat and sew it inside the pillow on which your victim usually sleeps. He will get no sleep, just as if he were wearing the whole bat as an amulet*
>
> (**Africanus** *Cestoi* 1.17).

· XXII ·

PROPHECY

*The best prophet is the one who guesses well (Eurip-
ides frg. 973).* Alexander the Great quoted this
verse to the Chaldaean soothsayers who tried
to persuade him to postpone his entry into
Babylon
(**Appian** *Civil Wars* **2.153); he ignored them,
and died there.**

*The philosopher Favorinus thought that the most intolerable thing about
astrologers is their notion that heaven above exercises control not only over
things that happen to us through external agencies, but also over our own
personal plans and opinions, our arbitrary and sudden changes of mind.
Suppose you intended to go to the baths, then decided not to, then changed
your mind again: Are we to suppose that this happens not through some
vacillating mental state, but through some fateful alignment of the planets,
leaving mankind not as rational beings but as silly and ridiculous pup-
pets? (Aulus Gellius Attic Nights 14.1.23).*

*If the time, the manner, and the cause of every person's life and death,
along with all human affairs, are determined by the stars in heaven, what
do the astrologers have to say about flies, and worms, and sea urchins, and
all the many other tiny creatures living on the land and in the sea? Are
they also born and destroyed by the same laws as humans are? Either frogs*

and gnats are assigned their destinies by the movements of the stars in heaven just as we are, or, if astrologers do not believe this, why is it that the stars should have influence over humans, but not over other animals? (Aulus Gellius *Attic Nights* 14.1.31).

George the Monk lists a wide range of objects and phenomena used by pagans to predict the future (*Chronicle* 238):

flour	*barley*
oak trees	*entrails*
the flight and the cries of birds	*chance utterances*
sneezing	*thunder*
mice	*weasels*
the creaking of planks	*ringing in the ears*
twitching of the body	*the names of the dead, of stars, and of rivers*

When the Spartans consulted the oracle of Jupiter at Dodona before the Battle of Leuctra in 371 B.C., *the urn containing the lots and the other things necessary for the consultation were knocked over and scattered by the king of the Molossians' pet monkey* (Cicero *On Divination* 1.76). The Spartans went on to suffer a defeat that marked the beginning of the end of their supremacy in Greece. A monkey wrought equally ominous havoc in the temple of Ceres at Rome just before the Battle of Actium in 31 B.C. (Cassius Dio *Roman History* 50.8).

Questions submitted to the oracle of Zeus and the ancient goddess Dione at Dodona, near Ioannina, in the western mountains of Greece:

> *Reveal to me, O Zeus, whether it is better for me to give my daughter in marriage to Theodorus or to Tessias.*

> *Cleoutas asks Zeus and Dione if it is profitable and beneficial for him to graze sheep.*

> *Lysanias asks Zeus and Dione whether he is the father of the baby borne by Annyla.*

A terra-cotta monkey-faced cup.

Agis asks Zeus and Dione about the sheets and pillows which he lost, whether one of those from outside stole them.

Should I enquire at an oracle elsewhere?

Nicias kept a soothsayer in his household, ostensibly to make enquiries about public affairs, but in fact he consulted him mostly about his own business, especially about his silver mines (Plutarch *Life of Nicias* 4).

While an astrologer sat on a hilltop during the night watching the stars, his associate waited with the woman in labor and, as soon as she gave birth, he would send a signal by striking a gong. When the astrologer on the hilltop heard the gong, he would note the rising zodiacal sign as being in the ascendancy. In the daytime, he would study both the ascendant stars and the movements of the sun (Sextus Empiricus *Against the Professors of Liberal Studies* 5.27). "Horoscope" means literally "watching the hour," referring particularly to the hour of a person's birth.

Here is how charlatans make a skull seem to speak as an oracle. The skull itself is made of the stomach membrane of a cow, wrapped around and molded onto a base of wax and chalk, so as to give the appearance of a skull. The windpipe of a crane or some other such long-necked creature is secretly attached to the skull by the oracle-monger's accomplice, who can then speak through it, saying whatever he wishes to say (Hippolytus *Refutation of All Heresies* 4.41).

Orpheus's head prophesying.

Hierius, the son of Plutarch, who studied philosophy under Proclus, saw in the so-called house of Quirinus a human head exactly like a chickpea in size and appearance. Hence it was called "The Chickpea." In other respects, however, it was just like a human head, with eyes, a face, hair, a mouth, and its voice was as loud as the voices of a thousand people (Damascius *Philosophical History frg.* 63*b* Athanassiadi). Photius quotes this passage as an example of Damascius's credulity, without telling us what the head actually talked about, but it is likely enough that it issued prophecies.

> *Politicians depend on good guesswork, not on understanding, in steering the state on the right course. They are just like soothsayers and prophets, who say much that is true, but understand nothing of what they are saying*
>
> (Plato *Meno* 99*c*).

· XXIII ·

WORDS AND EXPRESSIONS

If I had taken Prodicus's fifty-drachma course on
etymology, I could have told you straightaway the
whole truth about words. But I didn't; I took only
the one drachma course, so I don't know about such
things

(Socrates at Plato *Cratylus* 384*b*).

After winning a victory at Olympia, Heracles paid homage to the river
Alpheus [the local river] *by naming the letter "alpha" after it and placing*
it at the start of the alphabet (Ptolemy the Quail in Photius *The Library*
190.151).

Describing a thing instead of naming it makes what you say the more
impressive. For example, say "a surface that extends equally in all direc-
tions," not just "a circle" (Aristotle *Rhetoric* 1407*b*).

Byzantium is the armpit of Greece (Athenaeus *Wise Men at Dinner*
351*c*). If this vigorous expression is intended to be an insult, it is difficult to understand. Chalcedon, founded not long before Byzantium
on the opposite (eastern) side of the Bosphorus, was known as the
"city of the blind" (Herodotus *Histories* 4.144), because its founding

fathers ignored the much more favorable location on the other shore. The inhabitants of European Istanbul still gaze across the Bosphorus with the same satisfaction.

They understood the imperfections of the soul, whether a person was addicted to drinking or a lover of pleasure with his brains in his genitals (Aelian *On Animals frg.* 284, quoted at Suda s.v. *craepalodes* ["hung over"], with no further context given for this memorably formulated phrase). Demosthenes uses a more decorous version of the expression when addressing the Athenian assembly: *Any Athenians who are shown to support Philip of Macedon rather than their own country should be utterly destroyed by you, if you have your brains in your heads, and not trodden underfoot at your heels* (*On Halonnesus* 45, a passage much quoted by later rhetoricians). Plato had observed that *the desire for sexual intercourse turns a man's penis into a disobedient thing with a mind of its own, like an animal that will not listen to reason; goaded by lust, it tries to take complete control* (*Timaeus* 91*b*).

There is a wide range of personal names derived from κόπρος (*kopros*, "excrement"). In some cases the name perhaps commemorates exposure at birth on a dunghill, as in the case of St. Copres. Sometimes, however, the name may be apotropaic, an attempt to protect the child from evil spirits through its apparent worthlessness.

Among the works of Pindar is found an ode containing no sigmas [written as σ or ς]. *Hermioneus also composed an ode without sigmas, and Lasus wrote a hymn to Demeter without sigmas* (Athenaeus *Wise Men at Dinner* 455*c*).

Bodmer Papyrus 28, a fragment of a satyr play by an unidentified author, has no sigmas in its sixty lines (eleven of which are complete). Sigma is one of the most frequent letters in the Greek alphabet, and 92 percent of iambic trimeters are said to have at least one sigma; the chances against this omission being coincidental have been calculated at one in 10^{30}.

"Exile" is a term of abuse, at least among foolish people, who also use "pauper" as an insult, and "bald," and "short," and (my God!) "foreigner," and "immigrant" (Plutarch *Exile* 607a).

When the word τύραννος (*tyrannos*) was first imported into Greek, probably from Lydian, it meant simply "ruler," with no negative connotations. By the 4th century B.C., however, the pejorative sense "tyrant" was firmly established. Plato calculates that the life of a king (βασιλεύς, *basileus*) is 729 times happier than that of a τύραννος (*Republic* 587e).

The philosopher/scientist Archytas, who ruled Tarentum in the 4th century B.C., *was very sensible and was especially careful not to say anything obscene. If ever he was forced to use strong language, he used to write it on the wall* (Aelian *Miscellaneous History* 14.19).

The philosopher Athenodorus said to Augustus: "Whenever you become angry, Caesar, don't say or do anything until you've recited the twenty-four letters of the [Greek] *alphabet to yourself"* (Plutarch *Sayings of Kings and Commanders* 207c).

The longest word in Latin from the classical period or earlier is the comic coinage *subductisupercilicarptor*, "a person who criticizes, drawing his eyebrows from below," a mere twenty-four letters. The longest word in Greek, which is much more given to compounding words, is also comic, an Aristophanic concoction, describing an indigestible gallimaufry of various types of food in 171 letters: λοπαδοτεμ αχοσελαχογαλεοκρανιολειψανοδριμυποτριμματοσιλφιολιπαρομε λιτοκατακεχυμενοκιχλεπικοσσυφοφαττοπεριστεραλεκτρυονοπτο πιφαλλι<δ>οκιγκλοπελειολαγῳοσιραιοβαφητραγανοπτερυγών (*Ecclesiazusae* 1169–75; this will certainly have tasted atrocious, since it consists of an indiscriminate mixture of meats and sweets).

The Lexicon of Greek Personal Names (http://www.lgpn.ox.ac.uk/) is gathering statistics on the occurrence of Greek names, drawing on evidence spanning more than a thousand years, from the earliest literacy to the late Roman period. Much the commonest name for men is Dionysius (our Denis/Dennis/Denys), followed by Apollonius and Demetrius. Far fewer women's names survive, and there is much more variation in popularity from one region to another than with men's names; the most frequent seems to be Zosime, followed by Eirene (i.e., Irene) and Demetria.

Many Greek verbs formed from place-names and ending in *zein* mean "to speak or behave like the inhabitants of" a particular place. Since xenophobia was endemic in Greece, it is not surprising that such verbs usually have negative connotations. For example:

- κρητίζειν (*kretizein*) "to act like a Cretan" means to tell lies, because *lying comes as naturally to Cretans as movement comes to every living thing* (Theognostus *On Spelling* 530) and because *when Idomeneus the Cretan was selected to divide up the booty from Troy for the Greeks, he reserved the best for himself* (Scholion to Callimachus *Hymn to Zeus* 8).
- λεσβιάζειν (*lesbiazein*) "to act like a person from Lesbos"; that is, to fellate. *Fellatio was invented by the women of Lesbos* (Scholion to Aristophanes *Wasps* 1346).
- σιφνιάζειν (*siphniazein*) "to act like a person from the island of Siphnos" originally meant to perform elaborate musical compositions in the manner of Philoxenides of Siphnos (Pollux *Onomasticon* 4.65), but it came to mean also *to touch someone on the buttocks with one's finger* (Photius *The Lexicon* 515).
- σολοικίζειν (*soloikizein*) "to act like a person from Soli [in Cilicia]"; that is, to speak or write incorrectly, to commit a solecism. It is ironic that Aratus, the author of the *Phaenomena*, a didactic poem greatly admired by contemporaries as the ne plus ultra of careful composition, was from Soli.
- συβαρίζειν (*sybarizein*) "to act like a person from Sybaris"; that is, to live decadently; see p. 249.

ΖΩΣΙΜΗ ΗΡΑΚΛΕΩΝΟΣ ΑΠΑΜΙΤΙΣ (*Zosime Herakleonos Apamitis*, "Zosime, daughter of Herakleon, from Apamea"). The hands symbolize her kinsmen's vow to avenge her violent death.

- φοινικίζειν (*phoinikizein*) "to act like a Phoenician." *When it comes to shameful acts, we are more disgusted by those who act like Phoenicians than like people from Lesbos* (Galen *On the Qualities and Powers of Herbs* 12.249, who unhelpfully, but no doubt quite reasonably, assumes that his readers know what precisely he is talking about).

LOST IN TRANSLATION

Some say that when Alexander arrived at the temple of Zeus Ammon, the high priest wished to make a gesture of friendship by addressing him in Greek with the words ὦ παιδίον [*O paidion,* "O my son"]. *His foreign accent made it sound like* ὦ παιδίος [*O paidios* (a meaningless word)], *but Alexander was delighted with his slip of the tongue, and a story was circulated that the priest had said* ὦ παῖ Διός [*O pai Dios,* "O son of Zeus"] (Plutarch *Life of Alexander* 27). A similar pun is preserved by Plutarch at *Life of Dion* 5, where Dionysius ridicules Gelon (Γέλων), one of his predecessors as tyrant of Syracuse, by calling him the γέλως (*gelos,* "laughing stock") of all Sicily.

Instead of simply giving a literal Greek translation of "hare" in Leviticus, the Hebrew scholars commissioned by Ptolemy Philadelphus to translate the Torah (see p. 150) wrote "the short-legged creature,"

The deified Alexander, displaying the ram's horns of Zeus Ammon. Being the son of Zeus was good propaganda, but not everyone went along with it: *Demosthenes said he had no objection if Alexander wished to be the son not only of Zeus but of Poseidon as well* (Hyperides *Against Demosthenes* 7). It would be interesting to hear more about Athenaeus's claim that *Alexander the Great took on the guise of so many gods, and even of the goddess Artemis* (*Wise Men at Dinner* 537f).

because Ptolemy's wife was named "Hare" and they did not want him to think they were mocking him by inserting his wife's name in a list of non-kosher animals (The Talmud Megillah 9). This is rather distorted. Not only is the Greek for "hare" λαγώς (*lagos*) not Λᾶγος (*Lagos*) (which has a different accent and a different length in both its vowels and belongs to a different declension), but Λᾶγος was actually the name of Philadelphus's grandfather and also of his half-brother; his wives were both called Arsinoe.

A man from Abdera [where the inhabitants were proverbially stupid] *owed someone a little donkey, but didn't have one to give, so he asked to be allowed to give two mules instead* (Philogelos *Joke Book* 127). This may be Philogelos's best joke, but the wit is lost in translation: a donkey is an ὄνος (*onos*), and a mule, bred from a donkey and a horse, is a ἡμίονος (*hemionos*, a "half-donkey").

Classical texts suffered particularly in the Victorian era from bowdlerization, expurgation, and other forms of censorship designed to protect delicate sensibilities, no matter what the cost to the actual content. Consider, for example, this version of Diogenes Laertius 6.94, from *The lives and opinions of eminent philosophers, by Diogenes Laërtius, Literally translated* by C. D. Yonge, London (1853):

> *Metrocles was the brother of Hipparchia, and though he had formerly been a pupil of Theophrastus, he had profited so little by his instructions that once, thinking that while listening to a lecture on philosophy he had disgraced himself by his inattention, he fell into despondency and shut himself up in his house, intending to starve himself to death. Accordingly, when Crates heard of it, he came to him, having been sent for, and eating a number of lupins on purpose, he persuaded him by numbers of arguments that he had done no harm; for that it was not to be expected that a man should not indulge his natural inclinations and habits; and he comforted him by showing him that he, in a similar case, would certainly have behaved in a similar manner. And after that he became a pupil of Crates and a man of great eminence as a philosopher.*

No one could be offended by this translation, but it is perhaps not quite literal enough to make any sense. The point may be clearer in this version:

> *Metrocles, Hipparchia's brother, was once a pupil of Theophrastus, the Peripatetic. One day, because he was ill, he farted during a lecture and was so depressed that he locked himself up at home, intending to starve himself to death. When Crates heard about the incident, he came to visit Metrocles. He deliberately ate some lupines and then tried to persuade him by various arguments that he had done nothing to be ashamed of; it would have been a miracle if he had not passed gas, for that was only natural. He finally managed to cheer Metrocles up by farting, consoling him by pointing out that they both did what they did for the same reason. Metrocles subsequently began to attend Crates's lectures and became quite a distinguished philosopher.*

Discussing this passage, the article on *Porde* ("Fart") in Pauly-Wissowa's *Realencyclopädie der classischen Altertumswissenschaft* observes that, while Metrocles was deep in philosophical thought, an a posteriori noise escaped him (Vol. 22.1 col. 237). I do not recall noticing any other such frivolous witticisms in over forty years of consulting this formidable work of scholarship. The updated, and much abbreviated (eighteen volumes as opposed to eighty-three), *Neue Pauly* is positively whimsical by comparison, even offering a hoax article on the nonexistent sport of *apopudobalia*, allegedly a prototype version of soccer.

In 1891, the 54th year of Queen Victoria's reign, an edition of the mimiambs of the almost entirely forgotten poet Herodas was published in England, based on a papyrus recently found in Egypt. In the sixth poem, and also, but less overtly, the seventh, two ladies discuss the purchase of a red leather dildo. Scholars of the period persuaded themselves that the object in question was a bodice, a hat, or a shoe, but M. S. Buck observed in his limited edition (New York 1921) that "this is *puris omnia pura* ['to the pure, all things are pure'] with a vengeance. It is to be hoped that these scholars, realizing the grave danger lurking in references of this sort, have long since turned their attention to butterflies and flowers."

Lysistrata: *Ladies, if we are going to force our men to make peace, we must refrain—*
Cleonice: *From what? Tell us.*
Lysistrata: *So you'll do it?*
Cleonice: *We'll do it, even if it means our death.*
Lysistrata: *Well then, we must refrain from cock.—Why do you turn away? Where are you off to? Why grimace like that and shake your heads?*
(Aristophanes *Lysistrata* 120–26)

In 1912 a reviewer of the latest edition of the widely read translation of Aristophanes by Benjamin Bickley Rogers observed: "Many things that stand unashamed in the Greek are decently clad or put away in the English." Rogers renders Lysistrata's decisive term as "the joys of Love." In that same year a version published anonymously (but supposed, though I do not know why, to be by Oscar Wilde, who had died in 1900) has "we must refrain from the male altogether. . . ." Aristophanes's term here, πέος (*peos*), has the same Indo-European root as "penis," but it is vulgar and obscene, occurring eighteen times in Aristophanes, but not even once in the very much larger corpus of Galen's medical writings. Galen even avoids the perfectly decorous, but rather direct, φαλλός (*phallos*), preferring the more delicate αἰδοῖον (*aedoeon*, "thing to be discreet about").

NAMES

Quite contrary to Greek custom, the Ptolemaic rulers of Hellenistic Egypt quickly adopted the pharaonic practice of marrying their sisters or close relatives. All fifteen of these Macedonian kings were called Ptolemy, and their consorts were all called Arsinoe, or Berenice, or Cleopatra. Ptolemy II Philadelphus ("Brother or, as here, Sister Loving"), for example, was married first to Arsinoe, the daughter of Lysimachus, the ruler of Macedon, but subsequently to Arsinoe, his

A woman tending her phallus-patch.

own full sister, who had been married to Lysimachus. (For this Lysimachus, see also p. 78.)

Lycophron was famous at that time not so much for his poetry as for his anagrams, such as Πτολεμαῖος ἀπὸ μέλιτος *(Ptolemaeos apo melitos, "Ptolemy = from honey"),* Ἀρσινόη ἴον Ἥρας *(Arsinoe ion Heras, "Arsinoe = violet of Hera") (Scholion to Lycophron* Alexandra ad init.*).* Πτολεμαῖ ος actually means "warlike," and Ἀρσινόη means "virile minded." The play on his name will have been the more appropriate if Ptolemy was aware that the bee was the hieroglyph denoting the ruler of Lower Egypt. It is not clear how much the new Macedonian rulers of Egypt knew about hieroglyphs, but six hundred years later the soldier-historian Ammianus Marcell-

Ptolemy II and Arsinoe II.

inus recorded that *the hieroglyphic system represents a king by the figure of a bee making honey, indicating thereby that a ruler should have stings and not just sweetness* (17.4).

Arsinoe, who was apparently prone to vomiting, will have felt rather less flattered by a guest of Lysimachus, her first husband, when he misquoted a line from an unknown tragedy, changing κακῶν κατάρχεις τήνδε μοῦσαν εἰσάγων "You begin troubles by bringing here this Muse [*tende Mousan*]" to κακῶν κατάρχεις τήνδ' ἐμοῦσαν εἰσάγων "You begin troubles by bringing here this vomiting woman [*tend' emousan*]" (Plutarch *Table Talk* 634e).

At the end of many of the biographies in his *Lives of the Philosophers*, Diogenes Laertius lists prominent intellectual figures with the same name as the philosopher whose life he has just recounted. There are, for example, four more Socrates (one a philosopher), four more Platos (three of whom were philosophers, including one who was a pupil of Aristotle), and seven more Aristotles. Four distinguished philosophers share the name Zeno: Zeno of Elea, famous for paradoxes (see p. 165); Zeno of Citium, the founder of Stoicism; Zeno of Sidon, also a Stoic; and another Zeno of Sidon, who may have been the head of the Epicurean school, the chief rival to Stoicism. A late 3rd-century B.C.

tragedian rejoiced in, or labored under, the name Homer, as also did a grammarian of uncertain date, who wrote poetry in many genres (Suda s.vv. *Myro, Sellius*).

Pygela is a city in Ionia, so called because some of Agamemnon's men stopped there when they were suffering from an ailment of the buttocks [πυγαί, *pygae*] (Theopompus *frg.* 59). This rather embarrassing name appears on the 5th-century Athenian tribute lists, but less than a century later the city's coins are stamped *Phygela*, and a new explanation is given for the new name: *Phygela, as the name suggests, was founded by fugitives* [Latin *fugitivi*, Greek φυγάδες (*phygades*)] (Pliny *Natural History* 5.114).

Agamemnon's men with sore buttocks are specified as "rowers" in a later version of the story (*Etymologicum Magnum* 695). Cushions came to be standard equipment on ships, with the technical name being ὑπηρέσιον (*hyperesion*, literally "the thing under the rower"). Early in the Peloponnesian War, the Spartans and their allies secretly crossed the Isthmus of Corinth, intending to man forty ships waiting in Megara harbor and make a surprise raid on Piraeus; each of the rowers carried across not just his oar and his rowlock strap, but also his cushion (Thucydides *History* 2.93). Broken planks and spars are mentioned as flotation devices after shipwrecks and sea battles, but not cushions.

There is an island called Pordoselene, with a city on it by the same name, and there is another island facing the city; it also has the same name. . . . Some people say that, for the sake of decency, these places should be called Poroselene (Strabo *Geography* 13.2). *Pordoselene* was thought to mean "Fart Moon." Strabo goes on to suggest adjustments to the names of several other places that might also be supposed to be derived from πέρδομαι (*perdomai*, "pass gas"; πέρδομαι and "fart" have the same Indo-European root). The larger island's modern Greek name is the much nicer *Moschonisi* ("Calf Island"); since it is now in Turkey, however, its official name is *Ali Bey Adasi* ("Ali Bey Island"), in honor of the Turkish general whose troops occupied it in the war of 1922–1923.

By the early 6th century B.C., Greek *poleis* large and small were beginning to mint their own coinage, often representing the names of their communities pictorially rather than, or as well as, in writing. For example:

- Aegospotami is denoted by a goat (αἴξ, *aix*).
- Ancyra, by an anchor (ἄγκυρα, *ancyra*).
- Alopeconnesus, by a fox (ἀλώπηξ, *alopex*).
- Aspendus, by a slinger (σφενδόνη, *sphendone*, "sling").
- Astacus, by a lobster (ἀστακός, *astacos*).
- Delphi, by a dolphin (δελφίς, *delphis*).
- Leontini, by a lion (λέων, *leon*).
- Meliteia, by a bee (μέλισσα, *melissa*).
- Melos, by an apple (μῆλον, *melon*).
- Phocaea, by a seal (φώκη, *phoce*).
- Rhodes, by a rose (ῥόδον, *rhodon*).
- Selinus, by a stalk of celery (σέλινον, *selinon*).
- Tauromenium, by a bull (ταῦρος, *tauros*).
- Trapezus, by a table (τράπεζα, *trapeza*).

Sparta, with its iron bars instead of coinage (see p. 71), plays with no such visual puns, and surviving coins from Phygela (see p. 240) make do with Artemis on the obverse and a bull on the reverse.

A rooster on a coin from the Sicilian city of Himera, probably punning on the resemblance between Ἱμέρα (*Himera*) and ἡμέρα (*hemera*, "day"), that is, alluding to a cock crowing at dawn.

Demosthenes as a herm.

Ephialtes is a not-uncommon masculine proper name meaning "nightmare." In postclassical and modern Greek, it retains the same meaning. Writing in the 7th century A.D., Paul of Aegina is uncertain whether *an* ephialtes *is so called after a man or because those who suffer nightmares imagine that someone is jumping on top of them* [ἐφάλλεσθαι (*ephallesthai*, "jump on")] (*Epitome of Medicine* 3.15). The man after whom nightmares may have been named is Ephialtes of Malis, the traitor who led Xerxes's ten thousand Immortals over a mountain path to seal the fate of the defenders at Thermopylae (Herodotus *Histories* 7.213).

Aeschines, Demosthenes's archenemy in the cut-and-thrust of 4th-century Athenian political debate, calls him "Batalos" and "Argas" (*On the Embassy* 99). An *argas* is a type of snake. At *Against Timarchus* 126,

Aeschines pretends to suppose that *Batalos* is an endearing diminutive ("Little Stutterer," from βατταρίζω [*battarizo*,"stutter"]), given to Demosthenes by his nurse, but Plutarch notes that *Batalos seems to be what the Athenians at that time called an unseemly part of the body* (*Life of Demosthenes* 4). After suggesting rather naively that "Batalos" refers to Demosthenes's large buttocks, the scholiast to *Against Timarchus* goes on to note the homosexual connotations of identifying βάταλος as a vulgar equivalent to πρωκτός (*proctos*, "rectum").

> *Demosthenes is a little chap, consisting of nothing*
> *but syllables and a tongue*
>
> (**Demades** *frg.* **89**).

· XXIV ·

THE *SOROS*

The word σωρός (*soros*) means "heap" and reflects the particularly miscellaneous nature of this final chapter's contents. Whatever seemed worth including in the book, but could not easily be presented elsewhere, is swept up here. This title may seem casual, but it has a fine precedent as the name of a collection of early Hellenistic epigrams, presumably exquisite in their composition, but now lost. This whole book is a fairly random collection, so lack of coherence may perhaps be excused.

Coherence and relevance were not always of prime concern to Greek authors. Pausanias, for example, is usually a fairly well-organized writer. He makes a very emphatic announcement that he has omitted the achievements of Diagoras and the other members of his athletic family (see p. 110), "for fear they should seem irrelevant" (*Guide to Greece* 4.24). Such information would not have been conspicuous by its absence. On the other hand, he cheerfully admits, "I have inserted into my account of Phocis [on the central Greek mainland] a long digression about Sardinia, because it is an island with which the Greeks are so unfamiliar" (10.17).

If you pluck one hair from a man's head, does he become bald? What about two hairs? Or three? The same question arises with a heap of wheat. What if one grain of the wheat is taken away, or two, and so on? It is not possible to state when it first stops being a heap (Aspasius *On Aristotle's* Nicomachean Ethics 56).

We should ignore the patently absurd theory that Hermes taught humans to speak. Nor should we heed those philosophers who maintain that names were given to things systematically, for that is ridiculous—or rather, it's more ridiculous than anything ridiculous. . . . At a time when no kings, no writing, no languages existed yet, no single individual could have gathered multitudes of people together and taught them the way an elementary schoolteacher does, touching each thing and saying, "let this be called a 'rock,' and this a 'stick,' and this a 'person,' or a 'dog,' or a 'cow,' or a 'donkey'" (Diogenes of Oenoanda *frg.* 12). This is part of an inscription created by Diogenes in his hometown in southwest Turkey. It contains various significant Epicurean tracts, and when intact, it was bigger than any other inscription known from antiquity, being almost ninety feet long and comprising some twenty-five thousand words. About one-third of it has been recovered so far, with substantial numbers of new fragments still being found every digging season.

Why doesn't everyone speak the same language? Is it because languages were first devised through the imitation of animal noises, the way little children imitate cows mooing and dogs barking, and because there are many noises produced by the same animal, different people chose to imitate different sounds? (Ps.-Alexander *Problems* 4.88).

The same collection raises many other such problems, with the questions often being interesting even without reference to the proposed answers. For example:

Why is it that, whereas practically all other such actions can take place equally well in the daytime or at night, we never sneeze during the night? (4.40)

Why does rubbing our eyes stop us from sneezing? (4.41)

Why is it that sneezing has a sacred significance, but other emissions of air, whether passing gas or belching, do not? (4.50)

Why do humans sneeze more than other animals? (4.51)

Why do people breathe less frequently in the winter than in the summer? (4.48)

Why do we hear better when we are holding our breath than when we are exhaling (which is why hunters urge one another not to pant)? (4.97)

Africanus devised a test that would detect thieves. Cut off and pickle tadpoles' tongues and then, as need arises, mix them up with barley and feed this to those who are suspected of having taken whatever is being looked for. He claims that the person who took it falls into a sort of trance and makes a clear admission of his guilt. He calls this food "thief detector" (Michael Psellus *On Strange Things* 32).

Here is how to make a fruit imitate the face of a person or of an animal. Make a model of the face, cover it all over with plaster or clay, and let it dry. Then cut it in two with a sharp tool, producing a front and back half that fit together. Dry them and bake them as you would a pot. When the fruit is half grown, put the molds round it and secure them carefully, so that they will not come apart as the fruit increases in size. Pears, apples, pomegranates, citrons all take on the features of such molds (*Farm Work* 10.9). My attempts to revive this lost art have met with very limited success.

Since the baths are of no practical value, we should avoid them. In the old days, people called them "human laundries," for they caused the body to wrinkle and grow old prematurely (St. Clement of Alexandria *Paedagogus* 3.9.46).

If we fail to pay the rent, the landlord removes the door and the roof-tiles and blocks up the well, and we vacate the house. Likewise, we vacate our little bodies when nature, our landlady, takes away our eyes, our ears, our hands, and our feet (Bion of Borysthenes *frg.* 68).

In contrast to the Athenians (see p. 59), the inhabitants of some cities, most notably Abdera and Cyme, were proverbially stupid:

> *A man from Abdera tried to hang himself, but the rope broke and he hurt his head. He got a bandage from the doctor and put it on the wound; then he went off and hanged himself again.* (Philogelos *Joke Book* 112)

Rather ironically, Abdera produced several very significant philosophers: Democritus, Protagoras, Anaxarchus, and Hecataeus the Skeptic.

> *The city of Cyme borrowed money, pledging its porticoes as security. When the loan was not repaid on time, the citizens were forbidden to stroll there. But when it rained, their creditors were embarrassed and had a herald announce that they were to go into the porticoes. So the herald declared, "Go into the porticoes," but a rumor spread that unless they were actually told to do so by a herald, the people of Cyme did not understand that they were to go into the porticoes when it rained. . . . The historian Ephorus from Cyme is also mocked. When he had no achievements of his native city to include in his account of great events in history, but even so was reluctant to leave Cyme unmentioned, he declared, "At this time the people of Cyme took no action."* (Strabo *Geography* 13.3.6)

Greeks were not above criticizing their own *polis*. Perhaps most famously, the poet Hesiod says of his hometown in Boeotia, "My father settled near Mt. Helicon, in a wretched village, Ascra, bad in winter, dreadful in summer, and never good" (*Works and Days* 639–640).

Only two epigrams are credited to Demodocus of Leros, an obscure island colonized from Miletus:

> *The people of Leros are bad: not just some and not others; all of them, except Procles—and Procles is a Lerian.* (*Greek Anthology* 11.235)

> *The people of Miletus are not stupid, but they do the sort of things that stupid people do.* (quoted at Aristotle *Nicomachean Ethics* 1151a)

SYBARIS

All the Sybarites cultivated a decadent and luxurious style of living, but Smindyrides [see also p. 6] *outdid everyone, drifting into particular voluptuousness; he fell asleep on a bed of rose petals, and when he got up he complained of blisters* (Aelian *Miscellaneous History* 9.24).

A wealthy Sybarite heard of someone rupturing himself while watching some men working. He said that it was not surprising, for he had a pain in the side just from hearing about it (Diodorus Siculus *The Library* 8.18).

The Sybarites invited women to banquets with a year's notice, so that they would have enough time to arrange to come in fine clothes and golden jewelry (Plutarch *The Banquet of the Seven Wise Men* 147e).

More Sybaritic decadence recorded at Athenaeus *Wise Men at Dinner* 518–21:

Noisy trades such as metalworking and carpentry were not permitted in Sybaris, to ensure that the citizens could sleep undisturbed.

Likewise, it was forbidden to keep roosters [since their crowing would rouse sleepers; the word for "rooster" (ἀλεκτρυών, *alektryon*) was derived from ἀ and λέκτρον (*a* and *lektron*, "not" and "bed")].

Wealthy Sybarites used to spend three days on a one-day journey, even though they were carried along in litters.

Even in the countryside, some of their roads were covered over, to provide shade and shelter.

They had wine piped from their estates to their villas by the sea.

They invented basins in which they took steam baths.

They also invented chamber pots, which they took with them to symposia.

If a chef created a particularly choice recipe, he alone was allowed to make that dish for a year, the purpose of this restriction being to encourage the other chefs to try to outdo one another with similar creations.

DATES

Time is a child playing checkers (Heraclitus *frg.* 52).

There was little uniformity among Greek *poleis* in the organization of the calendar. In Athens the year started after the summer solstice, in Sparta after the fall equinox, and in Thebes after the winter solstice. Most states seem to have operated on a twelve-month calendar, but the Arcadians divided the year into three months, the Acarnanians into six (Macrobius *Saturnalia* 1.12). Even when they shared the same twelve-month system, the various *poleis* did not begin the months on the same day or use the same names for them. The best known are the Athenian months, all apparently named after festivals held at that time of year, but the precise significance of some of the names was probably obscure already by the classical period:

Hecatombaeon	*Metageitnion*
Boedromion	*Pyanopsion*
Maimacterion	*Poseideon*
Gamelion	*Anthesterion*
Elaphebolion	*Mounychion*
Thargelion	*Scirophorion*

The inherent difficulty in this lack of consistency is apparent in Thucydides's attempt to date the beginning of the Peloponnesian War as precisely as possible: *In the fifteenth year of the Thirty Year Truce, in Chrysis's forty-eighth year as priestess in Argos, when Aenesias was Ephor in Sparta, two months from the end of Pythodorus's Archonship in Athens, eight months after the Battle of Potidaea, at the beginning of spring, a Theban force attacked Plataea* (*History* 2.2).

In Sparta the Ephor Plistolas begins the truce on the fourth day from the end of the month of Artemisium; in Athens the Archon Alcaeus begins it on the sixth day from the end of the month of Elaphebolion (Thucydides *History* 5.19, recording the Peace of Nicias in March 421 B.C.).

The Athenian month Thargelion began about the 20th of May. *It is said that the sixth day of that month brought many good things, not only to the Athenians, but to many other people also*:

- *The Persians were defeated at Marathon* [490 B.C.], *Plataea and Mycale* [479], *Gaugamela* [331].
- *Socrates was born* [ca. 469 B.C.].
- *Alexander the Great was born* [356 B.C.] *and died* [323 B.C.].

This information, given by Aelian at *Miscellaneous History* 2.25, is either wrong, unverifiable, or contradicted by other writers. But historians liked such coincidences. Plutarch (*Life of Camillus* 19) dates the fall of Troy to the 24th of Thargelion, the day on which Timoleon crushed the Carthaginians against all odds at the Crimissus [ca. 340 B.C.], and likewise he states that the battles of Chaeronea [338 B.C.] and Cranon [322 B.C.] took place on the 7th day of Metageitnion.

Plutarch adds that King Attalus of Pergamum (who bequeathed his kingdom to Rome) and Pompey the Great died on their birthdays; had he not had his head hacked off, this coincidence might have pleased Pompey, who loved to imitate Alexander the Great, who also died on his birthday (see above). Plato likewise died on his birthday (Seneca *Letters* 58), but may have been disappointed that he was born on the 7th of Thargelion (Diogenes Laertius *Lives of the Philosophers* 3.2) and therefore did not share a birthday with Socrates, who was born on the 6th. He did, however, share a birthday with Apollo (as Socrates did with Apollo's slightly older sister, Artemis [twins with different birthdays]). The birthdays of Socrates and Plato were still being celebrated in Athens in the 3rd century A.D. (Porphyry *Life of Plotinus* 2.39).

Timaeus the Sicilian calculates (I do not know on what criteria) that Rome was founded at the same time as Carthage, thirty-eight years before the first Olympiad [i.e., in 814 B.C.] (Dionysius of Halicarnassus *Roman Antiquities* 1.74). The canonical dating of the foundation of Rome to 753 B.C. was established by Dionysius's contemporary, Terentius Varro.

According to some sources, Euripides was born on the day the Battle of Salamis was fought (in 480 B.C.).

Recording the assassination of Caligula in Rome, Josephus notes that *it is agreed that King Philip of Macedon was killed on that same day by Pausanias, one of his companions, as he was entering the theater* (*Jewish Antiquities* 19.95). Suetonius adds that the same tragedy was being performed at the time of both assassinations (*Life of Caligula* 58).

Alexander the Great was born on the same day as the temple of Artemis at Ephesus [one of the Seven Wonders of the Ancient World] *was burnt down* (Plutarch *Life of Alexander* 3). The orator Hegestratus the Magnesian said that *it was hardly surprising that Artemis's temple burned down, since she* [as goddess of childbirth] *was distracted by the responsibility of watching over Alexander's birth*; Plutarch observes that *this remark was frigid enough to have put out the fire.*

Alexander the Great and Diogenes the Cynic are said to have died on the same day.

ARTIFACTS

Fragments of two cups found at Naucratis in Egypt and now in the Ashmolean Museum (*Oxford G.141.2* and *G.141.15*) are inscribed with the name Herodotus. This is a common name, but since they are both roughly contemporary with the historian Herodotus, who is known to have visited Egypt, scholars are tempted to link at least one of the cups with him. There are many graffiti inscribed by Greek and Roman

Ephesian Artemis. The "breasts" are thought by some scholars to be bulls' testicles, symbolizing fertility.

tourists in the tombs in the Valley of the Kings. One is signed by Herodotus, but the scholar who published the inscriptions believed it to be a modern hoax (*Mémoires de l'Institut français d'Archéologie orientale du Caire* 42 [1926] no. 1078*b*).

A 5th-century B.C. cup with "I am the property of Phidias" (see p. 193) scratched on the base has been found at Olympia.

A pot, datable to ca. 440 B.C. and inscribed with Euripides's name, has been found in a cave on the island of Salamis. Euripides was said to have composed his plays in just such a cave. Puzzlingly, however, his name seems to have been scratched on the pot more than two hundred years after his death.

Simon the shoemaker is not mentioned by either Plato or Xenophon, our best authorities for the life of Socrates. Diogenes Laertius, however, wrote a brief biography of him, in which he tells us that he used to record the discussions that Socrates (who almost always went barefoot) held in his shop in the Athenian agora (*Lives of the Philosophers* 2.122). A large number of hobnails, some rings that were probably eyelets for footwear, and the base of a cup (*Agora* P 22998) with the inscription ΣΙΜΩΝΟΣ (*SIMONOS*, "of Simon") have been found on the site of what must have been his shop.

Thirteen clay medicine bottles have been found in a building in the Athenian agora identified as the state prison. It has been speculated that they were used for the hemlock to be drunk by condemned criminals such as Socrates (a statuette of whom has been found in the same building).

A bucket found in Athens (*Kerameikos* 7357) has on it the helpful inscription ΚΑΔΟΣ ΕΙΜΙ (*KADOS EIMI*, "I am a bucket"), presumably punning on the conventional vase inscription, "So-and-so is handsome," by substituting ΚΑΔΟΣ for ΚΑΛΟΣ (see p. 96).

CHAMBER POTS

Socrates had two wives, Xanthippe and Myrto, Aristides's granddaughter. They quarreled frequently, and he regularly bantered them for arguing over him, even though he was very ugly, with a snub nose, a receding hairline, hairy shoulders, and bandy legs. They attacked him together, beating him severely and chasing him out of the house. On one occasion Xanthippe shouted abuse at him from an upper window and soaked him with the contents of a chamber pot. But he merely wiped his head dry and said, "I knew we were in for a shower after such a loud thunderstorm" (St. Jerome *Against Jovinian* 1.48).

My assailant began to sing, imitating roosters that have won a fight, and his friends started urging him to strike his elbows against his ribs like wings (Demosthenes *Against Conon* 9). The defendant and his gang were also alleged to have beaten up, emptied chamber pots over, and urinated on the slaves of the plaintiff and his friends.

When Demetrius of Phalerum fell from favor in Athens [in 307 B.C.], *he was condemned in absentia. Since they were not able to lay hold of Demetrius himself, his accusers vented their bile by pulling down his bronze statues. They sold some of them, others they threw into the sea, and others they cut up and turned into chamber pots* (Diogenes Laertius *Lives of the Philosophers* 5.76).

A fragment of a chamber pot found in the Athenian agora bears the inscription *ΑΜΙΣ ΝΙΚΟ**** (CHAMBER POT OF NICO[***]), scratched on it after firing (*Agora* P 28053).

It is downright ludicrous how men carry round their silver urinals and crystal chamber pots, as if they were their retinue of advisors, and how silly rich women have receptacles for excrement made of gold, as if they, being so wealthy, cannot relieve themselves without a display of magnificence (St. Clement of Alexandria *Paedagogus* 2.3.39).

The scholiast to this passage remarks rather primly on "crystal chamber pots": *If they are merely showing off their wealth, this criticism is fair enough; but if there is a medical reason, with the chance that a disease may be detected through the crystal, your mockery is unjustified.* Joannes Actuarius notes: *Chamber pots are made of fine white crystal, so that colors show through accurately* (*On Urine* 2.1.1, in a 13th-century Latin translation of a Greek tract).

Unless water was extremely cold, he said it was hot, he kept pushing his cloak off his chest, and he refused to allow his chamber pot to be warmed (Hippocrates *Epidemics* 7.1.84, of a feverish patient). I know no other evidence for the warming of Greek chamber pots before use. Instead of "chamber pot" (ἀμίδα, *amida*), some manuscripts report a second term for "cloak," the similar-sounding χλαμύδα (*chlamyda*).

The Athenians once ostracized Themistocles, but then they recalled him to run the government. He declared, "I don't think much of people who use the same jar both as their pisspot and as their wine jug" (Aelian *Miscellaneous History* 13.40). Themistocles uses a different image in making the same point more politely at Plutarch *Life of Themistocles* 18: *He used to say the Athenians did not really honor and admire him for himself, but treated him like a plane-tree, running under his branches for shelter during storms, but plucking his leaves and lopping his branches as soon as the weather was fair.*

Stamp your foot and wave your fist, shout aloud and cough heartily, shake your whole body and shit from your innermost being, delight your mind, and may your stomach never pain you when you enter my house (a four-line graffito, based mostly on Homeric phrases, found on the wall of a latrine near the marketplace in Ephesus [*Ephesus Inscriptions* 456]).

Strabo praises Smyrna as a beautiful city, with its streets laid out and paved exceptionally well, with large porticoes, a library, and a memorial to Homer, whom the citizens claim was born there. *Unfortunately, the architects made one rather significant mistake: when they laid out the*

streets, they did not include any drains, and so sewage floats along on the surface, especially when it rains (Geography 14.1.37).

Hegesander of Delphi says that the philosopher Prytanis once displayed some very expensive drinking cups to his guests at dinner. When the party was in full swing, the poet Euphorion, who was drunk, took one of the cups and urinated into it (Athenaeus Wise Men at Dinner 477e). Euphorion was one of the leading intellectuals of the 3rd century B.C., and his poetry, though now almost entirely lost, is known to have had a considerable influence on the greatest Roman poets.

A slave boy holds a wine jar for a man to urinate into.

This is the man who once threw a ludicrous missile at me, the foul-smelling pisspot, and he didn't miss; when it hit me on the head, it crashed in pieces, breathing on me not from a vessel smelling of myrrh (Aeschylus *frg.* 174, preserved by Athenaeus at *Wise Men at Dinner* 17c). Athenaeus also quotes an imitation of that passage in a satyr play by Sophocles, with the comment that Homer is more restrained: when the suitors are represented as being drunk, the most indecorous detail is the throwing of an ox-hoof at Odysseus (*Odyssey* 20.299).

Why do people yawn when other people yawn, and urinate when they see someone else urinating? Baggage animals are particularly prone to urinating in such circumstances (Ps.-Aristotle *Problems* 887a).

A child sitting on a potty, or perhaps in a high chair.

In Thebes, people banquet night and day, and everyone has a toilet near his door. There's no greater good for a mortal when he's full. It's comical to see someone striding along, sweating profusely, and biting his lip, when he wants to relieve himself (Eubulus *frg.* 53).

WEIGHT PROBLEMS

They say that Philitas of Cos was very skinny and that, since he might easily be tipped over, he had the soles of his shoes made of lead, so that the wind could not blow him down with a fierce gust. But if he was so weak that he could not withstand a breeze, how could he have been able to haul along such a heavy weight? I find this implausible, but I record it anyway (Aelian *Miscellaneous History* 9.14).

> *Skinny Marcus once bored a hole with his head right through to the middle of one of Epicurus's atoms.*
>
> *A mouse once came across little Macron sleeping in the summertime and dragged him into its hole by his little foot. But Macron throttled the mouse with his bare hands and said, "Father Zeus, you have a second Heracles."*
>
> *Gaius was so underweight that he could not dive into the water unless he attached a stone or a lump of lead to his foot.*
>
> *Epicurus wrote that the whole universe consists of atoms, for he thought that atoms are the smallest things that exist. But, if Diophantus had been living then, he would have written that everything is made up of Diophantus, who is much smaller than atoms, or he would have written that everything else is made up of atoms, but that atoms themselves are made up of Diophantus.*
>
> (Lucillius *Greek Anthology* 11.93, 11.95, 11.100, 11.103)

Dew has a naturally erosive quality, as is indicated by its making fat people thinner. Fat women at any rate soak up dew on their clothes or on soft tufts of wool and imagine that this causes their excess flesh to melt away (Plutarch *Natural Phenomena* 913f).

Even by itself, thinking can promote weight loss, but when combined with a modicum of exercise that involves enjoyable competition, it gives us the benefit of a healthy body and an intelligent mind (Galen *On Exercise with the Small Ball* 5.904).

There are many pleasures that lead us into doing the wrong thing and force us to give in to them even though they are harmful, and the pleasure of eating is probably the hardest of them all to resist. For we meet with the other pleasures less frequently and can steer away from some of them for months or even years at a time; but we are inevitably tempted by this one every single day, and often twice in a day, for we have to eat if we are to live. But the more often we are tempted by the pleasure of eating, the greater the temptations it poses (Musonius Rufus *frg.* 18*b*).

Hecuba: *Helen should not board the same ship as you.*
Menelaus: *Why is that? Has she put on weight since the last time she sailed?*
(*Trojan Women* 1049–50; Euripides can make jokes even in his darkest tragedies)

The people of Gordium in Phrygia [where Alexander cut the famous knot] *choose the fattest man among them as their king* (Ps.-Plutarch *Collection of Proverbs Current in Alexandria* 10).

Ptolemy VIII had the nickname *Physcon* ("Sausage Man") because of his obesity. *When the members of a Roman delegation arrived at Alexandria and were walking into the city, Ptolemy had considerable difficulty keeping up with them, on account of his slothfulness and corpulence. Scipio whispered quietly to Panaetius* [the Stoic philosopher]*: "The people of Alexandria have already benefited from our visit; thanks to us they have seen their king walking"* (Plutarch *Sayings of Kings and Commanders* 200*f*).

Physcon's younger son, Ptolemy X Alexander, was not very charming either. *The ruler of Egypt was hated by the masses, but his courtiers fawned on him, and he lived in luxury. He could not even relieve himself without two men to prop him up, but even so he used to leap down barefoot from*

his lofty couch at drinking parties and join in with the dancing more vigorously than the experts (Posidonius *frg.* 77).

Athenaeus mentions both Physcon and Alexander in a catalog of obese rulers that also includes Magas of Cyrene, who was choked to death by his own fat, and Dionysius of Heracleia, who gave audience to his subjects from behind a large box, with only his head showing (*Wise Men at Dinner* 549*a*).

SLAVES

A slave is a possession that is alive (Aristotle *Politics* 1253*b*).

Is it right and just that someone should be a slave, or is all slavery an offense against nature? This question is easy to answer both in theoretical and in practical terms. It is necessary and proper that some people should rule while others are ruled, and we are marked out at birth to be either the ruled or the rulers (Aristotle *Politics* 1254*a*).

The women in authority in a household used to pour figs, dates, nuts, and other such tidbits over the head of newly bought slaves, to show them the sweetness and pleasure of the life they were entering upon (Lexica Segueriana *Rhetorical Glosses* s.v. *catachysmata*).

Slaves should be punished as they deserve, not just given a warning, as if they were free people, for that gives them big ideas about themselves. Just about everything you say to a slave should be an order. Never joke in any way with slaves, whether female or male. Many people are foolish enough to spoil their slaves with that sort of treatment, but it simply makes life more difficult both for the slaves and for their owners (Plato *Laws* 777*e*).

Plato once wanted to punish one of his slaves and asked his nephew, Speusippus, to do the actual whipping, for he himself was angry, and anger was inappropriate for a philosopher (Seneca *On Anger* 3.12). When Plutarch was having one of his slaves whipped, the slave protested that this was inappropriate for a philosopher who had written a book on "Not Being Angry." Plutarch calmly replied that he was not angry and told his other slave who was administering the whipping to carry on while he and his philosophizing slave continued their discussion (Aulus Gellius *Attic Nights* 1.26).

I have never struck any of my slaves with my fist. I adopted this principle from my father, who criticized many of his friends when they suffered a bruised tendon through hitting slaves on the teeth. He used to say that they deserved to suffer spasms and death as a result of the consequent inflammation, when they could quite easily have beaten them with a stick or a strap (Galen *On the Diagnosis and Cure of Afflictions of the Mind* 4). Galen may have been antiquity's most influential doctor, but he occasionally says things that make us wonder about his bedside manner.

In Athens, slaves and resident aliens are quite out of control. You cannot strike them, and a slave will not stand aside for you. The reason for this is that, if it were legal for a free man to strike a slave, an alien, or a freedman, you would often strike an Athenian citizen on the assumption that he was a slave, for the clothing and personal appearance of citizens is no better than that of slaves or aliens (Ps.-Xenophon *The Athenian Constitution* 1.10).

They say that the citizens of the Tuscan city of Oenarea, fearing that someone might establish himself as tyrant, entrust the government to emancipated slaves, replacing them with other such freedmen every year (Ps.-Aristotle *On Marvelous Things Heard* 837b).

Slaves were often known rather unimaginatively by their nationality. These manumission records are typical: *a slave called Cyprius, from Cyprus; a slave called Judaeus, from Judaea; a slave called Libys, from Libya* (*Collection of Greek Dialect Inscriptions* 1749, 2029, 2175).

Poor people, since they have no slaves, have to use their wives and children as their servants (Aristotle *Politics* 1323a).

If a slave is lucky enough to win any event, a quarter of the prize money is to go to his fellow-competitors (Papers of the American School of Archaeology at Athens 3.275, from an inscription giving rules for an athletic festival in southwest Asia Minor).

ETIQUETTE

Manners for the dinner table, as prescribed by St. Clement of Alexandria (*Paedagogus* 2.7):

- *Do not lean over your food, guarding it the way wild animals do.*
- *Do not over-indulge in dainty dishes, for humans are by nature bread-eaters.*
- *Do not make smacking noises with your lips, or whistle, or click your fingers.*
- *Do not spit excessively, or clear your throat too violently, or wipe your nose, for that is to behave like cattle and donkeys, whose manger is also their dunghill.*
- *If you must sneeze or hiccup, do not make so much noise that you startle the person reclining next to you.*
- *Do not open your mouth as if you were wearing a tragic mask, but dissipate the eruction discretely, concealing anything else that the displacement of air may bring up with it.*
- *Picking one's teeth until they bleed is disgusting.*
- *Scratching one's ears and sneezing unduly are swinish gestures, associated with unrestrained sexual activity.*

Even nowadays, the Persians regard it as shameful to spit, or to wipe one's nose, or to show signs of being flatulent, or to be noticed going away to urinate or for any other such purpose. They could not achieve this level of discretion if they did not follow a reasonable diet and work off the moisture in the body in other ways (Xenophon Education of Cyrus 1.2.16).

I have written to you in discreet terms about things that the Stoics discuss quite openly—but then, the Stoics say that people should pass gas as freely

A slave boy steadies an old man's head as he vomits.

as they belch (Cicero *Letters to His Friends* 9.22, concluding a lively discussion of verbal taboos).

Proclus can't wipe his nose with his arm, for his arm is shorter than his nose. Nor does he say, "Excuse me," if he sneezes: he can't hear his nose, for it's so far from his ears (Anonymous *Greek Anthology* 11.268).

With other diseases of the soul, such as love of money, love of glory, love of pleasure, there is the possibility that the person afflicted might obtain what he desires, but this is very difficult for people who chatter idly. They long for listeners, but cannot find any. Everyone runs headlong away. If people are sitting in a public park or strolling in a colonnade and see a chatterer approaching, they quickly pass the signal round for breaking camp. And just as they say that Hermes has joined the group if a sudden silence falls

at a meeting, so when a chatterer arrives at a symposium or other gathering of friends, everyone stops talking, so as not to give him a handle on any conversation (Plutarch *On Talkativeness* 502e).

When it comes to nosy people, everyone is defensive and circumspect. People do not like to do or say anything when a busybody might see or hear them. If such a person turns up while something is being discussed, the business is put to one side, just as food is taken away and hidden when a weasel runs by (Plutarch *On Curiosity* 519d). Weasels, and even snakes, rather than cats, which seem to have been uncommon in Greece, were kept domestically to control vermin.

Characteristics of an inconsiderate person, according to Ariston of Ceos, as quoted by Philodemus *On Vices* 10 (*Herculaneum Papyrus* 1008):

- *He asks the attendant for more hot or cold water without consulting fellow bathers.*
- *When he buys a slave, he neither asks what his name is nor gives him a name himself, but just calls him "boy."*
- *He does not rub oil on anyone who has rubbed oil on him.*
- *He does not reciprocate invitations.*
- *When he knocks at someone's door and is asked, "Who is it?" he does not respond until the person comes to the door.*

There are three ways to answer questions: the barely adequate way, the polite way, and the superfluous way. For example, in response to the question, "Is Socrates at home?":

> *The first person replies reluctantly and grudgingly, "Not at home," and if he wants to imitate the Spartans, he can leave out the "at home" and utter just the negative. That's what the Spartans did when Philip of Macedon wrote to ask if they would admit him into their city: they wrote "NO" in big letters on a piece of papyrus and sent it to him.*

> *The second person replies more politely, "He's not at home; he's at the bank," and if he wants to expatiate on that, he adds, "waiting for some visitors."*

The third person, who chatters excessively, replies, "He's not at home; he's at the bank, waiting for some visitors from Ionia, about whom he's had a letter from Alcibiades, who's spending his time near Miletus with Tissaphernes, the satrap of the king of Persia, who used to help the Spartans, but now, thanks to Alcibiades, is siding with the Athenians. Alcibiades wants a recall from exile, and that's why he's getting Tissaphernes to change sides," and he'll go right on reciting the whole of Thucydides's eighth book, inundating the person who asked the question.

(Plutarch *On Talkativeness* 513a)

Plato's companions used to imitate his stooping posture, Aristotle's, his lisp, Alexander's, the inclination of his neck and his gravelly voice (Plutarch *How to Distinguish a Flatterer from a Friend* 53d).

Starting at *Wise Men at Dinner* 248c, Athenaeus provides a long catalog of court flatterers. For example:

When Philip of Macedon had his eye knocked out, Cleisophus went about with him with a bandage on the same eye, and when Philip was wounded in the leg, Cleisophus limped around with him. If ever Philip ate something bitter, he would twist up his own features as if he were eating it as well.

Dionysius I, the tyrant of Syracuse, was laughing with a group of friends, and his flatterer Cheirisophus started laughing too, even though he was too far away to have heard the joke: when Dionysius asked him later why he had laughed, Cheirisophus replied, "I'm sure I can rely on you, that what was said was funny."

His son, also called Dionysius, maintained a large number of flatterers. Since he was shortsighted, they pretended that they also had poor vision. At dinner, they groped for the food set before them, as if they could not see it, until he steered their hands to the dishes. Whenever Dionysius spat, they often offered him their faces to spit on. They would lick off his saliva, or even his vomit, and say that it was sweeter than honey.

RIDDLES

What creature is two-footed and yet also three-footed and four-footed? No one else could guess, but Oedipus solved the problem with the answer "man," for a human being goes about on all fours when he is an infant; as an adult, he is biped; but he has three feet when he is old, for then he uses a walking stick (Diodorus Siculus *The Library* 4.64). This is the riddle of the Theban Sphinx, who killed those who were unable to solve it.

A man who was not a man, but a man even so, hit a bird that was not a bird, but a bird even so, with a stone that was not a stone when it was sitting on a log that was not a log. This is a children's riddle, alluded to

Oedipus and the Sphinx.

by Plato at *Republic 479c* and quoted in full by the scholiast *ad loc.*, who also gives the answer: *a eunuch hit a bat sitting on a hollow fennel-stalk with a pumice stone.*

There are two sisters. One of them gives birth to the other, and she herself, having given birth, is given birth to by the other (Theodectas *frg.* 4). Answer: *night and day.*

Solving riddles is not so unlike philosophy. In olden times, people displayed their learning at symposia through riddles, a far cry from what drinkers do nowadays, asking each other what sexual position gives the most plea-sure, or what sort of fish tastes best or is in season (Athenaeus *Wise Men at Dinner 457d*, quoting from the first book of *On Proverbs* by Clearchus of Soli, a pupil of Aristotle).

WONDROUS WATERS

The Florentine Paradoxographer lists over forty springs with amazing qualities in *Marvelous Things about Water*. Somewhere in the Greek world there is a spring with the power to, for example,

- *dye in bright colors the fleeces of sheep that drink from it;*
- *cure wounds; if you break a stick and throw it in, it becomes a single stick again;*
- *turn to stone the stomach of anyone who drinks from it;*
- *make people drunk;*
- *cause those who drink from it to lose their front teeth;*
- *throw out onto the bank anyone who bathes in it.*

In the interior of Sicily there is a little lake, the size of a shield. If anyone gets into it to wash, it expands, and if a second person gets in, it expands even more. It increases to accommodate fifty men, but when it reaches that number the water seethes up from the depths and throws the bathers in the air so that they land on the dry ground. It then returns to its original size. This happens not just with people, but with any sort of quadruped as well (Ps.-Aristotle *On Amazing Things Heard 840b*).

They say that there is a strange river in northern Italy that flows along with its water raised up out of its bed into the air, so that people on the other bank cannot be seen (Ps.-Aristotle *On Amazing Things Heard* 837*b*).

Some springs purify themselves at regular intervals. The fountain Arethusa at Syracuse in Sicily does this every four years, during the Olympic Games. This gave rise to the belief that the river Alpheus flows under the sea all the way to Syracuse, and that the dung of sacrificial victims thrown into the river at Olympia floats to the surface again in the Arethusa fountain (Seneca *Natural Questions* 3.26).

Strabo mentions speculation on whether the River Cydnus (in Eastern Turkey) could possibly cut across the Euphrates and the Tigris and empty into the Choaspes (in Iran) (*Geography* 1.47).

On Taenarum there is a spring in the waters of which it used to be possible to see harbors and ships, but a woman put an end to this marvel when she washed dirty clothes in it (Pausanias *Guide to Greece* 3.25).

I have heard a tale about the river Selemnus, that its water is a cure for love, effective for both men and women. People who bathe in the river forget their passion. If there is any truth in this story, the water of the Selemnus is worth more to mankind than great riches (Pausanias *Guide to Greece* 7.23).

GREEKS AND BARBERS

Demosthenes had an underground study built that has been preserved to this day. He used to go down there every single day to practice his gestures and to train his voice. He often stayed there two or three months at a time, shaving one side of his head to ensure that he would be too ashamed to leave the study even when he felt a strong urge to do so (Plutarch *Life of*

Demosthenes 7). Somewhat comparably, when the youthful Origen was keen to rush off to suffer martyrdom with his father in the early 3rd century, *his mother hid all his clothes, thus compelling him to stay at home* (Eusebius *Ecclesiastical History* 6.2).

Theophrastus used to joke about barbershops, calling them "symposia without wine" because of the chattering of those who sat in them (Plutarch *Table Talk* 679a).

A talkative barber asked King Archelaus of Sparta how he would like his hair cut. He replied, "In silence" (Plutarch *Sayings of Kings and Commanders* 177a).

In a barber's shop, the conversation turned to Dionysius's tyranny, how solid and invulnerable it was. The barber laughed and said, "You may say that about Dionysius, but I have my razor at his throat every few days." When Dionysius heard this, he had the barber crucified (Plutarch *On Talkativeness* 508f).

A barber was the first to bring the news of the Athenian disaster in Sicily, after hearing it in Piraeus from a slave who was one of the survivors. He left his shop and hurried to bring the news to the upper city. Panic broke out; the people assembled and tried to trace the source of the rumor. The barber was brought forward and questioned, but he did not even know his informant's name and had to refer to his source as an anonymous and unknown person. There was outrage and uproar in the theater: "Torture the wretch on the rack! He's made it up! Who else has heard about this? Who else believes it?" The wheel was brought in, and the barber was attached to it. Meanwhile, people who had actually escaped from the disaster arrived with the news. The assembly dispersed, each man to his own private grief, leaving the poor barber tied to the wheel. When he was finally released near evening, he was eager to learn from the public executioner whether they had heard how Nicias, the commander of the expedition, had died. Such is the irresistible and incorrigible vice that habit makes of garrulity (Plutarch *On Talkativeness* 509a).

A scholar, a bald man, and a barber were traveling together. When they stopped for the night in a lonely spot, they agreed to keep watch over their belongings for four hours each. The barber took the first watch and, to amuse himself, he shaved the scholar's head as he slept. When his watch was over, he woke the scholar. The scholar scratched his head sleepily, and finding that he was hairless, said, "That barber is such a fool! He woke the bald man instead of me" (Philogelos *Joke Book* 56).

If you burn a hedgehog and then mix the ashes with pitch and smear the concoction over hairless patches, the runaways (to make a little joke) will sprout again (Aelian *On Animals* 14.4).

Why do eunuchs not become bald? Is it because they have large brains? This happens because they have nothing to do with women, for semen comes down the spine from the brain (Ps.-Aristotle *Problems* 897b).

Indians dye their beards a variety of colors; some make their white beards as white as possible, others prefer dark blue, or crimson, or purple, or green (Arrian *History of India* 16.4).

Whenever something unfortunate is going to happen to the Pedasians, who live upcountry from Halicarnassus, the priestess of Athena grows a bushy beard. This has happened three times (Herodotus *Histories* 1.175).

MYTH BUSTERS

Pandora, who famously unleashed evils on the world from a jar she should not have opened, was usually said to have been fashioned from mud by Hephaestus and given to mankind bearing gifts (*dora*) from all (*pantes*) the gods. Palaephatus (*On Incredible Tales* 34) suggests that she was actually a very rich Greek woman who invented the mud pack to improve her complexion.

The birth of Athena, fully armed, from the head of Zeus.

They say that a monster used to come out of the sea to attack the Trojans. If they gave it young girls to eat, it would go away, but otherwise it would ravage their land. Who could fail to see that it is silly to suppose that people could strike a bargain with a fish? (Palaephatus *On Incredible Tales* 37).

Conventional mythology tells how Medea killed Pelias, who had deprived Jason of the kingship in Thessaly, by inducing his daughters to chop him up and throw him into a cauldron of boiling water, under the illusion that this would rejuvenate him. *But here is what actually happened. Medea discovered black and red dyes and was therefore able to make gray-haired old men appear to have dark or red hair. She also invented steam baths, which were a great benefit to mankind, but she made those whom she bathed swear to tell no one about the technique, in case any of the doctors found out about it. Anyone who underwent the steam treatment became lighter and healthier, but those who saw her cauldrons and the fire were convinced that she was boiling people. Pelias died while in the steam bath, but only because he was old and weak* (Palaephatus *On Incredible Tales* 43).

They say that when Narcissus looked into the water, he did not realize he was gazing at his own reflection, so he fell in love with himself and died of love at the spring. This is absolutely simpleminded: how could a person old enough to fall in love be incapable of distinguishing a real person from a reflection? (Pausanias *Guide to Greece* 9.31.7).

> *A writer was reading some long passages from his book; when he was approaching the end, Diogenes the Cynic saw that there was a blank column and shouted out, "Cheer up, everyone! Land ahoy!"*
>
> **(Diogenes Laertius *Lives of the Philosophers* 6.38).**

GLOSSARY

IN EXPLAINING why he considers performances of old comedy, written six hundred years earlier, to be unsuitable entertainment at dinner parties, Plutarch observes that *just as every guest at an important person's dinner party has his own personal wine-waiter, so each of us would need his own scholar to explain the allusions, and our symposium would turn into a classroom or else the jokes would be flat and pointless* (*Tabletalk* 712a). Such problems are obviously greater for us nowadays; no professional classicist would claim to be familiar even with the names of all the thousands of authors whose works have come down to us, whether in their entirety or, as is far more often the case, in tantalizing fragments. In lieu of explanatory footnotes accompanying the text, this glossary defines briefly some of the people, places, events, and institutions referred to most often and most prominently in the book. It is not comprehensive; further information is readily available in reference sources such as the *Oxford Classical Dictionary* (Oxford University Press, 4th ed., 2012).

Abdera: Greek city on the coast of Thrace.

Acragas: Greek city on the southwest coast of Sicily.

Actium: city in western Greece, where Octavian defeated Antony and Cleopatra in 31 B.C.

Aegina: island fifteen miles off the Attic coast.

Aelian (Claudius Aelianus ca. A.D. 165–ca. 235): author of *On Animals* and *Miscellaneous History*, rich sources of curious lore.

Aelius Aristides (A.D. 117–ca. 185): sophist and man of letters, author of a wide range of prose works, much admired in antiquity, but often rather boring.

Aeneas: Trojan prince and son of the goddess Venus; legendary founder of the Roman people.

Aeschylus: with Sophocles and Euripides, the greatest of the 5th-century Athenian tragedians.

Aesop: the semilegendary composer of fables.

Agora: the central focus of public life in a Greek community.

Alcibiades (451/450–404/403 B.C.): aristocratic Athenian politician and general.

Alexander the Great (356–323 B.C.): king of Macedon and conqueror of the Persian empire.

Alexandria: city founded by Alexander at the western edge of the Nile delta in 331 B.C., a great cosmopolitan center of learning and culture.

Ammianus Marcellinus (ca. A.D. 325–after 391): the last great Roman historian.

Anacharsis: semilegendary wise barbarian, said to have traveled in Greece in the 6th century B.C.

Anaximander of Miletus: 6th-century B.C. natural philosopher.

Anaximenes of Lampsacus: 4th-century B.C. historian and rhetorician.

Anaximenes of Miletus: follower of Anaximander.

Apelles of Colophon: 4th-century B.C. painter.

Apollonius of Rhodes: 3rd-century B.C. head of the Library at Alexandria, author of the epic *Argonautica*.

Appian (ca. A.D. 95–ca. 165): author of a history of Rome in Greek.

Archimedes of Syracuse (ca. 287–212/211 B.C.): mathematician and inventor.

Archytas: 4th-century B.C. Pythagorean philosopher, ruler of the Greek city of Tarentum in southern Italy.

Argos: city in the northeastern Peloponnese.

Aristides: 5th-century B.C. Athenian politician and general.

Aristophanes (ca. 455–ca. 388 B.C.): Athenian writer of comedies.

Aristotle of Stagira (384–322 B.C.): incalculably influential scientist and philosopher.

Arrian (Lucius Flavius Arrianus ca. A.D. 86–160): philosopher and historian.

Artemidorus of Daldis: 2nd-century A.D. author of *The Interpretation of Dreams*.

Aspasia: mistress of Pericles.

Athenaeus of Naucratis: late 2nd-century A.D. author of *Wise Men at Dinner*, a ragbag of discussions on literature, philosophy, law, medicine, and other topics.

Athos: headland on the coast of Macedonia.

Attica: the hinterland of Athens.

Aulus Gellius (ca. A.D. 125–after 180): author of the *Attic Nights*, a collection of quotations and discussions on wide-ranging and miscellaneous topics.

Bion of Borysthenes (ca. 335–ca. 245 B.C): popular philosopher, rather in the manner of Diogenes the Cynic.

Boeotia: region in central Greece, north of Attica.

Callimachus of Cyrene: 3rd-century B.C. scholar and poet in the Library at Alexandria and at the Ptolemaic court.

Caria: region in southwest Asia Minor (Turkey).

Carthage: located on the outskirts of modern Tunis, destroyed by Rome in 146 B.C.

Cassius Dio (ca. A.D. 160–ca. 230): author of a history of Rome in Greek.

Ceramicus: the potters' quarter in Athens, including the agora.

Charon: the ferryman who transported the dead across the River Styx to the Underworld.

Chios: Greek island off the coast of Asia Minor (Turkey).

Chrysippus of Soli (ca. 280–ca. 207 B.C.): philosopher, head of the Stoa.

Cicero (Marcus Tullius Cicero 106–43 B.C.): the greatest Roman orator.

Circe: beautiful witch who transformed Odysseus's men into pigs.

Claudius Ptolemy: 2nd-century A.D. author of works on geography, mathematics, astronomy, and astrology.

Cleon (?–422 B.C.): Athenian popularist politician.

Corinth: city on the isthmus joining the Peloponnese to central Greece.

Croton: Greek city in southern Italy.

Cyme: Greek city on the west coast of Asia Minor (Turkey).

Cyranides: a treatise on medical magic lore, probably first collected in the 4th century A.D.

Cyrene: Greek city in Libya.

Delos: island in the central Aegean, birthplace of Apollo and Artemis.

Democritus of Abdera (ca. 460–? B.C.): atomist philosopher.

Demosthenes (384–322 B.C.): the greatest Athenian orator.

Dio Chrysostom (ca. A.D. 45–after 110): orator and popular philosopher.

Diodorus Siculus (ca. 90–ca. 27 B.C.): author of a universal history in Greek.

Diogenes Laertius: 3rd-century A.D. compiler of biographies of early philosophers.

Diogenes the Cynic (ca. 410–ca. 324 B.C.): philosopher who questioned the conventions of life through his outrageous behavior and wit.

Dionysius of Halicarnassus (ca. 60–after 7 B.C.): Greek author of a history of Rome and of various treatises on rhetoric.

Dionysius I (ca. 430–367 B.C.): tyrant of Syracuse.

Dioscorides of Anazarbus: 1st-century A.D. author of *Medical Material*, a five-book study of the plants used in medicine.

Dodona: sanctuary and oracle of Zeus in the western mountains of Greece.

Drachma: basic unit of Greek coinage, of varying value in different *poleis*.

Elis: region in the northwest Peloponnese.

Elysium: home of the happy dead.

Empedocles of Acragas (ca. 492–432 B.C.): natural philosopher.

Ephesus: Greek city on the west coast of Asia Minor (Turkey).

Ephors: Spartan civil magistrates.

Epictetus: 1st/2nd-century A.D. Stoic philosopher, a slave in his early life.

Epicurus of Samos (341–270 B.C.): moral and natural philosopher.

Etymologicum Magnum: 12th-century lexical encyclopedia.

Eubulus: 4th-century B.C. Athenian writer of comedies.

Eupolis: 5th-century B.C. Athenian writer of comedies.

Euripides: with Aeschylus and Sophocles, the greatest of the 5th-century Athenian tragedians.

Eustathius: 12th-century Byzantine scholar and priest, compiler of commentaries on Homer and other authors.

Farm Work: 10th-century Byzantine compilation on agriculture.

Florentine Paradoxographer: one of several collections of strange stories, of uncertain date.

Galen of Pergamum (Claudius Galenus ca. A.D. 129–ca. 212): the most influential of ancient doctors, magnificently opinionated.

Gauls: the people of modern France and surrounding regions.

Gnomologium Vaticanum: 14th-century compilation of wise sayings, drawn mostly from classical sources.

Halicarnassus: Greek city in southwest Asia Minor (Turkey).

Hecuba: wife of Priam, the last king of Troy.

Helots: slave population exploited by Sparta.

Heraclitus: 6th/5th-century B.C. philosopher.

Herodotus of Halicarnassus (?–ca. 425 B.C.): author of the *Histories*, an account of the Persian Wars and the peoples involved.

Herophilus of Chalcedon (ca. 330–260 B.C.): physician at Alexandria.

Hesiod: 8th/7th-century B.C. author of the *Works and Days* and the *Theogony*, as well as much other poetry, now mostly lost.

Hippocrates of Cos (ca. 470–ca. 400 B.C.): father of Western medicine, but a shadowy figure.

Iamblichus of Chalcis (ca. A.D. 245–ca. 325): Neoplatonist philosopher.

Iphigenia: daughter of Agamemnon and Clytemnestra.

Isocrates (438–336 B.C.): Athenian orator.

Johannes Malalas (ca. A.D. 480–ca. 570): author of a chronicle of world history.

Josephus (Titus Flavius Josephus, A.D. 37–after 100): author of the *Jewish Wars* and *Jewish Antiquities*.

Julius Africanus: 2nd-century A.D. author of a chronicle of world history and of the *Cestoi*, a wide-ranging collection of miscellaneous information.

Lampsacus: Greek city in northwest Asia Minor (Turkey).

Leucadia: island off the west coast of Greece.

Lucian of Samosata: 2nd-century A.D. author of essays, dialogues, and narratives commenting wittily and satirically on literature and contemporary culture.

Lycurgus: semilegendary Spartan legislator.

Lysias (ca. 459–ca. 380 B.C.): resident alien in Athens, writer of speeches.

Machon: 3rd-century B.C. writer of comedies in Alexandria.

Marathon: region in Attica, site of the unexpected victory of the Athenians and Plataeans over the Persians in 490 B.C.

Marcus Aurelius (Marcus Aurelius Antoninus Augustus A.D. 121–180): Stoic philosopher and Roman emperor (ruled A.D. 161–180).

Medusa: mythical monster, celebrated mainly for her decapitation by Perseus.

Megara: city near the Isthmus of Corinth.

Menander (ca. 344/292/291 B.C.): Athenian writer of comedies.

Michael Psellus (A.D. 1018–after 1081): prolific author of works on history, philosophy, rhetoric, science, and literature.

Miletus: Greek city on the west coast of Asia Minor (Turkey).

Musonius Rufus: 1st-century A.D. Stoic philosopher.

Mytilene: the largest city on the island of Lesbos.

Obol: one-sixth of a drachma.

Orestes: son of Agamemnon and Clytemnestra.

Origen of Alexandria (ca. A.D. 185–ca. 255): Christian scholar and apologist.

Oxyrhynchus: city near the Upper Nile, source of almost three-quarters of all Greek literary papyri.

Palaephatus: author of a collection of rationalized versions of myths, originally written perhaps in the 4th century B.C., but surviving only in abbreviated form.

Parasite: literally "feeder beside," a companion to a social superior.

Patras: city on the north coast of the Peloponnese.

Pausanias of Magnesia: 2nd-century A.D. author of *Description of Greece*, a detailed account of most of the regions in the Roman province of Achaea.

Peloponnesian War: fought in 431–404 B.C. by Sparta and its allies against Athens and its allies.

Pentheus: legendary king of Thebes.

Perdiccas (?–321 B.C.): one of Alexander the Great's generals.

Pergamum: Greek city near the west coast of Asia Minor (Turkey).

Pericles (ca. 495–429 B.C.): Athenian political and military leader.

Phidias: 5th-century Athenian sculptor.

Philip II (382–336 B.C.): king of Macedon, father of Alexander the Great.

Philitas of Cos (ca. 340–? B.C.): poet and scholar at Alexandria.

Philo of Alexandria: 1st-century A.D. biblical scholar and philosopher.

Philodemus of Gadara (ca. 110–ca. 38 B.C.): philosopher and poet.

Philogelos: late antique collection of jokes mocking characters and professions, rather than individuals.

Philostratus: the name of three or possibly four authors from the same family who wrote on a wide spectrum of themes, including Homeric heroes, gymnastics, art collections, and biographies.

Photius (ca. A.D 810–ca. 893): patriarch of Constantinople and author of *The Library*, 280 chapters providing accounts of books he had read.

Phryne (literally "Toad"): the name or nom de guerre of several famous prostitutes.

Pindar (ca. 518–ca. 438 B.C.): Boeotian lyric poet.

Piraeus: port of Athens.

Pisa: district around Olympia in the northwest Peloponnese.

Plataea: town in southeast Boeotia.

Plato (ca. 429–347 B.C.): the philosopher to whom the European philosophical tradition is a series of footnotes.

Pliny the Elder (Gaius Plinius Secundus A.D. 23–79): author of the *Natural History*, an endlessly fascinating encyclopedia, conveying (by Pliny's computation) twenty thousand facts. Modern scholars would boost that total to approximately thirty-seven thousand.

Plutarch (ca. A.D. 45–127): as well as biographies of prominent Greeks and Romans, he also wrote the *Moralia*, essays on a wide range of philosophical, religious, and literary topics.

***Polis*:** the Greek city-state.

Pollux: 2nd-century A.D. lexicographer.

Polybius (ca. 203–120 B.C.): author of the *Histories*, an account in Greek of Rome's expansion in 220–146 B.C.

Porphyry of Tyre: 3rd-century A.D. Neoplatonist philosopher.

Posidonius of Apamea (ca. 135–ca. 50 B.C): Stoic philosopher, scientist, and historian.

Praxiteles: 3rd-century B.C. Athenian sculptor.

Priam: the last king of Troy.

Procopius of Caesarea: 6th-century A.D. historian.

Prodicus of Ceos: 5th-century B.C. sophist and rhetorician.

Protagoras of Abdera (ca. 490–420 B.C.): philosopher and sophist.

Ps.: pseudo, as in, for example, Ps.-Aristotle, author of a work falsely attributed to Aristotle.

Ptolemy I Savior (367/366–282 B.C.): one of Alexander's generals, subsequently ruler of Egypt.

Ptolemy II Philadelphus (308–246 B.C.): son of Ptolemy I.

Pyrrhus (319/318–272 B.C.): king of Epirus in western Greece, who invaded Italy in 280 to fight the Romans.

Pythagoras of Samos: 6th-century B.C. philosopher.

Pytheas of Massilia: 4th-century B.C. astronomer and geographer.

Pythia: the priestess through whom Apollo delivered his oracles at Delphi.

Quadrireme: ship with four banks of oars.

Quintilian (Marcus Fabius Quintilianus ca. A.D. 35–ca. 100): author of *The Education of the Orator*, a highly influential treatise on rhetoric.

Salamis: island off the coast of Attica, site of the Greek naval victory over Xerxes in 480 B.C.

Samos: island off the west coast of Asia Minor (Turkey).

Sappho of Lesbos: 7th-century B.C. lyric poetess.

Satrap: governor of a province in the Persian empire.

Scholia: explanatory notes written as commentaries to texts.

Scylla: a beautiful woman whose waist was encircled with ravening hounds that snatched sailors from passing ships.

Scythians: barbarians living north and east of the Danube.

Seleucus I: one of Alexander's generals, subsequently founder of a dynasty of kings ruling much of the Middle East.

Semonides of Amorgos: poet, probably 7th century B.C.

Sextus Empiricus: Skeptic philosopher, probably 2nd century A.D.

Sicyon: city near the Isthmus of Corinth.

Smyrna: Greek city on the west coast of Asia Minor (Turkey).

Sophist: itinerant professor of higher education.

Sophocles: with Aeschylus and Euripides, the greatest of the 5th-century Athenian tragedians.

St. Clement of Alexandria (ca. A.D. 150–ca. 212): Christian apologist and philosopher.

Stobaeus (Iohannes Stobaeus [John of Stobi (in Macedonia)]): probably 5th-century A.D. author of an anthology of extracts from prose and poetry on many topics.

Strabo (?64 B.C.–A.D.? 24): author of a voluminous treatise in Greek, the *Geography*.

Suda: 10th-century Byzantine historical encyclopedia.

Suetonius (Gaius Suetonius Tranquillus ca. A.D. 70–after 130): author of biographies of Julius Caesar and the first eleven emperors, as well as of poets, rhetoricians, and teachers.

Sybaris: Greek city in southern Italy.

Synesius (ca. A.D. 370–ca. 413): Neoplatonist philosopher and Christian bishop.

Syracuse: Greek city on the east coast of Sicily.

Talent: the largest unit of Greek money, worth six thousand drachmas.

Thales of Miletus: 6th-century B.C. scientist and philosopher.

Thasos: island in the north Aegean.

Thebes: city in Boeotia.

Themistocles (ca. 524–459 B.C.): Athenian politician and architect of the Greek victory at Salamis.

Theocritus of Syracuse: 3rd-century B.C. poet.

Theophrastus (ca. 370–ca. 287 B.C.): successor to Aristotle as head of the Lyceum.

Thermopylae: pass between the mountains and the sea in central Greece, where the Spartans and their allies delayed the Persian army in 480 B.C.

Thucydides (ca. 455–ca. 400 B.C.): Athenian admiral and author of an account of the Peloponnesian War.

Timotheus of Gaza: 5th/6th-century A.D. grammarian.

Tiresias: legendary Theban prophet.

Trireme: ship with three banks of oars.

Valerius Maximus: early 1st-century A.D. author of a collection of *Famous Deeds and Sayings*.

Vettius Valens of Antioch (A.D. 120–?): author of a treatise on astrology.

Vitruvius ([Marcus Vitruvius Pollio] ? before 70–ca. 25 B.C.): author of a highly influential treatise on architecture.

Xenocrates of Chalcedon (ca. 396–ca. 314 B.C.): head of the Academic school of philosophy at Athens.

Xenophanes of Colophon: 6th-century B.C. natural philosopher and poet.

Xenophon (ca. 430–354 B.C.): Athenian soldier and writer on philosophy, politics, history, hunting, and horses.

Xerxes I: King of Persia 486–465 B.C.

Zeno of Citium (335–263 B.C.): founder of Stoicism.

THE COIN IMAGES

All images of coins, at the chapter heads and throughout the interior, are reproduced courtesy of Classical Numismatic Group, Inc., http://www.cngcoins.com/.

Chapter I: Wild celery on a 6th-century B.C. didrachm from Selinus ("Celery Town") in Sicily.

Chapter II: Pegasus on a 4th-century B.C. stater from Syracuse.

Chapter III: A bee on a 4th-century B.C. tetradrachm from Ephesus.

Chapter IV: A satyr and a nymph on a late 5th-century B.C. stater from Thasos.

Chapter V: Athena in an elephant chariot on a drachm minted by Seleucus I Nicator of Syria. Seleucus was given five hundred war elephants by the Indian emperor Chandragupta under the terms of a peace treaty in 305 B.C.

Chapter VI: An owl on an Athenian tetradrachm minted in the second half of the 5th century B.C.

Chapter VII: Heracles on a tetrobol minted at Sparta in the first half of the 1st century B.C.

Chapter VIII: Alexander the Great/Heracles in a lion's skin, minted soon after Alexander's death in 323 B.C.

Chapter IX: Young man on a dolphin, minted at Tarentum in the mid-3rd century B.C.

Chapter X: An unidentified Achaemenid king on a 4th-century B.C. Persian daric.

Chapter XI: Zeus on an early 3rd-century B.C. tetradrachm minted by King Pyrrhus of Epirus.

Chapter XII: Hera on a stater minted at Elis in 376 B.C. to celebrate the 101st Olympic Games.

Chapter XIII: Two heads on a 4th-century B.C. drachm from Istros on the Black Sea.

Chapter XIV: Medusa on a 4th-century B.C. hemidrachm from Parion on the Hellespont.

Chapter XV: Apollo on a 4th-century B.C. tetradrachm minted by Mausolus of Caria.

Chapter XVI: Artemis the Savior on a bronze coin of Agathocles, tyrant of Syracuse (ruled 317–289 B.C.).

Chapter XVII: Arethusa, nymph of the spring in Syracuse, on a decadrachm minted in Syracuse at the end of the 5th century B.C.

Chapter XVIII: A crab on a 5th-century B.C. tetradrachm fom Acragas in Sicily.

Chapter XIX: A triform male head on an early 3rd-century B.C. obol from Cilicia.

Chapter XX: A winged thunderbolt on a coin from Syracuse minted just before the city fell to the Romans in 211 B.C.

Chapter XXI: Helios, the sun god, on a didrachm from Rhodes minted soon after Helios was depicted as the Colossus of Rhodes, set up to commemorate the failed siege of the city by Demetrius I of Macedon in 305 B.C.

Chapter XXII: Apollo, the god of prophecy, on a 4th-century B.C. tetradrachm from Rhegium in south Italy.

Chapter XXIII: A lion's head on a 5th-century B.C. teradrachm from Leontini in Sicily, punning on the city's name.

Chapter XXIV: A wolf's head on a late 2nd- or early 1st-century B.C. triobol from Argos.

ILLUSTRATION CREDITS